# PAINTING AND PERSONALITY

# PAINTING
# AND PERSONALITY

## *A STUDY OF YOUNG CHILDREN*

---

*Revised, Abridged Edition*

---

ROSE H. ALSCHULER

*&*

LA BERTA WEISS HATTWICK

---

THE UNIVERSITY OF CHICAGO PRESS
CHICAGO AND LONDON

*Library of Congress Catalog Card Number: 75-75966*

THE UNIVERSITY OF CHICAGO PRESS, CHICAGO 60637
THE UNIVERSITY OF CHICAGO PRESS, LTD., LONDON W.C. 1

© *1947 by The University of Chicago. Published 1947*
*Revised, abridged edition* © *1969 by The University of Chicago*
*Published 1969. All rights reserved*
*Printed in the United States of America*

# CONTENTS

# PLATES
*Following page 110*

## AUTHORS' NOTE TO REVISED EDITION

PAINTING AND PERSONALITY: *A Study of Young Children* was first published in two volumes by the University of Chicago Press in 1947. In essence, volume 1 is here reproduced. It represents our findings based on records, observations, and staff meetings that covered the daily lives of 150 children, white and black, over a year's time.

When published, more than twenty years ago, it seemed essential to validate our material. Accordingly we included our "Aims and Method," one complete case analysis, various record forms, biographical summaries of all the children involved, and fifty-six tables of quantitative findings. The tabulated material was of special interest to us because it validated our qualitative analyses.

Through the years, volume 1 has been consistently sought after, used, and found valuable in the understanding and guidance of young children. All too often owners of the original two-volume edition have complained that they loaned volume 1 to "someone" and it was never returned—would it be possible to get another volume 1?

The authors believe that, as here presented in one volume, *Painting and Personality* continues to have a real function and will fulfill an otherwise unmet need in the rapidly enlarging ranks of teachers of young children. A supplementary bibliography (1947–68) has been appended.

Today, as it was twenty years ago, children's growth and development, their passing problems as well as their basic conflicts, are reflected frequently in their paintings, just as they are in such other creative media as blocks, clay, and crayons.

It is with confidence and high hope for its continued usefulness that the authors see their study go forth in its present form.

ROSE H. ALSCHULER
LA BERTA WEISS HATTWICK

# INTRODUCTION TO REVISED EDITION

FROM TIME to time there comes into the body of professional literature in a given field a work which, by its insight and its clear presentation, is recognized as that most elusive of literary phenomena, a "classic." Such a book gives to each reader some new clue or idea by which certain aspects of his work or interest become infinitely clearer. Such a book, for many in the field of early childhood education, is *Painting and Personality*.

At the time of first publication, in 1947, many of the findings in *Painting and Personality* were so new that, as Mrs. Alschuler points out, "undoubtedly some informed readers might well have wondered how the authors arrived at their conclusions." Since 1947, however, additional studies have served to corroborate many of these findings; and teachers of young children, as well as researchers in the field of children's creativity, have accepted and utilized them.

In recent years the interest of the federal government in preschool education, through the Head Start and Child Development programs, has fostered study of the young child and his development. Many young people are attracted to this particular field because of the growing realization of the importance of the first years of the individual's life. Workers with young children need to know the findings of past experiences and research. *Painting and Personality* reflects children's personalities not only as they are expressed through their paintings but also as expressed through such other media as blocks, crayons, and dramatic play. To his interpretation of what he reads, each teacher will add his own observations as they derive from his daily experience.

It was because of this ever-continuing need that the Board of Directors of the Chicago Association for the Education of Young Children urged the republication of *Painting and Personality: A Study of Young Children*. In consultation with the authors, it was agreed that an abridged edition would be of value to today's students and teachers, and that those who might wish to explore the subject more fully would seek out the original edition as well as the Supplemental Bibliography in the revised edition.

In encouraging republication, the Chicago Association for the Education of Young Children has been conscious of three factors: the value of the work itself as a method of evaluating and understanding the paintings produced by young children; the stimulus it offers teachers and workers in the field to evaluate and seek constantly for a better understanding of the children in their care; and its commission to value each child as a person of creative potential and integrity. The last of these factors—the worth of individual creativity—speaks loudly to all of us who would give a moment to listen to the authors' statement "If we stop to ponder the matter, we realize that creative quality springs from some universal human disposition that is distilled differently by every individual." It applies to every child in every setting, and it speaks not only of the more fortunate children (by material measure) but of those in our society whose background makes them less able in the fields of language and verbalized concept formation.

The authors present a unique challenge and example in the second of these factors—the need for constant evaluation of all programs designed for the young. Rose Alschuler and La Berta Hattwick, who worked for ten years on this study, represent a fortunate combination of abilities. (Mrs. Alschuler has commented: "I could not have imagined a better colleague or co-worker.") Mrs. Alschuler's is the wide-ranging and imaginative mind that can see the possibilities for study in a given situation or a given body of ideas; Dr. Hattwick's is the ability to develop such possibilities into an organized study. The book they produced—with the co-operation of the many workers mentioned in the Foreword to the first edition—has evoked, in Mrs. Alschuler's words, "a response not only from professionals interested in the field of child development but from artists and other adults who found interesting implications as they viewed their own paintings and those of others, as well as the paintings of young children." Characteristically she adds, "Throughout the text will be found materials based on the analysis of both qualitative and quantitative factors." If only for this reason—her clear insistence on the evaluation of any program through continuous research—do Dr. Hattwick and the Board of Directors of the Chicago Association for the Education of Young Children feel that, in many ways, this particular work stands as a monument to the life of Rose Alschuler.

At a dinner given by the Association at the Art Institute of Chicago in June 1967, letters from many people who had worked with Mrs. Alschuler since 1926 were read by Dr. Frances Horwich. In 1926 Mrs. Alschuler was organizer and staff director of the Franklin Public School Nursery School, the first nursery school located in a public school in the United States. She held the same position in two nursery schools established in the Garden Apartments (1927–33), the Winnetka Public School Nursery and Junior Kindergarten (1927–41), and some twenty-three WPA-sponsored nursery schools (1933–41). In October 1941 she was invited to Washington, D.C., as chairman of the National Commission for Young Children (1941–43). While there she served as consultant to the Federal Public Housing Authority (1942–43). In the latter capacity she helped to plan and equip some seven hundred to eight hundred nursery school units established in connection with war housing. Mrs. Alschuler served as a member of the executive boards of the Progressive Education Association and the National Association for Nursery Education (now the National Association for the Education of Young Children). She is a member of the American Educational Research Association. In addition to *Painting and Personality*, Mrs. Alschuler is the author, with associates, of *Two to Six; Children's Centers; Play—the Child's Response to Life;* and many articles. She has lectured to university students in Oslo and London, at the Anglo-Indian Teachers College in Calcutta, and at the Albert Lasker Clinic in Jerusalem; has given a series of lectures at Mills College (1940) and at Indiana University (1960); and has given courses in child development and nursery education at San Francisco State College (1949). In 1965, Mrs. Alschuler was instrumental in organizing the Horizon House program in Chicago, a preschool center associated with the Head Start and Child Development programs of the Office of Economic Opportunity. Indeed, as was stated on the program for the dinner in her honor in June 1967: "Seldom do we have the history of a life which is also the history of a movement."

It is for these reasons—the continuing value of *Painting and Personality* for its insight and help to all of those interested in the development of the young child, and the testimony it gives to the life and work of a remarkable individual—that the Board of Directors of the Chicago Association for the Education of Young Children wishes to express its deep appreciation to Rose Alschuler and La Berta Hattwick for their gracious help in arranging for the one-volume edition of *Painting and Personality*.

CHARLOTTE CORNISH COLLIER

Chicago Association for the Education of Young Children

# FOREWORD TO ORIGINAL EDITION

A DECADE ago, in August, 1935, a group of American and Mexican educators held a conference in Mexico City under the auspices of the New Education Fellowship. As so frequently happens at conferences, the unrecorded and chance meetings proved particularly fruitful.

Among those participating in the conference was Dr. Edward Liss, New York City psychiatrist, who for many years has given generously, of both his time and his knowledge, to education. One evening Dr. Liss and one of the authors were looking at a series of water-color illustrations for a Mexican folk tale. Quite without realizing it, not only had the artist illuminated the folk tale, but, as Dr. Liss pointed out, he had revealed much about himself. The discussion drifted to the meaningfulness of young children's paintings. It was that discussion with Dr. Liss on a summer evening in Mexico that stimulated the present study. From time to time, especially in the early phases of the work, Dr. Liss met with us, discussed our findings, and stimulated our thinking in helpful fashion. We acknowledge with deep appreciation our indebtedness to him.

During the school year 1937–38 we did some preliminary experimentation in order to establish methods of investigation. That year also served to clarify and extend our thinking. We concluded that what we wanted to know could best be learned in the natural setting of the school rather than in any series of closely defined test situations. As discussions proceeded, it was decided that a study of children's choice of materials and their behavior during usage were essential to any understanding of the significance of the final products. We also realized that, inasmuch as the core of personality is constantly reflected in all of children's activities, we should study as many aspects of behavior and activity as might throw additional light on their paintings. Accordingly, study of their crayon work, clay, block building, and dramatic play was undertaken, along with study of their paintings. Our method for studying individual children had been established through many years of nursery-school experience, during which we had worked thoughtfully with individual children and their families. The staff that had helped to develop our particular methods and techniques continued to work together on this study.

Besides the authors, who served, respectively, as staff director and psychologist in the five nurseries under observation, the nuclear staff included

Edna Mohr, nutritionist of the Elizabeth McCormick Memorial Fund. Miss Mohr interpreted her function in terms that were unusual. With the full support of Mary E. Murphy, director of the Elizabeth McCormick Memorial Fund, Miss Mohr organized and operated the health program in the five nursery schools in which the children were studied. Throughout the period of the study we met weekly and sometimes several times a week to discuss the children, their development, and their needs. Along with the children, the research material was subject to continuous discussion. We were particularly eager to know whether or not the findings in the research material negated or validated our understanding of the children as we knew them in the groups. Staff discussions of the children and the research findings were one test of the validity of our analyses. In the course of our discussions it became obvious that quality of health, home attitudes, and habits of eating, sleeping, and elimination all were aspects of the health program that had bearing on the paintings and other products which we were examining. Miss Murphy's continuing interest and the high standards that she held for her staff and all who worked with them helped to give quality to the study. Miss Mohr's observations and her steadfast and able co-operation were invaluable to us.

This Foreword might well be entitled "Sine qua non" because without the co-operation of almost innumerable individuals and organizations we would not have initiated the study nor could we have carried it to completion. The quantity of time and the quality of thought and effort that the teachers on our staff gave to this study made possible our results. Margaret McFarland, Ethel Wright Kunkle, Frances Horwich, Antoinette Brown Suter, and Liesl May Schoen, all of them at that time staff members of the Winnetka Public School Nurseries, helped us during the first year of formulating methods, as well as through the succeeding years of observations.

Other teachers who contributed thoughtfully to our materials were Eleanor Lichty, Harriet Harris, and Helene Alschuler, of the Winnetka Nurseries; Josephine Prescott, Helen K. Smith, and Geneva Foster, of Baptist Missionary Training School; and Gwendolyn Oakes and Leona McGovern, of Howell House Nursery School. To add daily observations to their regular teaching assignments meant a kind of devotion that is all too rarely found.

In order to learn as much as possible about the children and their daily activities we tried to have two observers besides the teachers present in each group every day throughout the period of the study. Eight observers, all of them with professional standards and considerable experience, gave their services. These included Mary Aldrich, Clare Bernhardt, Mary Boyer, Martha Drake, Mary Harris, Martha Loewenstein, Teresa Jackson, and

Rosette Lowenstein (who had given her services to our nursery schools in Chicago and Winnetka for many years before this study was initiated). The conscientiousness with which they stayed on the job and the sensitive quality of their observations belie all that is usually said about volunteers. Our paid observers, who, like all the rest, gave much that they were not paid to give, included Emily Allen, Bertha Ferguson, Mae Schiffman Maizlish, and Ruth Townsend.

We shall remember Catherine Fulton and Alice Topper sitting at their desks "spinning figures" as long as we remember the process by which we obtained some of the answers. Dorothy Jones, Signe Fagerstrom, Alice Nafftz Woodruff, and Clara A. Schiff were others whose analysis of the research material was most helpful. Outstanding among clerical helpers were Lillian Peterson and Florence Olsen.

William H. Pemberton, clinical psychologist of San Francisco, came to Chicago in 1940 in order to give Rorschach tests to thirty of our children, some of whom by this time were in the first grade. His findings and observations corresponded in a high degree to many of our own. For us the Rorschach tests were but another way of cutting across and testing the validity of our findings. We considered the use of the Rorschach tests not only as a direct contribution to our study but also as an experiment in method for the study of personality. At a future date we hope to make some report on this aspect of our work.

Anni Weiss-Frankl developed her own play-interview technique for the understanding and guidance of children. She had play interviews with approximately thirty children. Her observations on these children contributed to our understanding of them. Mrs. Frankl was also exceedingly helpful in the training of observers.

Our appreciation goes to Leslie Bennett, who throughout most of one school year went from one to another of the nurseries where we were observing to get a photographic record of activities. Mr. Bennett was thoroughly co-operative, sensitive, and very successful in getting photographic material that greatly supplemented our other records.

During our first year of analyzing the material we were particularly fortunate in having Maria Weigl Piers, who had taken her doctorate in Vienna on "Symbolism in Primitive Art." In making qualitative analyses of each child's paintings and in our first formulations concerning the meaning of color and form, as well as in the relating of these to the behavior of children, Mrs. Piers gave us inestimable help.

To the superintendents of the two public school systems in which we worked goes our appreciation. Both were most generous in giving us work-

ing space, and both aided us in every possible way. Our thanks to Edward
Johnson, of Chicago, and Carleton Washburne, of Winnetka. Mr. Washburne occasionally sat with us at research staff meetings and brought questions and stimulus to our work.

For years it has been the fashion to berate and belittle the Work Projects
Administration. When the record is some day complete, it will become clear
that this study and innumerable larger and more important works could
not have been done without the facilities of W.P.A. Personnel whose vision
and understanding of our objectives helped to make possible this study included Florence Kerr, then regional supervisor of Professional and Service
Projects; Mary G. Moon, then state director of Professional and Service
Projects for Illinois; Harry J. Fultz, who succeeded Mrs. Moon; and H. K.
Seltzer, district director in Chicago. All those named and countless others
who were serving W.P.A. at that time did everything possible to facilitate
our work. A number of the persons named in this Foreword, including
teachers, observers, and research workers, as well as the authors, worked
interchangeably in W.P.A. and the Winnetka Nursery Schools. Paid and
unpaid, city and suburban, colored and white, we worked as one staff. The
co-operative spirit that characterized the work throughout made possible
the results obtained. We hope that these findings, along with those already
published and some still in process of formulation, will justify the time, effort,
and funds that have gone into this research.

To Alma Cronin, our particular thanks for her continuous and sensitive response to our material as well as for her efficient secretarial services.
Doubtless we have omitted a number of persons whose thinking and as-
sistance had a real place in our study. To them and to all whom we have
named above go our deep-felt appreciation.

R. H. A.

La B. W. H.

PAINTING AND PERSONALITY

# CHAPTER I

## THE BASES OF UNDERSTANDING

I F WE stop to ponder the matter, we realize that creative quality springs from some universal human disposition that is distilled differently by every individual. This creative quality derives in large part from the inner drives and feelings which underlie and are the dynamics of human behavior. Among two-, three-, and four-year-old children these drives and feelings tend to find relatively direct expression in overt behavior and are manifest in almost everything that children do. We should accordingly expect young children's paintings, which are a projection of creative quality, to reflect their inner lives in very direct fashion.

Continued observation of the paintings of two-, three-, and four-year-old children makes obvious certain aspects of creative quality. Each child has his own palette (i.e., each child has certain preferred colors and certain ways of combining these colors), as well as his own individual pattern of expression, characterized not by any particular realistic pictorial representation but rather by his characteristic and unique abstract use of color, line, form, and space.

This study was initiated to explore the possibility that each child's paintings tended to be both individual and directly expressive and to determine to what extent, if any, a systematic study of the paintings of individual children would reveal the effect of each child's specific and ever changing experiences on his particular nature and development. Systematic observations, we realized, must include, along with every child's paintings, the background of his life, the dynamic forces that were currently affecting him, and whatever else we could learn of his day-to-day experiences, together with his reactions to them. We hoped, through such study, to come to a heightened understanding of children, as well as to a more sensitive and discriminating awareness of whatever meaning the paintings in themselves might convey. We proposed to investigate the paintings through an analysis of those separate factors that together make up the final creative product, namely, color, line, form, and space usage.

Accordingly, case studies and daily observations of the activities of one hundred and fifty children were made during one entire school year. Twenty of the same children were observed daily throughout a second year.

THE UNIVERSAL AND THE PARTICULAR

The approach through individual case studies not only has given further insights into the highly individual quality of each child's work but has revealed that there is a very general, and perhaps even universal, tendency for all sorts of individuals to express similar feelings, reactions, and problems in like, or at least comparable, fashion. This likeness is evidenced sometimes in choice of color and sometimes in similarity of form, line, and/or space usage. Apparently, just as creative activity itself springs from some unexplained universal tendency, so the expression of certain universal experiences frequently takes on comparable form.

Certainly, such similarity of expression was definitely observed among the children studied, who not only were having widely diverse nursery experiences in five separate nursery schools but came from quite different social and economic levels, as well as from varied racial and national backgrounds. In their usage of color, line, form, and space, these children expressed, on the one hand, their individualized, highly subjective experiences, and, on the other hand, in these same paintings their responses were in many respects so basically similar as to suggest that their origin, to some extent at least, lay deep in the history of the human race and in the constitution of the human organism.

In order to arrive at some definition of these similarities and differences of expression and their probable meanings, an attempt was made, first, to analyze and relate individual behavior and painting tendencies and then to make a like study of the group painting tendencies with reference to behavior. Obviously, all the relationships suggested in individual case analysis could not be included in our group comparisons. However, the group comparisons which have been included have to an extraordinary degree harmonized with individual case findings and have provided a framework around which our discussion of the direct expressive qualities of paintings will be built.

EXCEPTIONS

The generalized framework which we shall present must be considered in a far more tentative manner than the individual case findings. Findings given are true in terms of our study; but, like other generalizations, they cannot be indiscriminately applied to individual cases. Many of the generalizations will fail to hold for a particular child for such reasons as those suggested below.

1. Our findings support the belief that two-, three-, and four-year-old children tend to express the same feelings through creative media that they express in overt behavior. However, even during these years, we find that some children conceal their true feelings in their overt behavior but express

them in their easel painting. In such cases, paintings and overt behavior are likely to reflect contrasting, rather than similar, drives.

2. During these early years we have found that some children's paintings tend frequently, if not persistently, to be copies of external stimuli rather than reflections of self.

3. Our generalized statement of relationships is based upon findings that relate to each separate factor or aspect of children's paintings, for example, an emphasis on red considered by itself; a tendency to work all over or cover the entire page considered by itself; an emphasis on circle painting or some other specific form, again analyzed as a separate factor. In order to understand the potential significance of every aspect, each one was, of necessity, studied by itself without regard to the way in which that aspect of painting might be related to other aspects. But in the analysis and interpretation of a given painting it is more often in the interrelationships of several aspects than in any single characteristic that the distinctive and telling qualities of the child's products are likely to lie. It is only through careful consideration of these interrelationships that sound interpretation can be made. Such consideration or analysis, as a rule, involves some adaptation of the generalized trends here stated.

As the discussion of findings develops, it will be important constantly to be aware of the dangers in wholesale application of generalized tendencies and to keep in mind, at the same time, the need for basing individual interpretations upon a detailed analysis of all available information concerning each individual child.

Before considering the various aspects of children's paintings and what each one has to contribute to keener discrimination and clearer understanding both of children and of painting, let us examine some of the current concepts and attitudes that concern children's work.

### THOSE MEANINGLESS DAUBS

Most casual observers would classify the paintings and drawings of two-, three-, and four-year-old children as "meaningless daubs." According to usual aesthetic standards, they rate low, and with little or no thought they are crushed into wastebaskets. Even if most adults paused long enough to examine them carefully, they still would be likely to characterize them in some such fashion as "smears" or "messes." Although it may be difficult to realize, it is nonetheless true that almost every drawing and painting made by a young child is meaningful and in some measure expresses the child who did it. Curiously enough, it is just because they are not planned but are the spontaneous results of free manipulation and of sheer experimentation with color and form that young children's pictures are meaningful.

When an adult, by some mistaken impulse, asks a youngster, on looking at one of his creations, what he has been painting, the child's answer may or may not be relevant to what he has produced. If he wants to be polite, he may look intently at his painting for a moment and then give some name suggested by the form in front of him—or he may be so absorbed in what he is doing that he will go right on painting and not respond at all. Most likely, the child has never thought of his painting as the representation of an object. If he is like the majority of two-, three-, and four-year-olds, his painting has come from those depths of his being from which feelings flow outward in generalized, rather than representative, form. Although the child has probably painted something he has been feeling keenly about, it is doubtful if he could put into words just what it was that he had felt the need to express. In other words, children can use paints and crayons to express absorbing experiences and preoccupations which they are not yet able to express in words. Sometimes this may be because the experiences are still at a *feeling* level not sufficiently clarified to express in words, or again it may be that children of this age have not yet sufficient vocabulary to express their feelings which are, nevertheless, impelling and forceful.

So long as we continue to see and appraise young children's paintings and their crayon drawings by usual adult standards, so long shall we fail to understand their meaning and diagnostic value. But even more important than understanding the diagnostic possibilities in their paintings and drawings is the realization that if we are to encourage, rather than inhibit, children's free creative potentialities, we must see the paintings and drawings through the children's eyes and, as far as possible, get an understanding of their feelings at the time when they produced them. When we look at the paintings of adult artists, we disparage exact reproductions. Yet the more exactly children reproduce given objects, the higher are we, with our lack of insight, likely to rate their artistic ability. In the very act of imitating or painting what they see rather than what they feel, children stifle their creative impulses. Two- to five-year-old children, and to some degree children up to the age of nine, if left quite free and particularly if encouraged to do so, will express not what they see but whatever it is that at the moment they happen to be feeling and experiencing most keenly. They paint to express those emotions and experiences that are stirring within them, that are welling up and pushing for expression.

That painting is a particularly good medium for expressing the artist's emotional drive is not a new viewpoint. The poet Strindberg is said to have turned to painting when he found himself unable to express satisfactorily what he had to say in words. Herbert Read, in *The Meaning of Art*,[1] states that if we wish to communicate ideas, words are the proper medium; but if we wish to convey feelings or emotions, we can do no better than to use the plastic arts, particularly painting. Louis Danz[2] in a recent novel offers similar recognition of the meaning of painting to the artist. He writes: "All my life I have felt something different about painting and now for the first time I understand. Painting isn't something you just see with your eyes. It's something you feel with your whole body. It is the design of your hurt or your happiness and when other people see it, they feel the hurt or the happiness just as you did." Although the concept is not new and although we find it reiterated from time to time, there is still amazingly slight recognition of the fact that painting is a deeply emotional experience to every artist who paints what he feels and not merely what he sees. In like fashion it is difficult for adults to realize that when little children paint, they, too, are expressing the "hurt and happiness of life."

### CHILDREN'S EARLIEST HUMAN REPRESENTATIONS

To recognize the validity of the above statement, one has but to look at a series of children's earliest human representations. At three and one-half to four years of age, as a rule children for the first time attempt with paints and crayons to represent human figures. On careful examination we find that they have most likely made human representations that somehow express themselves. They have painted themselves as they feel themselves from within. "Crying Eyes" (Pl. 1) was painted by an unhappy child who cried, screamed, and talked a great deal. Note the tears streaming from her eyes and her wide-open mouth. *Shirley*, another unhappy child, painted a similar self-expressive version of "Crying Eyes," as did A. A. (Pl. 93) just two days before a new baby was born into his family. *Jean* and *Elinor*, like most other children who had curls, represented all female figures with lots of hair. *Brian*, who had a defective foot, produced a human figure with one leg that had an excessive number of appendages on the side corresponding to the one on which he had a defect (Pl. 2). *Loretta*, inseparable from her pocketbook, produced girls carrying pocketbooks. Each child, in his paintings and drawings, accentuates those parts of his body which he has experienced most keenly. Löwenfeld in his study of the near-blind was impressed by the overemphasis which blind children, working with crayons and clay, gave to eyes[3] and to those other parts of the body that had particular emotional connotations.

[1] London: Faber & Faber, Ltd., 1936.

[2] *It Is Still the Morning* (New York: William Morrow & Co., 1943).

[3] Viktor Löwenfeld, *The Nature of Creative Activity* (New York: Harcourt, Brace & Co., 1939), pp. 121 ff.

The developmental order in which children add details to their portrayals of human figures also reflects the fact that children tend to draw and paint what they are feeling and experiencing rather than what they see. The first human representations tend to be mostly head or are simply delineated heads and legs. Apparently, these are the parts of the body which first impress themselves on children's consciousness. Through sight, hearing, taste, smell, and by crying and thereby getting what he wants, the child is well aware of his head. From his pictures it would seem that legs, which help him get where he wants to go, come next into his awareness. Arms then appear, and fingers become differentiated somewhat later. Although legs often expressing action are added early in drawing and painting experiences, toes, which are less functional than fingers, are rarely pictured. The trunk tends to appear later than these other more keenly realized members of the body.

Clothing and other details are usually added in accordance with the degree to which they have been actively experienced. Goodenough noted that hats are drawn before hair[4]—doubtless because most children have got the feel of hats by helping to put on and take off their head coverings. They evidently have not become equally aware of their hair. Children tend to emphasize buttons at the time that they are learning to manage their buttons. Armholes tend to be exaggerated while children are learning to negotiate arms in and out of armholes.[5] Perrine's observations, like Goodenough's and our own, underline the fact that details in children's drawings are emphasized in proportion to the intensity with which they have been or are being experienced.

Perrine[6] tells of a drawing by Pat, in which eyes were remarkably expressive, while hands and feet were disproportionate, crude, and schematic. Perrine, who was studying children and trying to understand how best to encourage their creative faculties, commented to Pat about the expressive eyes she had drawn, but he made no remark about the less well-drawn hands and feet. Questioned by a visitor for overlooking an opportunity to improve Pat's representation of arms and legs, Perrine replied that Pat had drawn the eyes expressively because they were a meaningful sense organ to her. He explained that when Pat's own experiences became sufficiently deep-felt, she would naturally develop awareness and perception about the forms of hands and feet. The soundness of Perrine's judgment

---

[4] Florence Goodenough, *Measurement of Intelligence by Drawing* (Yonkers: World Book Co., 1926).

[5] E. B. Hurlock and J. L. Thomson, "Children's Drawings: An Experimental Study of Perception," *Child Development*, June, 1934, pp. 127–38.

[6] V. D. Perrine, *Let the Child Draw* (New York: F. A. Stokes & Co., 1936).

was borne out later in the year. Through swimming and diving, hands became important moving forces to Pat. Interestingly enough, in a single drawing, we see and feel with Pat the meaning of her diving to her. The hands of the child who is standing on the diving board retain the purely schematic sunflower shape of her earlier drawings, while the hands of the child just ready to strike the water assume an expressive functional quality. To quote Perrine: "Creative quality out of its awareness of functional need, spontaneously builds a better hand than a negative criticism could and has left intact and operative a highly efficient creative faculty."[7]

### OLDER CHILDREN'S PAINTINGS ARE LIKELY TO BE LESS SELF-EXPRESSIVE

If we follow young children's drawings and paintings over a period of years, we note that as children grow older their drawings and paintings become less and less self-expressive. Children tend gradually to portray the realistic details of seen objects or to adopt popular schematic or usual pictorial methods of depicting them. By the time children are nine or ten years of age, they have, as a rule, been so thoroughly imbued with the need for reproducing exactly what they see that their own natural modes of self-expression have been blocked off and the earlier impulses to paint and express themselves from within have very largely been stifled.

Löwenfeld[8,] reports an interesting experiment which indicates that nine-year-olds tend to find it more difficult to express themselves spontaneously in drawings than do younger children. Approximately four hundred children, ranging in age from five to fifteen, were given the same problem, namely, that of depicting the picking of a much desired apple from a branch that was well out of reach. Five- to seven-year-olds made the human figures with which they apparently felt identified larger and more important than the tree with which they felt little concern. The picking arm was disproportionately long as compared to the unused arm. They thereby conveyed their feeling of stretch. In contrast to the younger children, the nine- and ten-year-olds depicted both trees and figures in more stylized, conventional fashion. Arms were raised, but no relationship between arms and apple was projected. Drawings were schematized according to set ideas of how they should look rather than derived and drawn from inner experience. Apparently, the children had lost the spontaneous ability to portray the stretching arm in self-expressive form, and they did not yet have sufficient skill to depict an outstretched arm in realistic or conventional fashion. Most children between seven and ten years of age have been indoctrinated by older sisters, brothers, teachers, and parents concerning how given objects should be depicted; and accordingly they have, to a great extent, lost

---

[7] *Ibid.*  [8] *Op. cit.*, p. 77.

their ability to invent, to create, to experiment, and to express themselves directly from their own experiences.

Several art teachers with whom the authors have spoken support the observation that it is particularly difficult to evoke self-expressive creative products from nine- and ten-year-old children. To what extent this decrease in self-expressive quality is the result of instructions given and to what extent it reflects general developmental changes is difficult to say. It is true that between the ages of five and ten, children become increasingly concerned with the world about them and less absorbed and preoccupied with their inner selves. Only at adolescence do most children once more tend to have preoccupations with self and evidence urges to project their inner thoughts and emotions much as they did during their first four to five years. But by the time they are adolescent their natural responses have been so thoroughly overlaid and conditioned by the circumstances of living that it would, as a rule, be difficult to derive the dynamics of behavior from their paintings and drawings. Accordingly, it is to the spontaneous drawings and paintings of young children that we return for study of basic drives, needs, and feelings.

### YOUNG CHILDREN'S PAINTINGS REFLECT THEIR DEVELOPMENT

As we begin to analyze their earliest drawings and paintings, we note that the very features which we at first regarded as meaningless errors—the exaggerations in size or number; the omissions; the unrealistic, sometimes persistent, use of one or another color; and the seemingly strange, meaningless forms—become the most revealing aspects of each child's products. Those features of the drawing or painting that are most highly individual and are peculiar to any given child's work become our clues to understanding the child's inner life and the dynamics of his behavior.

Children of two, three, and four use conventional forms (i.e., the usually accepted modes of representing, let us say, a person or a house) only as far as these forms have been artificially stimulated or superimposed. They deviate from conventionalized representation and paint abstract masses and forms when they attempt to express their reactions to their own particular deep-felt experiences. It is with the deviations from conventionalized or schematized forms that this study will very largely deal.

The fact that spontaneously produced drawings and paintings of two-, three-, and four-year-olds should be revelatory to an extraordinary degree conforms with other known facts about children of these ages. Gesell[9] notes that during these years children function on an impulsive, feeling,

[9] Arnold L. Gesell and others, *The First Five Years of Life: A Guide to the Study of the Preschool Child* (New York: Harper & Bros., 1940).

self-expressive level. They are more intent on expressing what they feel than in responding as others desire or expect them to do. Inasmuch as they are, in general, operating on an impulsive level, quite naturally the drawings and paintings of this period express their impulses, their natural drives, and their obvious frustrations.

### ABSTRACT PAINTINGS AND DRAWINGS OFTEN MORE EXPRESSIVE THAN REPRESENTATIVE PRODUCTS

As we examine *Aileen*'s work, we realize that young children's abstract paintings may reveal far more concerning the dynamic aspects of their personalities than do their recognizable pictorial forms. Although it may be difficult to accept on first observation, it is nevertheless true that Aileen's pedestaled abstraction (Pl. 9) is a more profound expression of her personality than is the readily recognized self-portrait, "Crying Eyes" (Pl. 1).

Aileen was a moody, unhappy child, who screamed and cried a great deal. She tended to withdraw from others and frequently adopted an aloof attitude toward them. Hers was an emotional and fanciful, rather than a realistic and objective, approach to life. When upset, Aileen was likely to climb up onto a window seat or retreat to the tree-house or to some other elevated place. Her block structures most frequently were thrones or platforms, on which she would stand or sit. Sometimes she built pedestals on which she placed miniature toys (Pl. 11). One of Aileen's most absorbing experiences with clay, one to which she gave an unusually long period of concentrated interest, resulted in a carefully modeled figure of a woman seated on a pedestal. As Aileen grew older and more frequently entered into social relationships with other children, it became apparent that she was happy only when she held an autocratic, domineering role. Psychically, as well as physically, she had to feel above others in order to feel equal to them.

In her pedestaled abstraction (Pl. 9), Aileen expressed her aloof, removed attitude toward life as she could not, at that period, have expressed it either in words or in realistic, pictorial painting. Yet even this symbolic abstraction made when she was five years of age is not so deeply revealing as is the ovular red pattern that characterized Aileen's paintings when she was three.

The ovular red mass (Pls. 3 and 4) was painted persistently throughout the first year of observations. As we followed her development over a period of years, it was noted that Aileen periodically reverted to this same pattern when she was upset and unhappy (Pl. 5). As her work became pictorial, we find this pattern incorporated in more conventionalized and decorative form (see Pls. 10 and 12).

Evidence strongly suggests that Aileen's ovular red mass was associated with her feelings about home. At such times as she talked about her paintings, she tended to refer to the red mass as "house." More than a year after entrance into the group and after some months of different and varied cativities, one day when Aileen was particularly depressed and unhappy she again painted the ovular red mass (Pl. 5). She then went directly to the blocks and built a structure and remarked with considerable feeling as she did so: "This is a house. Nobody can live in it. This is a house only for my people who haven't any other place to stay." In the latest painting obtained (Pl. 12), we find approximately the same enclosed red pattern specifically associated with the house theme. During that entire year (she was then in third grade), Aileen's teacher reported that she showed unusual concern about home.

As we look into her background, we understand Aileen's driving preoccupation with "house" and "home"—Aileen was the only child of divorced parents, both of whom were remarried. Aileen shuttled between their homes, and frequently she stayed with her grandparents. In none of these homes did Aileen receive enough affection to meet her needs.[10] Her mother, by her own statement, had various interests outside of the home. Aileen's father, during this period, had a child by his second wife. While Aileen was in her second year at nursery school, her grandfather, who had taken considerable responsibility for her, suddenly died. The grandmother, despondent and ill, made two attempts to take her life. Three different pets during this period were "loved to death."

It is not difficult to understand Aileen's unhappiness and her constant anxiety about "home." Her grandmother reported that Aileen frequently asked about home. Her mother asked counsel because "Aileen says she doesn't want to go home when she is at home and occasionally she asks if we are at home when we are."

In her persistent painting of the ovular red mass, as the full data substantiate,[11] Aileen was expressing her need and deep craving for a home which would give her adequate protection and love. These earliest abstrac-

[10] This does not reflect on what the family tried to give the child. But when the world is made insecure through a broken family situation, children's affectional needs in many instances remain unsatisfied.

[11] As we look into the generalized findings (chaps. ii, iii, and iv), we see how Aileen's closed red mass relates to her behavior pattern and her needs. Work within carefully defined, restricted space frequently has been produced by children who felt shut off, alone, insecure. A tendency to fill in outlined forms has been found in the work of children absorbed in their own feelings. Emphasis on red has been found in the work of children greatly involved in their own emotions either of love and affection or of aggression and hate.

tions of Aileen's bring us closer to her basic needs and drives than does any of her subsequent work.[12]

Abstract or pre-representative paintings and drawings can be, and often are, more expressive of inner feeling than are representative products because the very process of representation involves a conscious awareness of outside stimuli and a reaction to those stimuli rather than a direct expression of self. Even though the child in making a representative drawing may express his own feelings about the objects depicted, still the act of representation involves ideas and awareness of objects outside of himself. It is as the child uses creative media freely without intent to represent that he is most likely to express pure feelings quite free from external factors. It is, accordingly, children's abstract products which most truly reflect their free flow of feelings unbounded by ideas.

In somewhat parallel fashion it is the abstract qualities in the Rorschach ink-blots which evoke deep-seated emotional reactions on the part of Rorschach subjects. Likewise, Ernst Harms[13] found that when he could get juvenile or adult patients to break away from doing representative work and could get them to express themselves in abstractions, painted or drawn, he could obtain insights which had not been apparent in these patients' more realistic pictorial work.

In both the Rorschach and the Harms experimental situations these responses were evoked by *planned* methods and devices. In contrast to this, we have but to observe and analyze the *spontaneous* responses of two-, three-, and four-year-old children in their ordinary daily life to find that they express themselves constantly in abstract and meaningful ways through such varied media as drawing, painting, clay modeling, block building, and dramatic play.

Aileen's self-expression through painting is not, in other words, unique. *Archie's* and *Elinor's* paintings (Pls. 13 through 21,) as well as all the children described in following chapters, suggest how other children over a period of time persistently express the forces that motivate their lives. Anyone willing to pause long enough to make day-by-day observations of children's paintings in a nursery school will discover that each child's

[12] If we are to understand why children paint as they do, we must know something about their background and behavior. Accordingly, a biographical summary is included of each child whose art work is used as illustration. As a clue to understanding, and perhaps to formulation of new hypotheses, readers are urged to refer to each child's biography as they look at his paintings and read about him in the text. Biographical summaries appear in alphabetical order at the end of the book.

[13] "Child Art as an Aid in the Diagnosis of Juvenile Neuroses," *American Journal of Orthopsychiatry*, I (April, 1941), 192–309.

paintings are highly individual and uniquely his own. The differences observed between the paintings of various individuals at the nursery-school level are not likely to be in recognizable subject matter but rather in the abstract treatment of color, space, line, and form. How these aspects of painting will be handled by an individual child seems to be largely out of the conscious control of the individual and to reflect general, and perhaps universal, tendencies. Each aspect also seems to make its own specific contribution to the expression of personality. Our findings lead us to the following conclusions:

*a*) Color tends to give the clearest clues as to the nature and degree of intensity of the child's emotional life.

*b*) Line and form tend to give the most intelligible clues to (1) the amount of energy the child is expending, (2) the degree of control the child is exercising, (3) the direction in which that control is operating.

Color and line and form considered together are likely to indicate the balance which exists between the child's impulsive drives, on the one hand, and his overt, controlled behavior, on the other hand.

*c*) Space usage and spatial pattern tend to give less a picture of the child's inner life than a picture of the child as he relates, and is reacting, to his environment.[14]

We shall gain further insights into children and their paintings as we systematically investigate different individuals' treatment of color, space, line, and form.

---

[14] Too free application of the generalized framework here offered can to a large extent be avoided if (*a*) the generalized tendencies are treated as tentative findings subject to further study, (*b*) the individual's painting characteristics are studied in relation to one another, and (*c*) the painting characteristics are studied in relation to all other known reactions of the child. Equally as important as the study of products is the study of behavior while painting. Such behavior, when compared with behavior in other situations, often gives a significant clue to the value of the painting medium for the given child. Comparison of products with overt reactions, both while painting and in other situations, frequently provides a basis for discovering whether there is harmony or conflict between the child's natural drives and those stimulated by outside forces. Children's verbalizations while painting many times offer invaluable clues. Free association, in particular (in contrast to purposive naming) has repeatedly supplied the missing element needed to bring the other phases of the child's activities into focus. Further findings will substantiate and make more meaningful this footnote, which is here set forth to curb too quick acceptance and application of the general findings offered.

# CHAPTER II

## INDIVIDUAL DYNAMICS EXPRESSED THROUGH
## COLOR USAGE

COLOR more than any other single aspect of painting has been of particular value in offering clues to the nature and the degree of intensity of children's emotional life. One of the most readily perceived trends in children's paintings is that strong interest in using color tends to be paralleled by strong emotional drives.

*The parallelism between color emphasis and strong emotions* is supported by the following findings:

*a*) Children tend to express a primary interest in color (in contrast to line and form) during that stage of development when they are operating largely at an impulsive level. Their expressed interest in color decreases as their impulsive emotional drives become tempered and as controlled adaptive behavior comes to the fore.[1]

*b*) Color tends to be more intense and persistent among girls than among boys. Here, again, a parallelism with emotions is reflected, for girls have been found by many investigators to manifest emotion more than do boys.[2]

*c*) When a group of children who emphasized color was compared with a group of children who focused largely on line and form, the latter group stood out for their greater self-control, their greater concern with external stimuli, and their higher frequency of reasoned (in contrast to impulsive) behavior.

The parallelism between color emphasis and strong emotional drives becomes even more obvious as we turn from generalized comparisons to the

---

[1] Not only is this finding supported by our data, but Perrine (*Let the Child Draw* [New York: F. L. Stokes & Co., 1936]) makes a similar observation: "At three or four years of age sensitiveness to color perception is at its height. From that time forward, unless developed, it tends to give way to advancing intellect. This one may note in any exhibit of work showing upper and lower grades. By beginning at the upper grades and proceeding downward toward the kindergarten, one invariably feels an increasing predominance of the color appeal."

[2] See chap. v; see also Florence Goodenough, *Measurement of Intelligence by Drawing* (Yonkers: World Book Co., 1926); La Berta W. Hattwick, "Sex Differences in Behavior of Preschool Children," *Child Development*, December, 1937; and Bruno Klopfer, "Rorschach Reactions in Early Childhood," *Rorschach Reserve Exchange*, V (1940), 1–23.

study of individual children. Repeatedly in the course of the study it will be noted:

*a*) That those individual children who had strong emotional drives which were evidenced in their easel paintings tended also to exhibit strong preferences for certain colors and to express themselves with color and mass effects rather than through line and form. Among such children were *Aileen, Angela,* and *Elaine.*[3]

*b*) That children like *Ann, Alan, Albert,* and *Archie,*[4] who were fighting against the expression of strong emotional drives, tended by one means or another to avoid the warm colors (red, yellow, and orange) which were, in turn, most closely identified with the expression of strong emotions. Ann usually used one of the warmer colors but almost always overlaid it with blue and green. Alan and Albert avoided color emphasis by turning early in their school experiences to focus on line and form. Archie avoided warm colors almost altogether, emphasizing black and green instead.

*c*) That children like *Aileen* and *Andy,* who were emotionally involved and who found an outlet for their feelings through painting, tended to cling to the color-mass method of expressing themselves long after other children of their age and of comparable development had moved on to more representative and more realistic drawing and painting.

*d*) That as children who were ordinarily repressed or restrained broke into freer activity, they tended to show freer color usage in their painting and crayon work. *Ann* and *Albert* exemplified this finding. Griffiths made a similar observation: "Degree of freedom in drawing in general and in color use seems closely related to the degree of emotional inhibition present as well as to intellectual development. In one case, breaking into color use was accompanied by increase of monologue and greater pleasure in general, all pointing to loosening of inhibitions."[5]

*e*) That older children like *Aileen, Andy,* and *Gilbert,* as observed during later years in our follow-up study, inclined periodically when they became emotionally disturbed to revert to the color-mass method of expressing themselves. This was true even though they were past the impulsive stage of development and were customarily expressing themselves through representative form drawing. The need of these children to express themselves through color-mass painting was in some cases particularly marked be-

[3] Aileen, Pls. 3–12; Angela, Pls. 22–33; Elaine, Pls. 68–74.

[4] Ann, Pls. 51–55; Alan, Pls. 64–67; Archie, Pls. 13–17.

[5] Ruth Griffiths, *A Study of Imagination in Early Childhood* (London: Kegan Paul, Trench, Trubner & Co., 1935), p. 347.

cause the children spontaneously returned to the easels, although they had shown no interest in painting for some time past.

A most striking example of this was *Angela*, who during our two years of observation reverted three times to color-mass painting while absorbed in a deep-felt emotional problem concerning the birth of a sibling. Each time, as soon as the problem was resolved, Angela began to express herself at a higher level of representative work than she had previously used (see Pls. 22–33).

Although these parallels between color and emotional sensitivity definitely suggest a close association between the two, far stronger evidence of such relationship was obtained through study of the usage of specific colors as these related to the emotional lives of individual children.

There is something fantastic about the notion that among young children the use of red connotes one emotional state, the use of yellow a different one, and the use of black means something different again. Although to an amazing extent this was found to be true, a bald statement of this kind smacks of charlatanism. A nondiscriminating use of the facts which we shall present would be just that.

Yet systematic and objective investigation of the present field brought us to the conclusion that color, spontaneously used by young children of the age range studied, quite specifically seems to be a language of the feelings for which there tends to be, in our culture at least, a quite general, if not universal, code. Once children begin to use colors realistically rather than symbolically, they take on different meanings or values than are found in the early years of abstract color usage.

Support for the foregoing statements derives both from individual case studies and from quantitative group analyses. Evidence will be presented in the rough framework suggested by the quantitative analyses.

### DIFFERENCES IN THE USE OF WARM AND COLD COLORS

As one observes children's paintings, one discovers that some children consistently choose warm colors, such as red, yellow, and orange, whereas others choose cooler colors, such as blue, black, green, and brown.

Those children who consistently favored warm colors tended, for the most part, to manifest the free emotional behavior, the warm affectionate relations, and the self-centered orientation natural for children of this age. Typical behavior was characterized as "sympathetic with others," "dependent on others for affection," "co-operative in play," "good adjustment." Such exceptions as were found had various implications but were in keeping with the general trend toward free emotional behavior, as, for example, in the case of *Aileen*, in whom unusually long preoccupation with red paralleled self-centered orientation and an absorption in her own highly operative emotions.[6]

The relatively free and easy emotional pattern exhibited by most of the children who used warm colors, together with age data, indicate that warm colors are the expected **color** preference of nursery-school children who are developing in usual or typical fashion.[7]

Those children who consistently favored cold colors tended as a group to stand out for their highly controlled, overadaptive behavior. They were likely to be critical, assertive, and/or undemonstrative toward others. Typical behavior was characterized as "lead through ideas," "intellectual interests," "aggressive in contacts," "determined will," "selfish," "play alone," and "unaware and independent of adults."

Our observations suggest that individual nursery-school children who consistently focused on cold colors tended to be restraining or repressing their inner feelings. Their paintings were likely to reflect their overt behavior and often gave no clue as to their inner drives. For some children, as *Jill* (Pls. 60–62), high adult expectancies seemed to be a strong factor in this split between deeply felt personal desires and overt behavior. As a matter of fact, the children who used cold colors tended as a group to come from homes which exerted undue pressure toward control.[8] Specific fears at a given time, as in the case of *Elaine* (Pls. 68–74), or general fear and avoidance of all emotions because of previous painful associations, as apparently occurred in the case of *Alan* (Pls. 64–67), were among the factors which seemed to underlie focus on cold colors during the early years.

Developmental data also support the view that emphasis on cold colors is not natural for the two- to four-year-old child who is adjusting happily.[9] Once children have progressed naturally, as most of them do, from impulsive behavior to the level of conscious control and from mass techniques to

[6] Judgment as to whether a warm-color painting is the product of happy or of unhappy adjustment will depend upon various aspects of the painting and their interrelationships, rather than on color per se. The basis for this statement will become clearer when the significance of line and space usage is understood.

[7] This relationship holds true only at the nursery level (see chap. v).

[8] Children who develop freely and without undue pressure during the early years are more likely than others to lay a sound basis for understanding and sympathetic and friendly (or warm) relationships, while children who are pushed or forced toward control are more likely, in consequence, to develop avoiding reactions and dominating and competitive (or cold) attitudes toward others.

[9] See chap. v.

work with line and form, a preference for cold or cooler colors becomes natural, and such preference no longer reflects inadequate adjustment. In fact, for a child who has naturally progressed toward controlled behavior and toward work with line, form, and colder colors, a reversion to warm colors (and to mass technique) tends to occur, as previously indicated in the case of *Angela* and others, only at periods when emotional responses are heightened or disturbed.

### SYMBOLIC USE OF DIFFERENT COLORS
#### CHILDREN WHO PREFERRED RED

Those nursery-school children who outstandingly preferred to paint with red tended as a group to parallel in their behavior the children who preferred warm colors. As a group they inclined to react more freely (that is, as they felt) and to be less concerned with external standards than were the other children in the group. They showed relatively sound adjustment for their stage of development. Among these children were *Edith*, *Hope*, *Ray*, and *Stella*. Illustrative of the trends in their usual development were: "good relation with adults and children," "co-operative in play," "generally good adjustment."

A number of other children *not* ordinarily outgoing or easily affectionate in their relationships with adults and children—e.g., *Alan*, *Andrew*, *Edward*, *Esther*, *Floyd*, *Henry*, *Jimmy*, *Norman*, and *Ross*—were found to use red much more frequently and more freely than was their wont during certain periods when they were observed to be more sociable, happy, and outgoing than usual.

But, even during the nursery-school years, focus on red did not always reflect happy adjustment. When it was observed (*a*) in a highly repetitive pattern and to the relative exclusion of other colors or (*b*) during a period when there was a brief but intensive drive to use red exclusively, it seemed more specifically related to personality problems than to usual developmental factors. In such instances, use of red tended to reflect an accute emotional experience which might be either hostile or affectionate in nature.

The particular way in which a given child used red frequently offered a clue as to which emotion he was expressing. *Anita* (Pl. 35), *Archie*, and various other children used red in *heavy, straight, often vertical strokes* at periods characterized by hostile, assertive behavior. In contrast, *Hope* and some other children used red in *light circular strokes* at times when they were having unusually pleasant, gentle, affectionate relationships with others.

*Red used to express feelings that have to do with affection.*—As noted both in the text and in her detailed biography, *Aileen*'s entire record and her paintings make evident her craving for red paint and also her unsatisfied desire for affection. Her carefully restricted masses, painted within definite limits, seemed symbolically to express the limited amount of affection that she thought was hers. It is of interest that on two different occasions when *Aileen* was observed at the easel directly following experiences that seemed to give her great emotional satisfaction she used red more lavishly than usual. Her records read:

1-11-38.  *Aileen* wanted red, but none was available. *George*, to whom she was at that time particularly attached, was using red on the opposite side of the double easel. He voluntarily gave his jar of red paint to Aileen. She said, and then repeated as though deeply stirred: "He let me have red, he let me have red." Her product that day was not so restricted as usual.

2-1-39.  *Aileen* spent a happy morning in dramatic play with *Perry* as bridegroom. They had a marriage ceremony and a reception that included dancing. From the doll corner, where they had been playing, Aileen went to the easel. This was her most expansive red painting of the year.

Similar expression was observed among other children who craved some demonstration of affection.

*Phoebe*, an adopted child rejected by her foster-mother, was by nature high spirited and impulsive. She did not paint very frequently but whenever she did, her product seemed to reflect her prevailing mood. She tended to use red following or accompanying experiences that brought her affectional satisfaction. Phoebe's mother ordinarily not only did not express affection for her but did not allow the housekeeper to do so. During November, Phoebe's foster-mother was out of the city, and the housekeeper was freely expressing affection for Phoebe, whose school behavior and activities reflected her greater ease. On 11-23-38 Phoebe played happily at school with *Paula*, who, as mother, gave Phoebe, "her baby," much attention and affection. Following this dramatic play, Phoebe went to the easel and produced a painting showing widespread use of red. This was in contrast to her rather somber paintings of preceding days. Five days later, on 11-28-38, there was another red painting under circumstances similar to the above. Within a few days Phoebe's mother returned to the city. On 12-2-38, when Phoebe did her first painting after her mother's return, she overlaid red with cold and somber colors.

*Gloria* evidenced a great desire for love and affection in her play activities. This seemingly stemmed from too early home stimulation toward self-reliance and control. Her desire for some demonstration of affection was revealed in her dramatic play and occasionally in her painting. Although she seldom used red, she frequently talked of it. Her verbalization, together with such incidents as are recounted below, suggest a very real feeling about red and its probable association with her desire for more evidence of affection than she was receiving. The records indicate that Gloria was more released while at finger painting on 10-22-37 and 11-13-37 than at any time earlier in the year. On these dates she first spontaneously sought red. On 11-17-37 Gloria drew concentric circles of red and yellow. The larger outer circles in red were named "Father" and "Mother." The smaller inner circle was entitled "Me." [10] On 3-14-38 it was noted that for some time past Gloria had been using

---

[10] Our later analysis of this drawing, supported by other material (see Griffiths, *op. cit.*, p. 305), indicates that *Gloria* was symbolically expressing her wish for security and her desire to be surrounded by love.

red paint in a closed ovular form. (Although in a different nursery school, her paintings of this period are rather like *Aileen's* closed red forms.) While painting, on the same date, Gloria said "Isn't this a beautiful shade of red? I love red." During this period of red easel painting, Gloria went one day to the clay and made an ovular form of which she said, "Little house, me inside." This, again, suggests her desire to feel surrounded and secure, and it reinforces our belief that Gloria's use of red was significant.

*Virginia* and *Harriet* used red in restricted masses, and each seemed to be craving additional dependence and affection.

*Red used to express hostility or aggression.*—In contrast to the foregoing, the following children used red during periods of hostile emotion, and they characteristically showed one or more of the following techniques at such times: (*a*) heavy, often vertical strokes; (*b*) long, wide strokes covering most or all of the painting page; (*c*) heavy strokes overlaying other colors.

*Sally* (8-24-38) overheard the teacher make a favorable remark to another child about her new dress. Always resentful of attention to others, Sally began to bite her nails, turned to the easel, and produced a painting in which red was painted over blue with such forceful scrubbing that the paper tore. 11-1-38, Sally turned to crayons, selected red in contrast to her customary use of cold colors, and began scribbling hard and fast. As she did so she exclaimed, "Dick ran into my leg and I am mad at him" (Pl. 34).

*Archie* (10-11-38) had been using blue paint. As he left the easel he carried the painting brush along with him and spattered the paint as he walked. The teacher quietly called this to his attention. Archie returned angrily to the easel. He dipped his brush in the red paint, covered his earlier work with long, vertical red strokes, and as he did so said, "Firecrackers."

*Quinton* (3-24-39) produced his first red painting of the year, his third painting of the given day. No specific behavior incident for this date is recorded, though Quinton was described around this time as becoming more assertive at school. Five days later Quinton used a shovel as a weapon against another child. This was his first real aggression at school. Here, as was frequently the case, a child's paintings expressed his generalized emotional state, which a bit later was crystallized into words or actions.

*Edward* (11-19-38) produced a painting in which red predominated. Blue, his usual color preference, did not appear. This was one of the rare days when Edward was aggressive. On the playground he hurt *Floyd* and then remarked: "I had to make Floyd cry."

*Louis* (12-2-38) produced his only all-red painting on this date, which was the only day on which overt anger was recorded at school.

*Anita* with great intensity produced some incrusted red paintings and some similar red-crayon drawings on 11-20-38 and 11-24-38. These followed her smearing of the furniture at home with red lipstick (11-7-38). Throughout this period her temper flared on the slightest provocation, and she made numerous destructive attacks on materials (Pl. 35).

While full-page strokes in red have most frequently been observed in the work of children who were exhibiting aggressive or hostile behavior, this relationship has not always held.

*Glen* was overtly one of the meekest, most infantile four-year-olds in his group, yet with both paints and crayons he usually produced heavy red, vertically stroked, full-page masses. His painting and crayon work of that period offered the only observable clue to the possibility that Glen had strong aggressive feelings smoldering inside of him. As Glen's school activities were followed in subsequent years, it was found that he had shed his submissive role and become the boisterous assertive boy one might have expected, had one tried during his nursery-school years to judge him solely from his paintings and drawings. Apparently, painting and drawing had been a real outlet and form of release for him during the earlier nursery years. He felt free to express with paints what he found impossible to express more overtly.

While Glen's use of paints was not entirely unusual, it was not typical. Although a number of children used easel paints to express feelings not otherwise revealed or released, most of those who were in conflict tended in their paintings to reflect in quite different or contrasting ways both their overt behavior pattern and their conflicting inner drives. Many children like Glen, who had strong emotional impulses which were not finding direct expression, tended first to use red and then overlay it with some colder color or colors.

The characteristic painting patterns of *Freda* and *Tilly* illustrate the tendency to overlay red when they were overtly repressing aggressive drives.

*Harriet*'s and *Jessica*'s paintings at certain specified times exemplified this finding. Harriet, ordinarily a reserved child, painted in what was, for her, unusual fashion on each of the two days during which she was having happy interplay with *Gloria*. On both of these days she produced three predominantly red paintings. On 5-3-38, Harriet arrived at school after a quarrel with Gloria. She went to the easel, painted with red, then overlaid the red with black. From the beginning of the school year, Jessica had been outstanding in the group for her aggressive defiant behavior. During November for a period of time it became evident that she was struggling against her too impulsive reactions and was trying to adapt herself to the group. A frequent plea during those days was "Will you play with me?" Up to this time she had usually worked at the easel with heavy, warm-colored strokes (most often red). On 11-28-38 she painted two short red strokes, then quickly covered them over and remarked "Bad paint."

Other children having assertive drives, which they covered over with overtly submissive behavior, have been observed to use red very little but to verbalize about it in meaningful fashion.

*Bert*, a boy who was overtly too submissive, seldom used red. When he did so, he tended to overlay it with colder colors. It was Bert's verbalizations over a period of time which gave meaning to his use of red. Between 8-23-37 and 3-28-38 Bert used red paint only six times. In five of these paintings he overlaid red with colder colors, viz., blue or green. On 9-12-38 Bert commented "I'm covering red." In block building during this period he was using a red block as a traffic signal. He would frequently comment, "Red block says Stop." He was at the same time carrying on much fantasy concerning fire.[11] Typical remarks of this nature were: "I'm building a big tank. Nothing will catch on fire. This is where the

---

[11] "Fire" in young children's fantasy is frequently associated with red and with danger. Bert, like Angela, used red in association with concepts of fire. Both of these children frequently masturbated. Relatedness between masturbation, use of red, and fire fantasy has been suggested; this perhaps merits further investigation.

water finally goes. It will be really deep in a minute. Look at the furnace. Don't get too near my fire."

The only painting which Bert made during the afore-mentioned period in which red was not overlaid was paralleled by the assertive remark, "I want it to say Go." Only once after March did Bert use red, and then it was again placed on top of other colors. In this painting (made on 3-27-38), red was painted over yellow and green. This was the last painting Bert made during the school year. It is of interest to note that from that time on, Bert's behavior, like his painting, went into reverse. He became assertive and resistant. (In this situation, we again note that an inner generalized emotion was expressed through painting before it was crystallized in overt behavior.)

*Aldo*, whose mother died when he was born and whose father for a long time rejected him, was somewhat ambivalent about his masculinity and also was in considerable conflict between wanting to be infantile and wanting to grow up. Like *Bert*, Aldo was overtly submissive and like him, too, he spoke often of red (and yellow)—but rarely went into action with either color.

### CHILDREN WHO PREFERRED BLUE

Those two-, three-, and four-year-old children whom we observed to prefer blue in easel painting tended as a group to be in the process of developing away from impulsive emotional reactions toward controlled behavior.

Analyses of individual children suggest that emotional control at this level may or may not be in harmony with the child's basic drives. Two groups of children and two types of painting patterns that support this statement have been differentiated. The children of one group tended overtly to conform to external standards which they basically were not accepting. The children of the other group were also conforming to external standards, but they apparently were more ready and willing to accept them.[12]

The paintings of these two groups of children were characterized by quite different use of blue:

*a*) Blue paint was put on by the children in the one group with tense, sharp strokes, in concentrated masses, and it was often used to overlay warmer colors. The tense quality so obvious in many of the paintings, considered in relation to the children who did them, suggested the term "*controlled anxiety*."[13] This term actually characterized the status quo of those children at the particular times when the paintings were done.[14] The tense

[12] Children who emphasized blue and who were overtly conforming to external standards which they basically were not accepting were likely to be repressed and to have come from homes in which standards were exceedingly high. These children were inclined "to have no special friends," "to talk little," "to play alone," "to watch others." In contrast to them were the children who emphasized blue and showed more adaptive behavior. They tended to have "good relations with children," "interest in materials," "long attention span," "relevant verbalizations with others."

[13] E.g., see Pl. 36.

[14] Adults, we learned after our observations had been recorded, also tend to use *blue* under conditions of controlled anxiety (see Ernst Harms, "Child Art as an Aid in the Diagnosis of Juvenile Neuroses," *American Journal of Orthopsychiatry*, XI, No. 2 [April, 1944], 191–209).

stroking, the heavy restricted masses, and the use of blue (symbolic of control), all occurring together, suggest that, at the time of the painting at least, those children were emotionally driven rather than consciously controlled.

*b*) In antithesis to the foregoing, was the group of children who generally used blue to produce line and form rather than mass. They usually made representative constructive paintings, which frequently had delicate form quite in contrast to the mass effect previously described. Naming of their products was frequent among this group. The lighter tone quality, the directed type of activity, as well as the children's verbalizations and adaptive behavior, suggested the descriptive term "sublimated blue."

*Controlled-anxiety blue.*—Among the children observed who used blue in tensely stroked mass effects, the following are illustrative:

During the months when *Bert* used red very little and then practically always overlaid it with cold somber colors, he used much blue in tensely stroked masses. During this period he appeared withdrawn and worried. He was apparently expressing the conflict he felt between the family's overemotional concern, which drove him toward infantile behavior, and their high expectancies, which pushed him toward more control than he was ready to accept.

*Edward*'s paintings exemplified both controlled anxiety and sublimated blue. At the time when Edward was working in somber mass effects he was full of fears and took no part in play with others (Pl. 36). He often burst forth into a stream of unprovoked comments, such as "Don't put your face up to the window! The glass might cut you. . . . . You mustn't hurt the guinea pigs. You mustn't say Boo. It would scare them. . . . . I'm not going to scare them. . . . . I'm just going to sit and listen to them talking." Home observations revealed unusually high standards and continuous feeding of ideas, facts, and restrictions which were beyond his experience or emotional readiness. Edward spoke of and asked for blue more than for any other color. At the end of the year, when Edward produced "Spider Web on the Grass" (Pl. 37), he was showing less anxiety and better adaptation within the group. The following year his better adaptation continued, and his earlier focus on blue gave way to more balanced use of colors.

*Ruth* was similar to *Edward* in her spontaneous expression of anxieties and fears. She, too, often broke into unprovoked and irrelevant comments, such as "I didn't hit her." In painting, Ruth frequently used blue in tensely stroked, somber masses. Her verbal comments, such as "Girl crying," supported the impression created by the color-mass effect of her paintings.[15]

In addition to the consistent worriers whose anxiety-blue paintings expressed their controlled anxieties, there are many sporadic instances in which children's anxious, restrained behavior was paralleled by blue paintings that were in direct contrast to such children's usual painting patterns and their usual overt reactions:

[15] Other children who rather consistently used blue in tensely stroked, somber masses and were inclined to show (*a*) an overt pattern of restraint, (*b*) symptoms of emotional drives obviously in opposition to their controlled overt behavior, and (*c*) a general pattern of anxiety were Ann, Barbara, Clarence, Dora, Ethel, Elinor, Freda, Joe, Polly.

*Aileen* one day turned from her then characteristic red mass to the production of seven paintings which created the controlled-anxiety blue effect. Home reports around this date gave a picture of much family tension and of considerable crying and unhappiness on the part of Aileen's mother. On another occasion, Aileen turned to the controlled-anxiety use of blue on her return from an illness during which time her grandfather had died.

*Sidney*, immediately following a trip to the dentist, produced with crayons two intense purplish-blue masses that were in striking contrast to his other relatively pastel work.

Often these isolated instances of paintings done with anxiety-blue effects have occurred directly after children have had a protracted stay at home. As might be expected in the light of the foregoing, such children came from homes in which expectancies and demands were overhigh and where illness created more than needed anxiety in the child.

*Elinor* used the controlled-anxiety color-mass technique after a week at home with mother and grandmother. On the morning of her return she had had a tantrum before she came to school. Her mother told the teacher that Elinor was "emotionally disturbed." Elinor appropriately called the first of her paintings, "Clouds in Stormy Weather." She continued with this general effect for many days.

*Sandy* produced three paintings of heavy blue, overlaid on red, on her first day back after an extended illness. These were her only overlaid paintings of the year.[16]

*Sublimated blue.*—In contrast to the foregoing are the following examples of children who used blue for constructive outline patterns.[17] Many of them were in the process of making the swing toward adaptive behavior. They followed the back-and-forth swing that is characteristic of usual development. Changes in painting pattern paralleled changes in behavior.

*Barry* was a boy who willingly and consciously was trying to control his impulsive drive and to adapt himself to environmental situations and expectancies. He was consciously focused on blue (i.e., he asked for it) and used it freely. For the most part, blue was used to produce interrelated lines and forms. In the few instances when it was used to overlay warmer colors, his verbalizations suggest awareness or conscious intent: On 12-2-38, Barry painted heavy blue over red. He said: "I'm going to paint one color on top of another. I'm going to make a man. Now you can't see his leg. Look! I'm painting him red. My mommy would like to see him. She'll be awfully surprised to see him red. It is my mommy." (Note: Mother might indeed have "seen red," since red tends to reflect impulsive emotional responses and "Mommy," a professional woman, strongly stressed control.)

On 1-6-39, Barry again painted heavy blue on red. He said: "One is blue and one is red. I want to take it home after I've finished. This is swell." (In real life Barry, as well as his parents, was pleased with the subjugation of emotion to control, as suggested by this painting.) On 1-10-39, Barry used red, yellow, blue, and green with intermingled and overlaid techniques. Cold colors were predominantly on top. Barry said: "I have green. I'm using green. Joe, I'd like to paint blue over all the other colors."

On 1-21-39, Barry made a full-page mass of red, yellow, orange, blue, and green, all

---

[16] Sally and Phoebe also came from homes in which standards were high. Both of them tended to turn to somber mass use of blue following periods at home.

[17] Angela periodically illustrated this trend.

intermingled. He said, "I want to take this home to Mommy. I used orange.[18] I'm going to cover all the paper. I'm using blue. I like the orange color, too. After I paint, I'm going to wash my hands because I have paint on them. Mommy will like this. I don't know [he appeared concerned], I didn't leave any space. I covered it all up." Here his obvious concern over producing a controlled product, associated with "what Mommy will think," reached its clearest verbal level. The limiting of his comments on color to orange and blue, along with the verbal content, suggest that he was well on his way in his swing away from impulsive emotional reactions toward control. [19]

*Esther*, like Barry, was consciously and for the most part happily trying to adapt herself to the controlled, socially acceptable pattern which accorded with the family's standards. In painting during her first year in nursery school, Esther, then three years old, preferred blue to other colors available. Twenty-two of her thirty-six paintings were blue. Green, which to a large extent she used interchangeably with blue, was also a favorite color. A majority of Esther's products had delicate linear quality and received such "elevated" titles as "Rain Drops," "Moon in the Sky," "Moonlight on the Snow."

As frequently happened in this study, exceptions tended to prove the rule. During a two-month period Esther broke away from the above-described delicate linear pattern and took to making somber blue masses. During this time, Esther was unhappy and defenseless in the nursery group. She no longer played the big-sister role. Instead, her dramatic play during these months suggested fear—fear of bears and lions in particular. Home reports simultaneously indicated night waking and terrors.

As we reviewed Esther's paintings, we realized that her overt anxieties and fears had probably been foreshadowed in her earlier paintings entitled "Dog Chasing Kitty" (Pls. 38–42).

*George* alternated to and away from a controlled adaptive behavior pattern that was in each case paralleled by swings to and away from controlled constructive use of blue in outline form. The following three periods stand out in George's records:

*a*) A period from December 9 to January 10, in which George predominantly used blue for painting construction patterns. A recurrent name for his products during this period was "Sky." During this time, teachers reported that George, who had earlier delighted in attacking other children, almost never hurt children any more. During this period, also, for the first time, George began to relax at rest time.

*b*) During the next few months (January 10–April 6) warm colors became prevalent in George's paintings. Red ran through his work in a pronounced and persistent thread. At this time George became more assertive and gayer. He went through extremes of cruelty, teasing, and affectionate behavior.

*c*) From April 6 on, George went through another period of blue constructive painting. Teachers reported that he was more calm and quiet. His own intense drives were no longer apparent. He tended to adapt to the group.

So many children have been observed to turn toward constructive use of blue during their fourth to fifth year at the same time that they were nat-

[18] See discussion of the color orange, p. 41.

[19] Aspiration toward "high living" or a high standard of living took concrete form in block building with Barry as with various other children. Barry's verbalizations consistently emphasized the *high* element typical of his structures: "Big house. Look how high. Need a chimney. Tower forty feet high. The steeple. The elevator. 'Fraid it's going to fall. Not going to make it *so high* it will fall. See if you can reach *that high*. I built it *awfully high*."

urally making a transition toward controlled adaptive behavior that this may be considered as an expected tendency or pattern.[20] Other evidence that blue is associated with control is the fact that hyperactive children[21] have been observed to choose blue on their calmer, more co-operative days. The dearth of blue in the paintings of highly emotional children also supports this view.

Consistent with the parallel between blue linear work and adaptive behavior is the observed tendency for first representations to be done in blue.[22]

The only two recognizable form paintings made by *Edward* during the first year of observation were two "head-foot" men outlined in blue.

The only recognizable representation by *Henry* during his year in nursery school was a blue bus, quite in contrast to his usual brownish and heavily dotted mass.

The only human representation made by *Sidney* was in blue.

During observation in a nursery school located near New York, one of the authors observed a five-year-old painting a picture of a house. The teacher was excited because this was Bobby's first representative form painting. She pointed to his earlier work. They were all full-page masses of predominantly warm colors. The outlined house was blue.

The outstanding frequency with which children choose blue to make their first letters underlines the fact that use of blue parallels conscious control and aspiration:

*Elaine* tended to choose blue to write her initial.

*Ross* chose blue for his first attempt at writing and commented as he scribbled: "Writing I'm three years old."

*Esther, Patty,* and many others chose blue for similar first adventures in writing.

*Stanley* used blue to make a wavy horizontal line, with the comment, "My name on it."

*Specific conflicts associated with the use of blue.*—As we have studied the behavior of children of nursery-school age, we have found two types of conflict that recurrently are associated with use of blue:

*a)* One frequent conflict during these years is that between the desire to cling to the infantile role, on the one hand, and the desire to grow up, on the other hand. This conflict frequently becomes accentuated when a new baby arrives.

Children in the throes of this conflict have in many instances been observed to choose blue and yellow for their painting. Yellow is often used to express the desire to remain infantile,[23] while blue, as already indicated, is

---

[20] Children in addition to those already cited who also illustrated this trend were Alan, Andrew, Bee, Eric, Timothy.

[21] Illustrative are Andy, Anita, Jessica, Kenneth, Paul.

[22] "Consistent" because representations are in themselves the result of control and adaptation. They are adaptations to things seen.

[23] See discussion of the use of the color yellow, pp. 29–33.

used to express drives that have to do with being more "grown-up" and controlled. As a rule, the order in which the colors are put on tells the story of the child's overt behavior. If the child is really trying to grow up, blue is likely to be on top with yellow underneath, whereas if the desire to remain infantile is stronger, we find blue covered over and yellow on top.

Examples of this usage are given in a subsequent section.

*b*) A conflict which likewise reflects ambivalence has to do with the child's desire, on the one hand, to smear and be dirty and, on the other hand, to be clean in order to meet adult standards and to receive adult approval. This conflict is often a major one among young children.

Children in conflict between the desire to smear and the desire to meet cleanliness standards frequently show high usage of the colors blue and brown (or orangish-brown). Blue in these instances has been the color apparently associated with cleanliness; brown the color associated with the desire to smear. The two colors have in several instances been used in contrasting ways on the same product: in some paintings one color has been used to overlay the other, and in other paintings the colors have been applied quite differently on the separate halves of the painting page. The one color has been used perhaps in clean, clear strokes and the other to make smeary, dabby, dirty effects.[24]

*Danny*, four and one-half years old, produced anxiety-blue paintings at the time his parents and older brother were putting pressure on him to enforce bowel control. Danny was tense and resistant. After Danny's parents left for a holiday, Danny for the first time began to come to school alone, and he more or less got on his own. His quite evident emotional release was paralleled by his release (*a*) through smeary and dabbed use of blue and brown paints, (*b*) more frequent and aggressive use of clay, and (*c*) smearing with mud on the playground. Within a month he had voluntarily established defecation control. In painting he had worked away from mass use of blue and smeary browns to a clean, constructive pattern with varied use of color (see Pls. 43–46).

*David* and *Don*, like Danny, used brown and blue in contrasting ways while they were in conflict over establishing bowel control.

There were other children whose palettes showed some variation of the brown-blue combination, who evidenced great concern over cleanliness in general rather than a specific conflict over bowel control. These children tended in their overt behavior to put an undue amount of stress on neatness and orderliness. Problems in the area of elimination, if present, tended to be in the direction of constipation rather than lack of control. Only in their

[24] Another color combination used to reflect the desire to smear and be dirty, and also the more specific interest in elimination, was a muddy yellow-green. For examples of this see pp. 35–36, Fredrika (Pls. 56–59), and Jill (Pls. 60–67).

paintings, so far as we observed, could one catch the basic conflict between their desires and their overt behavior:

*Rita*'s paintings expressed a drive that was apparently quite at odds with her too clean and highly controlled behavior pattern. (This included a tendency toward constipation.) When Rita entered school, it was apparent that she had been continuously directed, not only in her routines but in her play activities, by a mother who was tense, anxious, and highly critical. The mother, interested in drawing, had taught Rita to draw alphabet letters and human representations. Particularly at first, Rita felt lost during periods of free play when no adult was directing her. In the course of the year it became clear that easel painting was her favorite activity. At first, Rita painted only human representations or alphabet letters. Blue was her most frequent color choice. As she became freer and happier at school, she broke away from the mother-taught, conventional forms, and her painting took on a left-right contrasting pattern. Blue, the color associated with control and learned responses, was most frequently used for painting clear-cut recognizable forms; brown and dirty orange were most often used to make smeary dabs. Rita sometimes expressed her conflict by using the right-left pattern (clear blue on the left, dabby brown and orange on the right), and at other times her conflict was expressed by smeary aggressive overpainting of her basic constructive pattern. That painting of this aggressive character offered release seems evident, as on different occasions both teachers and observers noted that Rita was more at ease and relaxed following such painting (Pls. 47–50).

*Dora*, *Jocelyn*, *Sidney*, and *Vera* were other children who came from homes in which cleanliness was particularly stressed. All of them showed parallelism between a too neat pattern in overt behavior and contrasting use of blue and brown in paint or crayon usage. Some of them, like Rita in her left-right paintings, seemed merely to be expressing their conflicts. Others, like Rita in her more heavily overlaid paintings, seemed actually to be working out at the easel the need to smear that they were not free to express in more overt behavior.

### CHILDREN WHO PREFERRED YELLOW

Group data and individual case analyses suggest that children who emphasized yellow tended to stand out because of their dependent, emotional behavior. Age data, together with observations, suggest that yellow may often be a reflection of the infantile stage of development. Characteristics associated with relatively free use of yellow are those of a happy, outgoing individual with such traits as "good relation with children," "sought," "popular," "initiates contacts."

It is as children get older and use yellow along with other colors that a variety of personality factors may be seen in the combined color usage. Yellow in combination with cold colors, particularly when used in contrast with blue, as was frequent, was likely to reveal, as we have seen, a child in conflict between the opposing drives to remain infantile and to grow up.

Children who preferred yellow to blue tended as a group to show more emotional dependence on adults, to have "better relations to adults," were more prone "to seek adult attention" and to be "disregarded by children." In contrast to this, children who preferred blue to yellow were likely to have a more mature objective orientation and more self-control. As a group they tended to be more "self-sufficient" and to show "more interest in materials." Staples'[25] study, like our own, indicated that the strongest interest in yellow was during infancy and the early nursery-school years. She, too, found that, with age, interest in yellow decreased and interest in blue increased.

It is but natural that in a study of two-, three-, and four-year-old children there should be voluminous records indicating how children are caught between the desire to remain infantile and the recognized need to grow up. This problem was repeatedly brought into focus on the arrival or expectancy of a new baby. Then the child, as a rule, felt driven by his own wishes to remain the cared-for baby and at the same time felt pushed toward maturity by the family's expectancies.

*Jimmy* began to overlay yellow with cold colors, especially blue, ten days before his baby brother was born. At the same time, his behavior pattern showed a corresponding change as he focused on oral and elimination interests. There was much spitting, infantile speech, nonsense language, and verbalization that centered around food, eating, and elimination. After three months the smeared and overlaid painting pattern took on more structuralized form, and his behavior returned to its earlier norm.

Because *Gilbert* usually played with blocks and infrequently painted, his paintings done at times of emotional crises were of special interest. Around the date of his brother's birth, Gilbert overlaid yellow with blue.

*Alvin,* usually happy and outgoing, turned to crayons and to a lesser degree to paints when he was upset. In both media, during a six weeks' period of tension following his sister's birth, Alvin consistently overlaid yellow with colder colors. Gradually paintings began to show circular forms and intermingled colors. At the same time Alvin began to play in the doll corner where he frequently named the doll after his sister. The home simultaneously reported him as more receptive to the baby sister.

*Tony* also showed reversal in his use of blue and yellow and a corresponding reversal in his behavior around the time his sister was born (1-28-39). Tony made 24 of his 28 paintings between 12-1-38 and 1-13-39. Red and yellow predominated in these paintings, and blue, when used, was overlaid by red or yellow. Circular strokes were pronounced, and circle-filling was frequent. Tony's overt behavior at this time was distinctly infantile. He carried on solitary play and was dependent on both adults and children. Tony made only four paintings after his sister's birth. Three of these were blue and yellow. The last, made eight months after the birth, was a mass of yellow overlaid by blue. In these last four paintings vertical strokes predominated. Tony's overt behavior became more controlled, more masculine and assertive, during the months following his sister's birth.

In a number of other children the conflict over infantilism seemed related not to the birth of a sibling but to the fact that these children felt a

[25] Ruth Staples, "The Responses of Infants to Color," *Journal of Experimental Psychology,* XV (1932), 119–41; also in *Psychology Bulletin,* XXVIII, No. 4 (April, 1931), 297–308.

lack of affectional satisfaction. Many of them tended to overlay yellow with blue, while their behavior suggested infantile desires, which to a greater or less extent were also overlaid—i.e., were restrained or repressed.

Overlaying of yellow with blue or green was recurrent in *Ethel's* paintings, most of which were done within the first four months of school. Ethel's family history revealed a striking lack of affection, and at school she seemed to be solitary and dejected a good deal of the time. She was happiest during play with finger paints, easel paints, clay, water, and during bathroom routines. All these activities require adult supervision and to a degree are associated with a smearing, infantile phase of development. Whenever possible, Ethel tried to secure adult help and attention.

*Andy*, during his second year at school, consistently overlaid his yellow smeary masses with blue or green. At home Andy was rejected and neglected. From time to time he ran away. At school he was unable to maintain warm affectionate relationships with children or adults. His pronounced baby talk, desire to be fed, and focus on oral processes in clay and dramatic play all suggest his strong desire and need for dependency and affection.

*Percy*, like Andy, was a rejected child with a conspicuous lack of interest in maintaining affectional relations with adults. In his few paintings and in his crayon work he consistently covered yellow with blue.

*Ann* was an adopted child who would not talk at home when guests were present, nor would she speak at all for many months after her entrance to nursery school. In her less guarded moments, however, one could note her eager absorbed interest in what others were doing. After months of observing her obvious interest in the crayon table, the director forcibly placed Ann in a chair at the table. Ann took up a crayon and went to work. For days thereafter she sought the crayons. She worked over and over the same circular restricted area. In these drawings, yellow and occasionally other warm colors were covered with blue and green. By the same technique of forcing her into situations in which she had betrayed interest, the teachers introduced her to blocks and clay, in both of which she obviously found satisfaction.[33] Having found the method successful, the teachers introduced Ann to easel painting in the same way.

Ann's first paintings were remarkably like her crayon drawings—a mass of yellow was covered with blue and then with green (sometimes the green and blue were put on in reverse order). For two months Ann persistently painted the same pattern—overlaying yellow with colder colors. Then one day, under rather dramatic circumstances, Ann began to talk. The next day she painted a more widespread mass of yellow—and *did not* cover it over. As soon as she began to talk, she exhibited teasing, negativistic, and other forms of hostile behavior. She was now acting as she basically felt. She no longer needed to cover her yellow. In fact, she now no longer felt the need to paint. Although Ann attended summer school, it was noted that she did not paint for some time. By fall the character of her painting palette had completely changed (see Pls. 51–55).

[33] Ann tended to pile blocks together to make a broad, solid surface on which she would sit or stand. She attempted to appropriate all the material and protected her work from others. Sometimes she sat on it and covered it with her skirt, or again she built an elaborate structure behind a plain wall of blocks (see Pl. 55). Ann liked to break clay into tiny pieces, which she piled one on top of the other. She persistently appropriated all available material and sometimes stayed at the clay table after the others had left so that she could combine everybody else's clay into her mound.

*Barbara* consistently overlaid yellow with blue or green. She was an only child of relatively older parents. Like several other children who overpainted yellow, she had been pushed too early toward patterns of control. Barbara was large for her age. She was quite at ease and adult-like in her reaction to adults. She took a moralistic attitude toward other children and was unable to play with them in natural, childlike fashion. She was highly verbal, precise, and orderly. Infantile drives had obviously been suppressed in actual life as they were symbolically covered over in easel painting. Barbara overlaid yellow with blue. She made clean, defined strokes. When she used green for overlaying, she usually daubed and smeared it.

*Philip*, with but one exception (a painting of red over blue), used yellow as his basic color. No particular color was used as overlay. Philip gave the impression of being unaware of children and adults. He seemed neither to want nor to have a close rapport with any other individual. He was restless and negativistic. He frequently wet himself. He keenly enjoyed water play and similar smeary, wet activities characteristic of an infantile stage of development. Philip's background suggested that his conflict over his long-continued infantilism reflected a situation which was *just the reverse* of those children who were rejected by their parents. Philip was kept infantile by the excessive attentions of his mother, sister, grandmother, maid, and nurse. It was only with great effort that he would in time reject the infantile role. Philip's desire to reject or cover over his infantile life-pattern was reflected in his covering over his yellow base.

*Arnold*, the youngest of four boys, felt under considerable pressure to grow up. He was inclined to be listless and disinterested in activities. He urinated with unusual frequency. During his happier periods, when he apparently felt freer to live out his role of youngest in the family, he used yellow. During other periods when the records indicated low energy and listlessness, Arnold painted with green.

Yellow has been discussed first in relation to other colors rather than by itself because in our observations it was most often found to be used in meaningful fashion in combination with other colors rather than by itself. It is nonetheless true that yellow, in and of itself, when freely used, tends to be associated with happiness, probably of a carefree, infantile type. "Infantile," as here used, connotes a period that is happy and carefree—a period when everything is given and nothing demanded.

Our clearest evidence that children who used yellow most freely (and without overlay) were happy and carefree has been found in the case studies of children who were for the most part unhappy. They were children who used yellow almost not at all but chose to use it during periods when they were particularly happy.

*Aileen* turned to the use of yellow during the week preceding her mother's second marriage, again before Christmas, and again on her birthday—all periods when records of various observers noted that she was unusually happy.

*Andy*, *Eric*, and *Louise*, like Aileen, chose yellow most conspicuously around their birth dates. (Such a choice accords with our foregoing generalization, for it is probable that at no other time after infancy is a child more completely the center of gifts and love and more generally satisfied and carefree than on his birthday.)[26]

*Bert*, *Betty*, *Jean*, and *Jeff*, who characteristically painted a cold palette, turned to yellow during the Christmas season. *Sally*, who had reached the stage of representative work but still chose her colors symbolically, tended to paint her Christmas trees not green but yellow. *Joe* was another child whose string of black, disturbed-looking paintings was broken by the appearance of yellow only around the time of his birthday and at Christmas time.

In children's thoughts, Christmas apparently stands next to birthdays as a happy, attention-getting, self-oriented period.

Consistent with this has been our observation that yellow tends to disappear from children's paintings or to be overlaid during unhappy periods.

*John*, ordinarily a happy child, went through a period of depression, during which time he frequently played at being dead in dramatic play. Simultaneously, he began to overpaint yellow at the easel. On one occasion, while overlaying yellow, he commented, "My daddy didn't like us so he ran away."

*Barry* and *Louise* as a rule were happy children. Both tended to have a thread of yellow running freely through their paintings. Both conspicuously and consistently omitted yellow on days when they were unhappy.

*Alan* and *Margaret* were the two most consistently unhappy children observed. The paintings of both children are characterized by a dearth of yellow.

Consistent with the foregoing trends were the tendencies of some children who put on an act of clownishness and gaiety to splash yellow on top of colder colors.

*Stanley* tended to paint yellow on top of cold colors and to be clownish and gay in the nursery-school groups. His history of tensions and night terrors suggest that there were hidden anxieties beneath his gay exterior.

*Hope* and *Howard* went through a period of teasing, clownish behavior during the spring of their year in nursery school. It was paralleled by a tendency to paint yellow on top of colder colors. [27]

*Ronny* ran smiling around school and often clowned, though his stuttering and other aspects of his behavior revealed him as an anxious child. He frequently splashed yellow over blue.

*Gertrude*, child of a tense, anxious mother, apparently was quite happy and well adjusted. Periodically she painted yellow over blue.

[26] The birthday experience has been for some unloved children the symbol of all they miss and want. Virginia, for example—a child from a broken home, whose craving for love and affection was comparable to Aileen's—made the birthday situation and particularly the Birthday Cake the symbol of her craving. She expressed this symbol again and again in all of her activities, but especially in painting, in clay, and in dramatic play.

[27] One further relationship between yellow and infantilism is suggested by certain data which indicate association between yellow and enuresis. Ann, Freda, and Jessica each used yellow in wet, drippy fashion during periods of enuresis. Other children, to be described later, used yellow with green while concerned with elimination processes.

### CHILDREN WHO PREFERRED GREEN

Those children at the nursery-school level whom we found consistently choosing green tended to show a perceptible lack of strong, overtly expressed emotions. Compared with the group of children who emphasized red, they were likely to be more "self-restrained." The highly controlled behavior of the children who emphasized green was reflected in such characteristics as "self-sufficient," "self-confident," "have ideas for play," "lead through ideas," "carry on relevant verbalizations," "co-operative in routines," "orderly," "careful."

Several of the persistent users of green (as *Alma, Ardis, Dora,* and *Priscilla*) were characterized by their tendency to go along tranquilly and inconspicuously in their groups. They seemed quite content when at play by themselves, yet accepted social relationships when advances were made to them. They belonged to that variety of children who are overlooked in many schoolrooms because they are self-reliant and inconspicuous.

Just as green (the cool color in a visual sense) complements red (the hot, vibrant color), so in terms of personality were the persistent users of green and red likely to be in contrast to one another. Children who predominantly used green appeared to be among the children who were least driven by their emotions. We have already noted that children who emphasized blue tended in their rather controlled emotional reactions to be in contrast with the more emotionally driven users of red. These observations suggest that blue and green may have been used in comparable, or even interchangeable fashion. This was apparently so in some cases, while in others blue and green were used in quite distinctive ways.

Studies of the children who made a distinctive use of blue and green suggest (*a*) that *emphasis on blue* may reflect a sublimation of strong basic feelings, while (*b*) *emphasis on green* may reflect a lack or conscious avoidance (as in *Alan*'s case) rather than a sublimation of strong emotional drives.

Evidence from case studies in support of suggestions *a* and *b* is not sufficiently specific to justify lengthy case presentations. Illustrative of the type of evidence, however, that prompted the foregoing tentative statements are the cases of (1) *Esther*, who pronouncedly preferred blue[28] and who was described by her teachers as capable of extraordinary sublimation for a child of her age, and (2) the serene, adaptive, and extraordinarily unemotional

---

[28] See Pls. 38–42.

behavior of *Alma* and *Priscilla*, each of whom markedly preferred green. We believe that further investigations along this line might be fruitful.

Case studies have revealed another tendency which seems associated with green but which tends to contrast with the characteristics associated with blue. Blue was used largely to depict clean, controlled situations, whereas green, often in combination with yellow, has been frequently sought by children interested in excrements and in allied smeary or dirty activities or processes.

*Fredrika* has given one of the clearest portrayals of the association of green with interest in excrements. Fredrika consistently used green, or a combination of green and yellow, on 14 out of 18 paintings which she made between November 2 and January 13 of her year in nursery school. During this period she carried on verbal interplay with other children, suggesting her interest in elimination and excrements. At clay, during this period, she openly voiced her interest in excrements. Although she did not express her interest in elimination as explicitly while easel painting as she did at clay, the types of products and comments which she made clearly suggest that the same interest was finding expression in somewhat symbolical or sublimated form.

On September 24, Fredrika made her first greenish painting. She called it "An Incinerator." It anticipated the pattern that was to appear in November and persist for some weeks thereafter. On November 15, Fredrika made a greenish mass in which red was slightly intermingled. She said, "Snow, funny snow." While painting and while making this comment, she snickered and made gestures to another child which suggested an association with elimination. On the following day Fredrika made a painting composed of green daubs and masses. The observer caught disjointed comments of "Bowel movement" and "Dog dirt." Playing out of doors earlier in the morning, Fredrika had let the sand trickle through her fingers and at the same time had talked of "pee wee." During these days while rolling the clay, she was overtly discussing "Bowel movements."

On November 18, in contrast to her predominantly green paintings, Fredrika made one in which green was overlaid with red. She commented: "My mother told me what those words mean—those bad words Gloria said." Note that Fredrika overlaid the green color (apparently weighted with dirty connotations) and at the same time suppressed the corresponding words that were socially unacceptable.

On January 4, Fredrika made a comment that was significant in the light of preceding and following episodes. She said: "I don't say those words any more. My mother says I can say them at home." The mother and teacher together had decided that Fredrika would be asked not to impose her interest on the other children at school but that she might express it as freely as she wished at home. From this time on, Fredrika's naming was a masked rather than a direct expression of her interest in elimination. Symbolical descriptive titles such as she had used at first now prevailed (for further details see Pls. 56–59).

Also suggestive of an association between green and smeary, soiling desires are the paintings of *Betty*, though here the associations must rest upon rather general parallels and conjectures, as we have no verbal comments to lend support to our analysis. Betty went through three distinct stages in easel paintings: (*a*) a period in which green was used in precise dotted designs; (*b*) a period of constructive patterns for which blue was chosen; (*c*) a final period in which green was consistently overlaid with blue.

When we first observed her, Betty was a dainty, highly feminine little girl, who was overly meticulous and clean. It was at this time that the precise green dotting prevailed. This gradually gave way to constructive use of blue. During the course of the school year Betty spent several weeks with her parents in Florida. When she returned, she was somewhat freer in social relationships, and the third painting pattern then appeared.

The insights that have been gained from other children's work with blue and green suggest that the three phases in Betty's painting might reflect the three following tendencies: (a) a highly sublimated expression of her suppressed desire to smear;[29] (b) a growth away from desires to smear and a willing acceptance of control; (c) an expression of the two conflicting drives (perhaps released while on the holiday), namely, the suppressed desire to smear and the overt pattern of control. Continued observations might have given evidence which would have verified or nullified the analysis here set forth. Unfortunately, such continued observations were not possible.

We have noted many other examples which suggest an association between choice of the color green and the desire to smear. Among them are the following:

When *Bert* could not find brown (a color also related to the smearing interest),[30] he chose green as a substitute.

During periods of free indulgence in mud play, *Kit* and *Archie* began to make smeary green masses in easel painting.

*Howard* went through a brief period of soiling himself following his sister's birth. His paintings at this time consisted of smeary masses and daubs of greens.

*Brian*, obsessed with the need for cleanliness in overt behavior, evidenced an aversion to green in painting. He not only avoided using it, but he specifically announced on one occasion, "I hate green." (Brian was a boy of strong emotional makeup. This may also accord with his dislike of green).

*Hugh* used green and brown to daub and dot. He described his work with the suggestive name of "Chickies peep peeps."

*Jill*, very orderly and neat, went through a painting period in which she seemed to secure greenish effects regardless of the colors used (Pls. 60–62).

Considering its association with soiling tendencies, muddy green would seem to be an expressive color to choose for smearing or soiling of constructive or representative work. We have observed a number of children, including *Alan, Arline, Carol, Gregory, Jill,* and *Ronny,* who rather consistently chose green with which to smear over their constructive patterns. These children came from homes in which standards were overhigh for young children. In smearing over their constructive patterns with green, they probably were symbolically expressing their desire to dirty or cover the orderly standards that had been superimposed on them. In some instances, as with Jill, painting was the only outlet noted that reflected a reaction against home standards. Other children, however, notably *Arline* and *Gregory,* not only reacted in painting but otherwise resisted the standards imposed on them.

[29] Form, as well as color, enters into this interpretation (see pp. 49, 51 ff.).

[30] See pp. 41–42.

### CHILDREN WHO PREFERRED BLACK

Children who over a period of time—sometimes long, sometimes short—consistently used black tended as a group to show a dearth of emotional behavior. Individual case analyses, as well as quantitative data, indicate that this lack of free emotional flow reflected children's repressions caused by fears and anxieties. As we shall see in the cases to be reported, the children were afraid either of individuals (a severe father) or of situations (other too high-powered children in the family, physical handicaps, broken homes) with which they felt unable to cope.

As a rule, these children repressed their feelings and anxieties. Some of them made overadaptive or excellent surface adjustments. They were "highly controlled" and "realistically oriented" (they felt they had to adapt or take the too painful consequences). Goaded by "too high standards" and "intellectual stimulation that exceeded emotional readiness," they absorbed themselves in work to which they gave "long attention span," "high control," and "intellectual interest." Because they felt forced to accept life, they were "co-operative in routines," "co-operative in social relations," "had good relations with adults and children," and were considered to be "generally well adjusted." Although described as "friendly," they did not have warm friendships. They tended to verbalize in high and varied fashion to escape their inner tensions. They were basically tense and anxious.

Some other users of black, also fearful and anxious, did not adapt as did the above-described children. They sometimes repressed their emotions and sometimes were aggressive in their nonacceptance. They often "played alone," unduly "protected themselves and their work," and were likely to be "upset by interference" with what they were doing.

*Alan, Archie, Elaine, Edward,* and *Joe* all were users of black who tended to adapt. *Gregory* and *Kenneth* belonged in the category designated as "solitary." They varied between aggressiveness and more or less solitary acceptance of life as they found it.

It seems worth noting that most of, though not all, these children had turned from mass technique of painting to more controlled usage (through line and form).[31]

---

[31] See chap. iii; also see Trude, Schmidl-Woehner, "Formal Criteria for the Analysis of Children's Drawings," *American Journal of Orthopsychiatry,* XII, No. 1 (1942), 95–103. In a study of school-aged children, "The color scale of neurotic depressives is different. They use very little yellow (this color is avoided) and little red. Most of them use mixtures and black. Many use blue, and use of pure white is somewhat increased."

As a younger child, *Edward* expressed his anxieties through his tensely stroked painting of blue masses and through repeated verbalizations weighted with fears (see Pl. 36 and p. 24). His adaptive behavior was reflected in Plate 37. In Plate 63 we note his continued underlying anxiety symbolically expressed both in his representative drawings done in black and in his verbalization.

*Alan* had a history of emotional upsets related to the separation and divorce of his parents. At school he was a verbalist and a perfectionist. Throughout his first year he played alone and cried loudly when anyone tried to join him or interfere with his chosen activity. He avoided close personal relations with adults as well as with children. At this time Alan did not paint, but crayon drawing was a favorite occupation. With crayons he made abstract structuralized patterns, in which cold colors, particularly purple and black, predominated. His history suggests that his behavior, including choice of cold colors, was an attempt to shut emotions out of his life. His early swing to line and form, his complete omission of mass painting, his preference for the more structural materials—crayons and blocks—all accord with his other reactions. He consistently tried to avoid situations that might involve his emotions and to seek situations that demanded organization and control. When Alan first began easel painting, a year and a half after his entrance to school, his paintings were similar to his early crayon drawings in their use of cold colors and of linear technique. Later, when, in spite of himself, he became emotionally involved at the time his mother expected another child (by her second husband), Alan expressed his disturbance in mass paintings. He continued to use black, and to outline his structural forms, but overlaid them (see Pls. 64–67).

*Archie*, a little Napoleon with a drive for power, was lacking to an extraordinary degree in warm, affectionate relationships and attitudes. Paralleling this was his emphasis on black and green and his avoidance of warm colors. Even when he painted a subject that ordinarily would evoke the use of warm colors, viz., a "Pot of Flowers," Archie chose black, white, and green, with just a touch of orange. Archie's great drive, expressed verbally as well as otherwise, was to be a "big man." Evidently his image of a big man was one who turned away from warm emotions. Follow-up observations made several years later revealed that Archie was still concerned about being a "big man," and that he still predominantly used cold colors, especially black.

*Gregory* and *Kenneth*, because of difficulties in their own lives, were unable to establish warm, personal relationships with others. Each at first had seemed desirous of making friends but, not knowing how to make a positive approach, had attempted contacts through teasing, annoying, and disruptive advances. Both were consequently rejected by others and came to be almost unanimously disliked in their respective groups. Gradually each in his turn became wary of others. It was at this point that each of them turned to the use of crayons and paints. Each used a predominance of black and other cold colors. Both were working toward line rather than mass techniques. (The boys attended different nursery schools.)

The children of the ages studied who used black for mass patterns and for overlay seemed to be in more immediate and acute emotional difficulties than were children who used black for line or form. Among such children was *Elaine*, who was preoccupied and very much disturbed by certain emotional problems. During the period when she apparently was most disturbed she persistently used black.

*Elaine* entered nursery school in mid-year. She had just moved into the neighborhood after three years of foreign travel. Lacking security and being inexperienced in play with other children, she tended to seek and to cling to solitary activities. Outdoors, the sandbox or the tricycle seemed best to meet her needs. Indoors, easel painting became her favorite occupation.

Elaine's first paintings consisted of heavy blue masses, such as have been described as "anxiety" blue (Pl. 68). This was a pattern which, as previously observed, we had seen in other anxious, too highly controlled children. There were various causes for Elaine's anxiety. There had been considerable traveling and moving about. Elaine's mother was rather tense and was pushing her toward high intellectual attainments. Among the many strains put upon Elaine was the expectation that she speak French, German, and English.

After several paintings, all made up of somber blue masses, Elaine went through a period when she did not use the easel at all. During part of this time she was at home with a cold, and it was then that she became aware of an expected baby. The mother reported that Elaine at first asked many questions about the baby and raised such queries as what would her mother do if Elaine fell out of a window or if something else happened to her. By the time she returned to school, the mother reported that Elaine was awakening often during the night, that she was masturbating, that she was showing fear of the dark, of dogs, of loud noises.

The first painting made upon Elaine's return to school (2-23-38) began with blue. Then Elaine said, "Have to have a little black, too." Before she had finished, she had practically covered the page. Thereafter, Elaine again was kept at home with a cold.

During this period Elaine's mother had a fall, which necessitated her staying in bed. Home reports indicated that Elaine was kept from the room during the day but was allowed in her mother's room to be calmed, if she awakened frightened at night. Shortly after her return to school, Elaine painted Plate 70 as described. She remarked that the blue angular shaped mass was "a wall." Several times at school, Elaine made walls with clay, and she repeated the wall pattern in three more paintings. In these she did not use black.

On her next return to school after a two-day absence at home (4-6-38), Elaine painted her third picture (Pl. 71). This was the beginning of her persistent black series. The day after this painting, the teacher informed Elaine and the other children that "Blackie," one of the school's pet rabbits, had been killed by a dog. Elaine had been attached to the rabbit to a marked degree. The news of "Blackie" seemed to heighten Elaine's need to paint and to use black, for on the following days she came to school with such remarks as, "I have to paint, I have to have black," and she painted several full-page paintings a day.

During this period, when Elaine was most intensively producing black paintings, she did not mention the coming baby. She frequently talked about the dead rabbit. She was also having night terrors, got up several times at night to go to the toilet, and wet herself frequently at school during the day. Once when her nurse reproached her for this latter behavior she remarked: "Well, babies do that."

On 4-22-38, Elaine produced the first break in her intensive black series (see Pl. 72). It seems significant that on this day, when she made her first overt comment about the baby, she first omitted black overlay. For another ten days Elaine focused on full-page paintings in black. Several of these paintings were made immediately after rest. Elaine on several occasions called her paintings "Night." Her enuresis and night terrors continued.

On 5-9-38, Elaine's painting was less heavily overlaid with black, and diary records suggested that she had been more expansive in her use of the underlying colors (blue, green, red, and yellow). On this day Elaine went from the easel to the doll corner, where she played house with Edward. She put the "baby" (the doll) in bed and covered it entirely, head and all, "so that the flies won't get the baby." Then she rushed to the bathroom, but she was already wet. From this point on, Elaine seemed to have little or no need to express herself through painting. Only two more paintings were made during the remainder of the year, and these were characterized by warm, varied colors and by sublimated naming (Pl. 73). Instead of painting, Elaine now was verbalizing and working out her problem at the more overt level of dramatic play. Her play always involved putting the "baby" to bed and keeping the "baby" in bed.

On 5-23-38, Elaine was talking freely about the expected baby. On this date she remarked during story period: "If the baby is a boy, I'll call him Blackie [the name of the dead rabbit], and if it's a girl, I'll call her Snow White [the name of the still living female rabbit" (Pl. 74).

While we lack the data necessary to give Elaine's work unified meaning, it seems evident that the full-page black paintings expressed her resistance against accepting the fact of the coming baby. Somehow one feels that the death of Blackie and her fear of night also were important factors in the situation. Painting probably enabled Elaine to express her generalized emotional disturbance. Pervaded by anxieties and fears which she was not yet ready to verbalize or otherwise work out overtly, she undoubtedly found in painting a very real release for her tensions. It is of interest to note that, once she could accept the baby's coming enough to talk about it, bit by bit she lost her need to paint. First she broke away from black, then from mass painting, and finally from painting altogether— for the time being at least.

*Ruth* was another child observed by us who tended to overlay warm colors with black. In the nursery school, observers noted her constantly worried expression. Sickness was a constant theme in her dramatic play, and crying was frequently dramatized. With paints, as well as with crayons, Ruth drew recognizable representations in cold colors. Her blue figures were frequently described as "Girls Crying." Her brown and black figures were "Bogey Men." She frequently smeared her representative figures with black.

As with *Elaine*, her home situation was not deeply enough probed to make possible a unified and coherent picture of the relationship of the factors that caused Ruth's worried mien, her black overlaid paintings, and her other "unhappy" play activities. But even from the relatively superficial level of school observations and information, we knew of the home atmosphere of anxiety and strife, of discord between parents, of the father's infidelity which was bitterly resented by the mother, and the mother's poor hearing, poor health, and pessimistic outlook. All these together were quite enough to disturb any child. As far as we were able to observe, painting for Ruth meant an expression of her problems rather than an active release from them.

*Margaret* characteristically painted with black and green to produce dirty, greenish-black effects (see Pl. 75). She was a dejected, unhappy child. Her paintings reflected her melancholic perspective on life.

Other children who tended to overlay different colors with black were *Eric* and *Joe* (II, 304, 329). Each of these children tended to show repression and restraint.[32] Home records for these children included such evidence of fear and anxiety as "fear of dark," "crying out in sleep," "night terrors," "insecurity in family relationships."[33]

[32] Eric, for instance, also showed a concealment, inclosure, or "covering-over" pattern with blocks. He became anxious and disturbed when his blocks fell or when toys were damaged in play. His black overlay frequently covered crosses.

[33] Other associations with black: Several children identified black with "dirty" or "naughty." Esther said: "Naughty black." Kit said: "Awful black, ickly black." Aldo said: "Black looks like dirty dirt." Fredrika said: "Dirty black" and sometimes used black and brown, as well as green, to express her elimination concern.

OTHER COLORS

Data on other colors than those described are too scant to be conclusive. The more pronounced trends, however, will be discussed.

*Orange.*—Orange was found in group analyses to characterize the work of a number of children who stood out for a relatively good adaptation to their environment. While warm emotional relationships were clearly present, such relationships were not excessive. Pleasant, well-tempered relationships seemed to prevail.

Ruby was one of the children who showed a strong liking for orange and who stood out for her placid, nonaggressive behavior.

Richard, another user of orange, was friendly and outgoing but in no way an aggressive child.[34]

Individual case records suggest that the timid child who feared strong emotional expression found outlet and satisfaction in the use of orange:

Bert, for instance, who overlaid red and who verbally identified red with danger ("Stop," "Fire," etc.), used orange freely in separate or intermingled color placement.

Individual records also indicate that a number of children who favored orange were children who took refuge from life in imaginative play. This association again suggests that orange is likely to parallel the less strong and direct rather than the assertive reactions reflected by emphasis on red.[35]

*Brown.*—This color was not persistently used by enough children to permit of group analyses. The instances in which we have found it contrasted with blue, however (see pp. 28–29), suggest its association with a desire to smear.

Most of the children who were observed to favor brown to a pronounced degree (as *Alan, Barbara, Carol, Danny, Darlene, Della, Dora, Jill, Ronny, Sara*) came from homes which overaccentuated cleanliness education in the form of too early bowel and bladder control and also restrictions in play with dirt or other smeary materials. The eagerness with which these children sought and smeared with brown in particular and with smeary media in general, once they had overcome their initial resistance, suggests that brown provided a real outlet for feelings and interests not permissible in overt behavior.

---

[34] We recall once more the physical qualities of colors. Orange, physically a tempered color, was frequently used to express tempered emotions.

[35] Other associations observed with orange: (a) Angela and Norman used this color frequently, and each showed tendencies toward fantasy and masturbation; (b) Don, Rita, and Sara used orange interchangeably with brown.

*Rita's* use of brown and/or orange, in contrast to blue, has already been described (I, 29). Illustrative notes from the records of other children mentioned follow.

*Della,* trained for bowel control at three months, excessively neat and orderly in overt behavior, repeatedly mixed whatever colors were available and almost inevitably achieved a muddy brown, which evidently gave her considerable satisfaction, as she frequently and with obvious pleasure called attention to her painting, remarking, "Painted brown."

*Alan* asked for brown for his first easel painting and likewise for his first finger painting. While finger painting, he exclaimed, "More brown! I want it." As we have already seen, Alan was another much too controlled, overclean, and orderly child.

*Margaret* delighted in brown effects in easel painting and finger painting during an interval when she was defying bowel control at home.

*Jill,* who seemingly never quite broke down her outer reserve of cleanliness and orderliness, was observed one day to take the brush from the jar of brown paint, wave it in front of the paper as though to paint, replace the brush and walk away, then return, select the brush from the jar of blue paint and finally paint with blue.[36]

*Purple.*—We have observed only a few children who showed a persistent interest in purple. Many showed an initial interest in experimenting with this color when first introduced to it, or around the Easter season when it was frequently seen coupled with yellow. Such interests, however, were of brief duration.

The children who showed the most persistent choice of purple in the present observations were *Alan, Percy,* and *Scott.* These children were rejected, unhappy boys. Some children, particularly *Brian, Ruth,* and *Ross,* tended to choose purple during unhappy periods. *Richard* produced his one purple product, a heavily and closely stroked mass done with a crayon, immediately following a painful bout with the dentist. Harms has noted that purple is a color choice of depressed patients.[37] These varied observations suggest that purple bears some association with dejected and unhappy moods.

It was also noted that, quite apart from the Easter season, several children were interested in using purple and yellow together—but in contrasting fashion. Such contrast is consistent with preceding generalizations inasmuch as yellow was most frequently associated with happy moods and experiences and purple with depressive or gloomy moods and experiences.

### COLOR PLACEMENT

Not only do the colors that children choose reflect moods and personality factors, but the ways in which they place those colors on the painting page

---

[36] Other aspects of behavior common to several of the children mentioned above and seemingly part of a repressed or sublimated desire to smear were: "history of constipation," "strong drive to collect objects," "use of dabbing and dotting techniques with paints and crayons," "emphasis on detail."

[37] Harms, *op. cit.*

are significant. Four frequent types of color placement have been noted for which parallels in behavior and personality factors have been observed: (1) overlay, (2) separate placement, (3) intermingling, (4) indiscriminate mixing.

### OVERLAY

The children observed who consistently overlaid one color with another tended as a group to be hiding strong personal feelings under some assumed pattern of overt behavior. The underlying colors in these cases were likely to suggest the quality of the hidden feelings. The colors used for overlay tended to reflect the overt pattern of behavior. Frequently, the overt behavior pattern was one of marked repression in all areas.[38] In a few instances the more basic emotions not only were underlying but were in conflict with the overt, expressed emotions. In these cases the actual dynamics of behavior were camouflaged or covered over in daily living.[39]

We have previously remarked (a) that a major and usual aspect of development during the nursery-school years is the transition from infantile to controlled behavior; (b) that many children who are pushed too hard or too fast through this transition (i.e., on whom demands for control are too stringent) tend to conform overtly while they conceal and/or camouflage their personal desires and drives; and (c) that a frequently observed painting pattern which parallels this sort of development is the overlaying of a warm color (particularly yellow) with a cooler color. [40]

In the course of our observations, where overlay was used, cold colors most frequently overlay warm ones.[41] It is of interest that, of all the cooler colors used, blue, which is most suggestive of control, was most often used for overlay. [42]

One aspect of this developmental adjustment, already noted as characterizing the nursery-school years, was the establishment of cleanliness habits, including the control of elimination.

Previous case descriptions have indicated that many children were inclined to hide their personal desires to smear and be dirty under an overt

---

[38] As in Ann's case, Pls. 51–55.

[39] See Stanley (p. 33).                    [40] See pp. 30–33.

[41] Cold overlay of warm colors was almost seven times as frequent as was the reverse. The exact ratio was 53:8.

[42] Blue was the predominant overlay color used by 18 of the 53 children whose paintings consistently showed overlay. Blue and green used interchangeably predominated in the paintings of 13 of these 53 children. Green only was used as overlay by 5 of the 53 children, while a miscellaneous, indiscriminate choice of blue, green, black, brown, or purple characterized the remaining cases.

pattern of neat, orderly, precise, controlled behavior.[43] As noted, these children tended to use blue and brown in contrasting ways. They did not always overlay brown with blue—the pattern which, from our observations, one might have expected. They frequently alternated clean use of blue with smeary use of brown,[44] or they devoted the major part of their painting time to smearing with brown. They not infrequently smeared brown over blue. In those instances the children seemed to be expressing not merely their problems in a general way but actually their inner drives, which were in conflict with external demands. The painting situation undoubtedly offered them a real outlet for basic feelings about which they probably could not have expressed themselves with words or in any other direct fashion.

As is well known, anxieties and fears frequently result during the early years from ineptly imposed or poorly accepted demands. A number of children observed expressed their hidden fears and anxieties through color overlay. Black used to overlay warmer colors seemed, in particular, to parallel hidden fears.[45] Several children also were observed who tended to cover black with warm colors. These children, their records indicated, were hiding their anxieties either under gay, clownish behavior or under an obviously forced bravado.[46]

Whereas overlay with cold colors usually paralleled obvious restraint or repression in overt behavior, overlay with warm colors more often reflected a behavior pattern of high activity. The two patterns suggested immediately above—i.e., (a) the pattern of gay, clownish, hyperactive behavior concealing deep anxieties and fears and (b) the pattern of bold, defiant, assertive behavior concealing timidities and fears—illustrate actual relationships observed. However, they occurred only spasmodically in our data and lacked the persistency and frequency found in the study of cold-overlay themes.

Just as the easily perceived alternating currents in *Angela*'s life served to illuminate and make meaningful the corresponding changes in her drawings and paintings, so do the alternating factors in *Phoebe*'s life highlight the significance in use of cold and warm overlay of colors.

*Phoebe*, one of two adopted children, was an impulsive, effervescent, high-spirited child. She was openly rejected by her foster-mother in favor of the adopted brother. The mother frequently spoke of Phoebe as "dumb," and once remarked to a teacher: "I wanted a daughter and I have a witch."

Phoebe's first period of cold overlay (1-30-39 and 2-1-39) was preceded by illness and a stay at home. During that time she was supervised by a housekeeper, who spanked her

---

[43] See pp. 28–29, 42.                    [45] See pp. 38–40.

[44] See Pls. 47–48.                       [46] See p. 33.

and who in general was an overstern disciplinarian. The foster-mother was also ill during part of this time. The four paintings which Phoebe made immediately after that stay at home consisted of black overlaid on red and orange. Of one of the paintings, Phoebe said: "This is night; it's dark." Phoebe was characterized as "tense, distractible" and "unassertive" at the time these paintings were made.

Phoebe's interest in painting then became spasmodic until March 6, when a concentrated period of warm-overlay painting began (3-6-39; 3-30-39). This period, too, was preceded by illness at home, but this time Phoebe returned in an assertive and defiant mood. Her mother reported that she was also quite aggressive at home. On March 7, she had thrown cereal at the cook and as punishment was kept at home for the day. She returned to school, announcing, "I wasn't sick yesterday, I was bad." During this period of warm overlay, Phoebe's foster-mother, father, and brother took a trip away from home (3-13 to 3-27). The housekeeper reported that Phoebe was relatively easy to handle during their absence. At school, Phoebe's outgoing tendencies shifted from aggression toward more sociable play. She frequently played happily in the doll corner, where she particularly enjoyed the baby role.[47] All the paintings of this period showed red overlaid on green, yellow, or blue with one exception described below.

(Note that the paintings just described support our previously suggested finding that red is used to express or symbolize heightened emotions and assertive behavior, sometimes of affectionate and sometimes of defiant nature. The earlier incidents of the period above-described suggest the parallelism between red overlay and defiant behavior. The later paintings and incidents suggest the parallelism between red overlay and affectionate relationships. During the period under discussion, when she overlaid with warm colors, Phoebe was overtly expressing her emotions. She was undoubtedly at the same time hiding the anxieties and fears which in the light of her home situation must have been ever present.

A single incident of 3-24-39 offers some basis for the assumption that Phoebe was in conflict during her assertive period and that the conflict was associated with home. On 3-24-39, Phoebe had a morning of happy dramatic play, during which she had the prized role of baby. She went from this play to the easel and began immediately to paint with red— without overlay. While she was painting, the nurse came to take her home. Phoebe quickly took to blue paint and overlaid the red with blue).

A second period of cold overlay became apparent in Phoebe's work on 3:29-39. On the preceding day, Phoebe's parents had returned home. Phoebe had refused breakfast on that day and had been kept home in punishment. The new period of cold overlay persisted through 4-25-39. Throughout this time Phoebe was tense, restless, excitable, unexpressive. On April 17, a new housekeeper arrived who took an immediate liking to Phoebe and who openly demonstrated her affection. Although the two paintings which followed the housekeeper's arrival continued to show cold overlay, both had a touch of red, the only red used by Phoebe during this interval of cold overlay.[48]

On April 25, Phoebe's mother reported that the housekeeper had been dismissed because "she would increase Phoebe's ego by playing favorites." Phoebe's painting of this date was of black on yellow. On this same date Phoebe spent considerable time sitting alone in the doll bed in the doll corner, looking downcast and dejected.[49]

[47] See p. 20.

[48] Here, as in the paintings following happy dramatic play, red seemed to reflect emotional satisfaction.

[49] For other tendencies comparable to overlay see smearing (p. 85) and over-and-over the same area (p. 99).

### SEPARATE PLACEMENT

Whereas the children who consistently overlaid colors tended to be concealing certain emotional reactions, the children who used colors separately were likely as a group to be directing their energies outward and to be adapting them to environmental expectancies. Their clear-cut, uncovered use of color suggests a direct expression of emotions. The care exercised in securing separation of colors suggests an effort at emotional control. Actually, a number of cases were noted in which children who persistently took great care to place their colors separately so that they might not touch one another were inclined to be too rigid in their conformance to environmental molds. As these children struck a better balance in living, they tended to intermingle and overlap colors (Pl. 76).

Separate color placement has been observed in many children who were just becoming consciously concerned with adapting to external demands.[50] It was as though, in their initial zeal and effort to adapt and conform, their controls became quite tense and rigid.

Children who used separate color placement but who otherwise did not have a rigid or fixed painting pattern have, in our observations, tended to show uncomplicated personality factors. Usually personal desires to conform with and be pleasing to the world about them have seemed stronger than any personal drives in the opposite direction. Imitation of others, particularly imitation of social amenities, has been frequent among these children. Although some of these children had strongly assertive personalities, our observations suggest that they faced the danger of losing their special and individual qualities because of their desire to be like others. Assertion among these children tended to take the form of bossing and dictatorial behavior rather than of self-expression.

When we have found separate placement of colors accompanied by a set or highly repetitive pattern, as was the case with *Jessica* and *Louis* (both used mass techniques to paint vertical blocks of color), conflicts have also been present.[51] Throughout this study, the factor of degree of persistence and repetitiveness of a given aspect or theme must be considered in the analysis of any specific theme or pattern.

[50] Bess, Diane, Robert, Roberta, Sara, Sheldon, and Stella illustrate this point.

[51] Both Jessica and Louis evidenced ambivalence about their sex roles. Jessica in clothing, behavior, and activities tried to be like a boy. Louis displayed many interests and reactions characteristic of girls. In both cases emphasis on color masses (suggestive of emotion, and of more feminine qualities) *combined with* emphasis on verticals (associated with assertive, masculine drives) suggest a clue to observed ambivalence (see pp. 72–74 for further notes on these children).

### INTERMINGLING OF COLORS

Our observations have shown that those children who consistently intermingled colors, i.e., whose paintings have kept the identity of the original colors but showed free overlapping or intermingling of these colors, seemed as a group to be freer in emotional expression than children with separate color placement and more outgoing than children with persistent overlay patterns.

Intermingling has often been observed in varicolored, full-page painting products made by four- and five-year-old children who were displaying colorful, outgoing personalities and who were adapting to environme tal demands within socially acceptable limits. Follow-up observations on these children indicated that they were fitting into their school groups with relative ease and were making real contributions to them (Pl. 77).[52]

### INDISCRIMINATE MIXING OF COLORS

Indiscriminate mixing of colors has seemed for the most part a characteristic of very young, immature children who were still functioning on a manipulative, smearing level and who probably had not yet fully developed sensitivity to color differences.[53] The children observed who long and regularly continued indiscriminate mixing of colors so that the identity of the separate colors was lost in a nondescript, often muddy-looking effect have inclined as a group to be outgoing in emotional expression but to lack the controlled adaptive qualities that characterized the group of children who intermingled colors.

Somewhat of an exception to the foregoing are the children who seemed to find in indiscriminate mixing of colors a means of expressing their desire to smear.[54] Yet these cases to some degree parallel the generalized trend, as they were children who apparently were expressing infantile desires which they had not been able to work out satisfactorily at the appropriate age.

[52] Loretta, Robert, Sara, and Stella illustrate this tendency. Their intermingling, varied use of colors and their wide use of space suggest their colorful, outgoing personalities. Filling of the page reflects both a recognition of external conditions and a tendency to adapt to them (i.e., space was neither sparsely used nor overflowed).

[53] Illustrative are Irving, Audrey, Andy, and Jeff, especially in the early stages of our observations of them.

[54] Illustrative are Anita, Carol, Jill, Margaret.

Individual palettes,[55] like choice and placement of colors, often seemed to provide clues to personality, mood, or passing phases of development. The following observations on individual cases (already discussed) suggest that further study along these lines might be fruitful:

Loretta, Robert, Sara, Stella, and many others who tended to produce multicolored paintings were notable for their outgoing personalities and their varied, balanced interests. Group data indicates an association between multicolored effects in painting and the type of personality suggested above.

Carol, Fredrika, and Jill tended to secure brownish or greenish effects regardless of the color of paint used. These children apparently found in painting an expression for their interest in elimination and for their desire to smear and dab. [56]

Alan's finished palette usually gave a nondescript yellow-green-brown effect no matter what colors were used. Margaret, likewise, achieved muddy nondescript effects regardless of choice or sequence of colors chosen. Each of these children was unhappy and melancholic.[57]

Louise alternated between moods of happiness and unhappiness. Her paintings showed parallel alternation between brilliant and dull color effects.

Frank went through an unhappy and tense period, during which time his paintings took on a blackish-bluish hue in spite of his use of a variety of colors.

As previously stated, almost all the children observed who showed strongly assertive, often masculine, behavior tended to paint with heavy strokes and strong color effects. Group data, as well as individual cases, support the parallelism between heavy strokes and assertive drives.

Louis's, Percy's, and Paul's paintings gave pastel rather than strong color effects. These boys all seemed overtly to reveal the delicate feelings and sensitivities which we usually associate with girls.

Jessica, who usually worked with heavy painting strokes and who was ordinarily assertive and boyish in behavior and even in way of dressing, produced a pastel painting on the day when she wore a dainty girlish dress to school for the first time.

Anita's paintings during one period were characterized by parsimonious use of color. She made a little go a long way and with a few scattered dabs managed to achieve a very smeared, messy effect. This seems in keeping with and paralleled her smearing upholstery and walls at home with a few well-directed dabs of lipstick and shoe polish. It also paralleled Anita's mother's withholding of affection and of food, for fear Anita would become "plump like her grandmother."

Hugh, Kit, Richard, Sara, Stella, and many other children have been observed consistently to use complementary colors, i.e., to balance warm and cold colors. These children were outstanding in their groups for their well-rounded development and excellent adjustment.

[55] Some children, regardless of colors used, always achieved a greenish effect and others a dull depressed effect, etc.

[56] For further details see pp. 35–36, 42.          [57] See Pl. 75.

Both *Danny* and *Fredrika* were observed to turn to varied, balanced use of colors as they worked out of their emotional problems and developed varied, outgoing interests in their environment. [58]

*George* used balanced color combinations and multicolored effects during the period when he was a popular outgoing leader in the group. He reverted to single-color painting when on being transferred to another group he felt strange and unable to adjust. George's swings from cold- to warm-color combinations were paralleled by cyclic changes from withdrawing to outgoing behavior.

*Aileen* turned from emphasis on red to more balanced use of colors with multicolored effects as she became somewhat better adjusted and better balanced during the second year of observation. Aileen—also *Alan* and *Jill*—produced paintings with varicolored borders at times when their daily records showed an increase in outgoing behavior. These children had all previously used a single color for outlining or making their borders. The transition from single to varicolored borders seems to reflect lessened sense of closure and in each case was paralleled by less restricted behavior.

*Norman* persistently used complementary or contrasting colors. He used them in highly repetitive, almost stereotyped, patterns throughout the first year. There was neither integration nor balance in the design of his paintings. Of all children observed, Norman most needed psychiatric care. He showed a definitely schizoid personality (it was later so diagnozed). His tendency to use contrasting colors, but never to blend or balance them, may have reflected his schizoid tendencies.

*Brian* showed alternating periods in his choice of colors. For a time he painted only with warm colors, using two or more on a given product. Then his choice would reverse, and he would choose two or more cold colors to produce a painting. Such alternation paralleled strong alternation in Brian's moods. It might be here noted that the balanced use of colors recorded above as characteristic of children who were disposed toward balance in their way of living was quite lacking in Brian's case.

*Bee* also went through periods when she alternated from use of cool to warm colors. Bee was a child with an intense, "one-track" personality. Her interest chart indicates exclusive preoccupation and interest in one creative medium at a time, e.g., she painted persistently for weeks and then gave that up for an exclusive interest in blocks.

*Carol*'s color choice and mood alternated in direct relationship with each other. Red and orange were her choice during periods of extreme attention-seeking, while green and blue were chosen during periods when she was trying to avoid attention. During the year observed, Carol's behavior tended to lack balance.

## PERSPECTIVE ON CHILDREN'S USE OF COLOR

The foregoing descriptions make clear that as yet relatively little is known about the infinite variety of ways in which children may express themselves through color choice and usage. It also is clear that if we would understand children, color usage must never be considered as an isolated aspect of their painting products. As previously stated, analysis and interpretation must rest upon a constellation of factors that characterizes the given individual and his work.

[58] See pp. 28 and 35–36, respectively.

In order to emphasize this concept, we have but to recall that, whereas emphasis on warm colors spread freely over the painting page tended to reflect relatively outgoing, freely flowing, and expressed drives, warm colors in restricted areas more often paralleled drives which were not finding full expression—drives which were being restrained or repressed. As we shall find in the coming discussions of line and space usage, consistent placement of a given color to the left or the right side of the painting page, along with the forms used, is likely to modify our interpretations.

We have observed that warm colors associated with circular strokes tend to parallel mild affectionate emotions, while warm colors used in long, heavy vertical strokes are more likely to parallel aggressive behavior—frequently anger, hostility, or both. As we proceed, we shall note that children preoccupied with personal conflicts involving assertive-submissive or masculine-feminine roles may consistently choose certain colors to express the vertical theme (i.e., the assertive drive) and other colors to express the circular theme (i.e., the passive drive). As the implications of these other aspects of painting become clearer, it will be quite obvious that analyses and judgment about color *must* be qualified by careful consideration of line and form.

Obviously, the process of understanding the significance of painting entails a step-by-step approach in which we examine first one and then another aspect of children's work. Our examination of color has shown how color choice may reveal much about the individual's emotional makeup. But colors, in themselves, do not indicate in what direction or within what limits the emotional drives are operating. As we have studied color usage, it has become ever more evident that over-all analysis and judgment, if it is to be sound, must be weighted in terms of every other phase of the painting experience. We wish to emphasize this because we recognize the danger in the unadapted application of the generalizations which our data suggest. In every individual case, as we have tried to demonstrate, the given generalization can be validated, negated, or modified only after due consideration of all aspects of the individual child's painting and the dynamics of his personality.

# CHAPTER III

## INDIVIDUAL DYNAMICS EXPRESSED THROUGH
## LINE AND FORM

OBSERVATIONS and analysis of children's characteristic use of line and form have, as previously stated, provided most helpful insights into (a) the amount of energy which the child had and was expending, (b) the degree of control which the child was exercising, and (c) the direction in which that control was operating, viz., toward or away from self. Insights in the color area, as we have seen, dealt largely with emotional responses. Understanding of children's use of line and form tends to supplement insights gained concerning their use of color.

We recognize that making lines and forms·requires more highly developed muscular co-ordination and physical control than does mass-painting technique. It is perhaps more difficult to realize that *line and form may express not only physical control but also emotional control or degree of self-control.*

We have observed that as most children in the natural process of development make the transition away from their first impulsive reactions toward more controlled adaptive behavior, they make a parallel transition in the use of the various media at their disposal, as clay, blocks, etc.[1] In working with paints this transition means that children ordinarily turn from painting mass effects to making lines and forms. At first, they are likely to make abstract, structured patterns. Later, a majority of children turn to painting representative figures.[2] Children's initial use of line and form, as a rule, parallels their increased interest in relationships outside of themselves. The children who showed greatest concern for form tended, as a group, to differ from the children primarily interested in color, in that the group interested in form exhibited more logical behavior and fewer impulsive reactions than did the group concerned with color. The group of children that preferred to work with line and form, in contrast to the group with long-continuing and persistent concern for color, tended toward more outward orientation, as indicated by such traits as tendency to seek attention, to compete, to initiate contacts. They generally had greater con-

---

[1] See pp. 101–3; also Dorothy Van Alstyne, *Play Behavior and Choice of Play Materials of Preschool Children* (Chicago: University of Chicago Press, 1932).

[2] See chap. v, p. 106.

trol, as indicated by their ideas for play, intellectual interests, planned purposive work. They also tended to show more adaptive behavior, as evidenced by their being sought after, popular, and co-operative in play.

There may well be very real constitutional and organic differences that
would account for these response differences. Our visual sense organs provide an obvious physical basis for color sensitivity and discrimination. Such
sensitivity can be observed far down in the ranks of animal life.[3] Among
primitive peoples and in the early months of human infancy, color discrimination is also to be found.[4] Line, however, is an abstraction. It represents an idea dependent upon associations and higher thought processes.
Löwenfeld, in his study of the near-blind, found that the haptic child who
functions on a feeling level was at an utter loss when he tried to work with
line.[5] Animals, such as those trained for circus acts, have no reaction to
line unless and until specifically trained. While color is likely to evoke
primitive impulses, line and form would seem, according to our present
knowledge, to evoke little, if any, response until higher mental processes
are brought into play.

In the course of our longitudinal studies of line and form in children's
paintings, a number of tendencies have appeared with sufficient frequency
to merit discussion. Some of them, we believe, hold clues to guidance.
Among the tendencies to be considered are the following:

1. We have found that some children as they turned to line and form
*moved quickly through abstractly patterned to representative work.* Usually these
children in their earliest and most frequent representations portrayed the
human figure. They showed a good degree of variety in both their painting
content and their pattern.

The children who turned quickly from abstractly patterned to representative form and who showed a preference for representation of the hu-

---

[3] Certain invertebrates, birds, fishes, and primates show color sensitivity. The color sensitivity
of fur-bearing mammals is still a question. For references see Carl Warden, Thomas Jenkins, and
Lucien H. Warner, *Comparative Psychology,* II (New York: Ronald Press, 1936), 685 ff.; also Ross
Stagner, "Visually Determined Reactions in the Vertebrates," *Psychological Bulletin,* XXVIII,
No. 2 (February, 1931), 99–129; also W. E. Walton, "Exploratory Experiments in Color Dis-
crimination," *Journal of Genetic Psychology,* XLVIII (1936), 221–22.

[4] For references to primitives see Grant Allen, *The Color Sense: Its Origin and Development* (London: Kegan Paul, French, Trubner & Co., 1892); and W. H. R. Rivers, "Primitive Color
Vision," *Popular Science Monthly,* LIX (1901), 44–59. For reference to infants see Ruth Staples,
"The Responses of Infants to Color," *Journal of Experimental Psychology,* XV (1932), 119–41;
also in *Psychological Bulletin,* XXVIII, No. 4 (April, 1931), 297–308.

[5] Viktor Löwenfeld, *The Nature of Creative Activity* (New York: Harcourt, Brace & Co., 1939),
p. 72.

man figure were inclined as a group to be interested in interaction and communication with others. They tended to be socially oriented. Probably because of their desire to communicate with others, they were likely to turn quickly to reading and writing skills, which would facilitate communication and interaction. Attempts to write often appeared in the nursery-school paintings of these children and even more often in their crayon products.

*Angela, Elinor, Patty, Rita,* and *Sally* all turned quickly to human representation, and each was primarily concerned with social intercommunications. *Loretta,* similarly oriented, was predominantly interested in making human representations during her kindergarten year. *Jay* had many ideas and was a forceful, though not always a constructive, leader. At an early age he turned to use of lines and to making easily recognized forms.

2. Other children, *instead of progressing quickly from pure experimentation with line and form to realistic representation, persisted in varied and increasingly intricate abstract or structural designs.* Careful study of these children suggests that they probably had special abilities along constructive lines.

*Neil* is illustrative of the children with a special and persistent interest in structural patterns. Throughout his stay in nursery school he showed predominant interest in construction rather than in representation. Neil's paintings showed much structural detail. Emphasis was on angular, rather than curved, forms. Products were detailed and additive rather than in general outlines. As he grew older, the development of his work was characterized by increased complexity of design rather than transition to representation. When he began to do representative work, he chose to represent boats, trains, and other mechanical inanimate objects rather than human beings.

Overtly, Neil was more interested in materials than in people or in human relationships. He showed almost no interest in dramatic play. When he occasionally engaged in dramatic play with others, it was secondary to his interest in construction, e.g., others joined him when they saw him "mixing cement" (gravel and water) and plastering bricks together "to make a wall." It was the children who actually injected the social dramatic-play element into his activity.

*Ross* also seemed to be expressing natural abilities in his focus on constructive, interrelated, and varicolored forms in easel painting. Ross used paints only during free, happy, outgoing periods. He was highly constructive in most of his activities. His interests, his well-channeled energies, and his skills were in keeping with those of his parents. His father was an expert watch repairer, and his mother was recognized in her community for her delicate needlework.

*Steven* persisted in painting structural patterns at an age when others were turning to representative work. Like *Ross,* he seemed to have both unusual interest and ability in this type of activity. His predominant interest was block building. Staff members sometimes characterized him as "the builder" of the group. When Steven turned to representation, the content of his work had to do with inanimate objects rather than human beings. "Streets," "Garages," "Gardens," are illustrative of Steven's representations. Like *Neil,* Steven showed more persistent interest in play with materials than with other children. He showed less interest in children than was usual for his age.

The authors have a fairly strong conviction that the work of *Neil, Ross, Steven,* and other children like them reflects special aptitudes and abilities that could later be channeled to advantage along engineering or research lines. Not only their special abilities but their reasons for avoiding human representation require further study. Additional investigations along these lines might, we believe, offer clues to educational guidance.

3. Some other children *persisted in abstract designs long after they might reasonably have been expected to be doing representative work, but their designs lacked the variety that characterized the work of the children just described,* and in overt behavior they were less well adjusted. Our analyses suggest that in seeking and clinging to abstract, linear techniques, these children were symbolically expressing their desire to escape their emotions.

*Alan, Albert, Ann,* and *Tilly* each used an abstract, structural pattern in crayoning at a period when they were represented and restrained in overt behavior and when they were apparently too tense to use the easel or to seek other creative media. Three of these children showed speech blocks during the time they were using crayons to draw structural patterns. All of these children broke away from the lines and forms used to draw or paint structural patterns as they became ready to work freely with color and mass. At the same time, each of them began to talk more easily and became freer in overt behavior.

4. When children remained *focused on one specific abstract pattern so persistently that their work took on a strongly repetitive or even stereotyped character,* they were found to be emotionally disturbed, and their painting pattern tended to be a symbolic expression of their specific conflicts. In their emotional disturbance and in the intensity of their focus on a particular painting pattern, these children are comparable to those who painted highly repetitive color masses. They seem to have substituted symbolism in line and form for color symbolism.[6]

The foregoing observations suggest that use of line and form offers some insights and clues to individual differences that have to do both with (*a*) general personal characteristics and (*b*) presence and sometimes specific nature of conflicts.

*a*) Through his use of line and form the individual gives some further clues to his personality. Strongly marked individual characteristics are evidenced in direction of strokes, length of strokes, intensity, and interrelationship of strokes. Persistent painting tendencies along these lines reflect those individual qualities that are constant.

*b*) The individual's characteristic use of line and form sometimes reveals the presence of conflict and even its specific nature. Children for whom this is true reveal a more complete and persistent focus on one particular form or pattern than do the children for whom a more varied use of line

[6] This subject will be clarified and supported by the discussion of symbolism in line and form which appears in a later section of this chapter.

and form is a general personality index. Line and form as used by children who are expressing conflicts is congruent with line and form as used by other children; but, to the extent that it is more stereotyped, it is also more specifically symbolical.

### POTENTIAL SIGNIFICANCE OF STRAIGHT-LINE, VERTICAL, OR ANGULAR STROKES IN CONTRAST TO CURVILINEAR OR CIRCULAR PAINTING

The study of those children who worked predominantly with straight lines versus those who worked largely with curvilinear forms, and particularly the study of those who characteristically stressed verticals as contrasted with those who stressed circles, proved significant because such study revealed not only personality factors but also symbolic expression of conflicts.

The persistent constellation of characteristics associated with each of these patterns and the marked contrasts between the two sets of characteristics seem of special interest when we realize that children's drawings, like all designs of nature, may be broken down into these two basic patterns—the straight and the curvilinear line.[7]

The children observed to work primarily in single straight-line strokes tended to stand out as a group for their relatively assertive, outgoing behavior. Typical of them were such traits as "realistic interests," "initiative for play," "aggressive," and "negativistic." By contrast, the children who worked with curved, continuous strokes tended to stand out as a group for their more dependent, more compliant, more emotionally toned reactions, viz., "affectionate," "lack confidence," "seek adult attention," "random work habits," and "fanciful imagination."

These differences became even more pronounced as comparison was made between specific forms. Children who emphasized circles tended as a group to be more dependent, more withdrawn, more submissive, more subjectively oriented than children who predominantly painted vertical, square, or rectangular forms. Among the characteristics illustrating the tendency to work in circles are "lack confidence," "lack ideas for play," "emotional interests," "imaginative interests," "follow," "imitate."

#### EMPHASIS ON CIRCLES

Emphasis on circles was likely to tie in somewhat with immaturity. As has been noted, a majority of children usually, during the nursery-school years, swing from egocentric, subjective, emotionally toned behavior toward a

---

[7] See James B. Pettigrew, *Design in Nature*, Vol. III (London: Longmans, Green, 1908); and Adolf Best Mangard, *Method for Creative Design* (New York: Knopf, 1927).

more externalized, organized, and objectively directed way of functioning. In our observations, emphasis on circles appeared to parallel the earlier phase of development, and it tended to decrease in favor of vertical and other straight-line or angular strokes as the child moved toward more outgoing and organized behavior.[8]

Emphasis on circles also seemed to tie in with a relatively feminine pattern of behavior. When we selected all the children who stood out most sharply in our observations for circular emphasis and whose painting showed a dearth of straight-line strokes, we found a group of 18 children. A majority of these were girls (13 girls to 5 boys). The girls[9] were among those who in their records and in staff meetings were characterized by one or more of the following phrases: "distinctly feminine," "soft," "withdrawing," "submissive," "self-contained," "insecure." The boys[10] also tended to fit these same descriptions. They were variously described by teachers and observers as "immature," "effeminate," "soft."[11]

Our group findings suggest that circular emphasis occurred in children who were relatively less secure than others. Comparable observations have been noted by others. Dummer's comments on this point are of particular interest:

(a) "Recent work with subnormal boys shows that through the use of primitive folk games, songs and dances one seems to reach back to their level of social development. They are happy and orderly in circle games, but not yet ready for forming in a line." (b) ". . . . order was secured in circle games before the boys were ready for a game played in a line, for this resulted in the end boys breaking away. Was this form a sense of security given by the unity of the circle, or did it reach some deep level of a social unconscious?"[12]

As we think over the individual children in the study, we find many whose general insecurity and withdrawing tendencies at given times were paralleled by a persistent circular or ovular pattern in easel painting. *Aileen, Ann, Gloria, Harriet, Sally, Tilly,* and *Virginia* are a few of such children.

In contrast to the children with circular emphasis, those whom we have found emphasizing verticals freely[13] have tended, as a group, to be more

[8] See chap. v, pp. 112–14.

[9] Alma and Ann (in first year of study), also Anita, Arline, Audrey, Betty, Gertrude, Gloria, Hope, Jean, Jill, Tilly, Rita, Virginia.

[10] Jeff, Andy (following a period when he did all-directional strokes), Erwin, Floyd, and Ralph.

[11] For quantitative study of sex differences in personality see p. 15, n. 2.

[12] Ethel S. Dummer, *Why I Think So: The Autobiography of an Hypothesis* (Chicago: Clark-McElroy Pub. Co., 1920), pp. 204 and 232 ff.

[13] We have considered "verticals freely used" when they were an outstanding feature of the child's painting product: (a) without any apparent attempts at concealment or obliteration, such as cutting off, crossing out, or smearing over; and (b) without any apparent confusion or contrasting with circular forms, such as consistent placing of each on its own side of the page, consistent production of each in its own distinctive color, or consistent overlaying of one with another.

self-reliant, more assertive, and more outgoing in interests and social relationships and generally better adjusted in the nursery-school setting.

### SWING FROM CIRCULAR TO VERTICAL PATTERNS

We have found, as suggested above, that emphasis on verticals tended to
increase with age during the nursery-school years. It increased as children
were making the shift from impulsive and subjective to more controlled,
more objective behavior.[14] This shift has been particularly marked in some
instances.

During a period when *Floyd*'s records describe him as "slow," "inclined to play alone in a
doll corner" (10-20-37), his paintings were characterized by circular work. However, his
painting pattern changed from circular to vertical, and the vertical theme predominated
during the last five months of the year, when teachers and observers noted that he was
"increasingly talkative," "becoming a real part of the group," "much more outgoing than
before."

*Benjy* changed during a three-month period from one of the shyest four-year-olds in the
group to the opposite extreme in aggressive behavior. His painting pattern showed a parallel
change from small, filled, circular masses to open interrelated square and rectangular constructions (see Pls. 78–79, and further mention, p. 89).

*Scott* changed from an overt pattern of solitary play, overdependence on adults, intervals
of inactivity, handling of sex organs, pronounced sensitivity, and a highly protective attitude toward his work to increased play with others and marked interest in construction
with blocks. A corresponding change in his painting pattern from filled circles to vertical
and horizontal strokes occurred within this same period.

At the times when *Barry, Catherine, Chris, David, Della, Dorothea,* and *Ralph* showed a
pronounced transition from infantile toward more reasoning, controlled behavior, they
showed corresponding shifts in easel painting from circular to straight-line or angular
(square or rectangular) forms.

In many children the transition toward vertical or angular strokes has
been paralleled by a pronounced heightening of ability in constructive use
of blocks, as well as an accelerated development of interest in space-and-
fact relationships.[15]

*Hugh* enjoyed construction with unit blocks and picture puzzles. Although paints and
crayons were not of major interest to him, all his paintings and drawings showed heavy
vertical strokes and well-structuralized designs.

When *Fredrika* turned away from her interest in smearing activities to constructive play,
particularly block building with a group of boys, her painting pattern showed a correspond-

---

[14] See chap. v.

[15] This finding—that there is a parallelism between children's more constructive use of blocks
and their better sense of spatial pattern (as reflected in their drawing and painting designs)—
is of special interest because it supports the theory of those teachers of modern architecture who
believe that actual handling of three-dimensional materials and fashioning them into furniture
and building models is basic to development of proper feeling for design.

ing change from smeary, greenish masses to structuralized patterns with interrelated squares and rectangles. Verbalizations indicated that her interest changed from elimination to machinery, building, shooting (see Pls. 56–59).

*Steven*, already described as a "builder" in his group, also showed a parallelism between his general construction interests and his work in vertical and horizontal strokes which resulted in interrelated structuralized forms, both in painting and in crayoning.

*Bee, Carol, Danny, Della, Diane, Eda, Esther*, and *Gloria* also illustrate a parallelism between development of more assertive, outgoing, realistic construction interests and the appearance of vertical and horizontal emphasis in easel painting.

### EMPHASIS ON VERTICALS

We have already commented on the fact that children who emphasized verticals in the present study were likely, as a group, to be assertive and outgoing, to show a constructive pattern in their activities, and to be rational in their thought processes. Among them, masculine, rather than feminine, interests predominated.[16]

Emphasis on verticals was pronounced in the more "typical" boys, i.e., in boys with outgoing, self-confident, assertive mannerisms, many of whom seemed already to have identified themselves with older boys or men.

*Sheldon* was a short, sturdy, "boyish" sort of boy. His pockets were always full of stones, string, screws, and the like. He showed a boyish tendency to spit. He was, as a rule, friendly, self-reliant, self-assured. Sheldon painted with well-defined vertical and horizontal strokes to produce full-page effects with blocks of different colors. Observers noted: "Each stroke is well-defined and deliberate, each important in the final product." Sheldon likewise drew verticals and horizontals with crayons to produce airplanes, streets, etc., with interrelated square and rectangular forms.

*Victor*, a tall boy with a fine physique, was the uncontested leader among the older boys in his group. He spent his time in motor activities, in block building, and in active dramatic play, where he assumed the dominant role of father, or sometimes engineer or bear. Except for a month during which both painting pattern and overt behavior changed,[17] Victor worked predominantly with vertical strokes at the easel.

*Walter* was a happy, self-confident, outgoing boy who attempted to exaggerate his strength and bigness by putting extra flourishes into all that he did. He would pile blocks high on his head and carry them with pronounced gusto, announce exaggerated intentions to the group, assume overly conspicuous leadership of younger boys. In easel painting, Walter used strong vertical strokes and ordinarily worked with warm colors. Emphasis was on the top of the page.

Parallels between masculine tendencies and vertical strokes have been particularly pronounced in children whose masculine, assertive drive has been heightened by environmental stimuli.

*Danny*, the youngest of three boys, played predominantly with boys at school in strongly competitive relationships and resisted any activity which he considered girlish. As Danny matured, vertical emphasis became increasingly pronounced in both his painting and his

[16] See p. 57, n. 17.          [17] See p. 135.

crayon work. Only two of his earliest paintings showed any attempt at curvilinear strokes.

*Archie*, whose consuming drive to be a big man has already been discussed, predominantly painted with vertical strokes and cold colors, often emphasizing the top of the page and announcing verbal content which suggested the element of height.

*Edward, Erwin, George*, and *Jeff* each showed a shift from effeminate toward masculine behavior during the course of observation, and each showed parallel changes from circular to vertical painting patterns.

The foregoing discussion is not meant to imply that vertical emphasis is limited to boys. The free use of verticals has been noted in the paintings of many girls who had strong assertive drives and who, for the most part, had no apparent conflicts over their assertive feelings.

*Sadie* was variously described by observers and teachers as "self-assured," "brazen," "decisive," "outspoken." Though frail and wiry in appearance, she had a strong, raucous voice. She defended her rights "with every fibre of her being. . . . ." "Even the huskiest and strongest cannot intimidate her." Sadie's 30 paintings were characterized by vertical, horizontal, or occasionally diagonal masses, each produced with short, staccato, back-and-forth strokes. Only 1 of the 30 paintings had even a suggestion of a curved stroke.

*Sara* was a strong-willed child who held a unique position of authority in her group and who spent her time giving expression to this recognized role. She also stood out for her keen interest in reasoning or, as one observer noted, "in putting two and two together in order to understand this world." Fifteen of Sara's 20 paintings consisted of sweeping, heavy verticals which completely covered the page.

*Shirley* was a talkative, self-assured, outgoing child with a wealth of ideas which were carried out in dramatic play, in which she took the lead. Shirley showed relatively little interest in painting. She used warm colors, and her products were consistently characterized by vertical and horizontal strokes often combined into squares.

SUGGESTED INTERRELATIONSHIPS BETWEEN BEHAVIOR AND USE OF CIRCULAR
AND/OR VERTICAL PATTERNS

Parallels between behavior and use of circular and/or vertical patterns suggest the following tentative conclusions:

*a) A maturity difference.*—Whereas circular emphasis seems to reflect and to be associated with relatively infantile (emotional, subjective, dependent) tendencies, vertical emphasis tends to reflect a relatively more mature (more rational, more objective, more self-reliant) pattern.

*b) A sex difference.*—Whereas circular emphasis reflects relatively feminine tendencies, vertical emphasis tends to reflect a more masculine pattern.

*c) A general personality difference.*—Whereas circular emphasis seems to reflect and to be associated with more self-centered, withdrawing, in-turned personality, vertical emphasis tends to reflect a more outgoing, assertive individual.

These suggested findings are but a partial picture of children's use of circular or vertical strokes. The paintings just described are those of children who freely emphasized one *or* the other pattern in easel painting. But at least as many more children were observed who painted highly repetitive patterns in which both *verticals and circles appeared* either in conflict, in contrast, or else alternated with each other.

Analysis of observations has suggested that the conflicting use of verticals and circles seems to parallel another conflict as prevalent during the nursery-school years as is that between cleanliness and smearing previously described. This conflict is the struggle between assertive and submissive drives. It has been reflected in various types of situations, viz., sometimes children's conflicting use of verticals and circles has seemed to mirror their ambivalent desire, on the one hand, to remain "the baby" and, on the other, to grow up; sometimes it has seemed to reflect ambivalent boy-girl drives; or again the conflicting use of verticals and circles has seemed to express definite identification with specific individuals, the verticals representing the person in the assertive dominant role, the circles symbolizing the submissive role.

Many times the conflict over submissive-assertive roles was precipitated by sibling rivalry or by the arrival of a new baby. In such cases the sibling was usually of the opposite sex from the (presumably disturbed, or at least concerned) nursery-school child. In these cases the conflict between assertive and submissive seemed to involve factors both of maturity and of sex.

SYMBOLIC USE OF VERTICALS AND CIRCLES TO EXPRESS CONFLICTS OVER BIRTH OF SIBLING

This conflict was well illustrated by the work and accompanying behavior of both *Howard* and *Frank.*

During the fall of the year, *Howard* was reported as "one of the happiest and most energetic children in the group." He showed a good sense of fun and often laughed heartily. He settled disputes and difficulties with artful and diplomatic techniques. He was interested in everything, but particularly in active play: in swinging, climbing, riding the bike, running, block building, loading the wagon, shoveling, etc.

Howard used the easel only three times during the first part of the school year and the crayons not at all. His first two paintings (10-11-37 and 11-12-37) consisted of swing scribblings with resultant mass. Interest seemed more in the activity than in product or content. Howard's third painting (11-23-37) seemed more like an expression of felt need to paint, a possible forecast of what was to come. On that date, as he approached the easel he said, "I want to paint now. I'm going to paint with red." He made a few daubs, then a circular sweep. "I'm through," he said, after being at the easel for one minute.

In January it was noted that Howard became increasingly tense. At the same time, a period of interest *in using crayons* began.[18] From crayoning, Howard shifted to an interest in

---

[18] Howard's most intensive period of crayoning was in January. Of 17 products made during the year, 10 were produced in January, 3 in February, 3 in March, 1 in April (see discussion of parallelism between tension and use of crayons, pp. 129–30).

easel painting.[19] During this period Howard's social interests and his entire overt pattern of play had changed. The following observations outline the change in his paintings as well as in his overt behavior and suggest the cause that probably underlay the changes: On January 4, Howard painted heavy, red, vertical strokes which he then crossed out and smeared. The crossing-out of verticals suggests a denial of the assertive or masculine role (see Pl. 80).

On January 16, Howard painted two circles, a small yellow circle on the left, a large blue circle on the right. This painting remained unsmeared (see Pl. 81).

Howard's choice of yellow for the smaller circle, probably symbolizing the baby, and the choice of blue for the large circle, symbolizing the mother, seem to accord with the earlier discussion of color significance and give further support to our interpretation. A verbalization at the crayon table at this time also suggests that yellow may have had symbolic meaning for Howard. He chose yellow and quickly drew circles. Then he exclaimed, "Oh, dis is no good." He put yellow back and selected another color.

On January 18, Howard arrived at school with news: *a baby sister had been born the night before.* For a long time on this day he played alone in the tree house. He seemed tense and excited. He went to adults saying, "I like you, I like you." He apparently wanted physical affection. He pushed the doll buggy for a long time. He did not paint. The next day (January 19) Howard played alone on the climbing apparatus. Indoors he had a doll party alone in the doll corner. He did not paint.

On January 23, records indicate, Howard again sought a great deal of affection from the teachers. He ran to them, clasped them about the neck, and kissed them. On January 24, Howard was still playing alone more than usual. His favorite spot continued at this time to be the tree house where he was up and off by himself.[20] On January 26, Howard was again described as seeking much physical affection from adults. Indoors he played at tea party with Hope. Playing party was a recurrent activity throughout this period. Various observations have suggested that during periods of tension, heightened oral activities (e.g., eating and thumb-sucking) may indicate a child's current need for increased support and affection.[21]

On January 27, Howard painted for the first time after his sister's birth. He made two paintings. The first painting consisted of yellow verticals on the left, red verticals on the right. The second painting consisted of yellow verticals crossed out on the left and a clear, unsmeared circle in red at the right (see Pl. 82).

The smearing of verticals, as illustrated in Plate 82, is a return to the pattern observed on 1-4. It suggests that a reaction against the masculine role was undoubtedly brought into focus and intensified by his sister's birth. The color placement, with yellow on the left, parallels the painting of 1-16 and suggests symbolic color usage. The smearing of verticals and the relatively unsmeared circles parallel the treatment of these two forms on 1-4 and 1-16 and again suggest that Howard was reacting against being masculine and against being pushed out of his "baby" place in the family. The feminine and baby role appears to have

---

[19] Howard's most intensive painting period was in January and February. Of 27 paintings, 3 were done in the fall, 19 in January and February (most of them were done between 1-27 and 2-6), 4 in March, and 5 in April. There were no paintings after April. Between 1-27 and 2-6, Howard made 2 or 3 paintings a day.

[20] Aileen and Sally, both very insecure, tended to seek high places where they could be apart from the group and aloof from social relationships.

[21] Aileen's and Virginia's histories support this observation.

been more desirable at that moment. The choice of red for the circular, "feminine" representation suggests that Howard's emotions were most strongly identified with the feminine role.[22]

On February 1, Howard trailed the teacher and tried to secure her attention in various ways. At the clay table he said to his cousin Hope, to whom he was devoted and with whom he played a great deal: "If you didn't have a ribbon and those yellow curls, you'd be a boy." Howard painted on this day. His product consisted of both circles and verticals, and both were crossed and smeared. He used red on the left, blue on the right, of his painting page (see Pl. 83).

From the foregoing we gather that Howard's inner conflict was evidently reaching a verbal level. His conversation at the clay table substantiates the view that he was concerned over the boy-girl problem. (It is also of interest to find that Howard first verbalized his conflict while playing with clay. In our observations, clay more than any of the other media used was likely to release or evoke free verbalization of underlying preoccupations or problems.)

As recorded, in his painting of February 1, Howard smeared both verticals and circles. The smearing of both symbols in his painting of 2-1 suggests that the inner conflict was still going on but that Howard's earlier interest in being a girl (expressed in unsmeared circles) and his resistance to his masculine role (expressed in smeared verticals) had been supplemented by a more evenly balanced conflict.

On February 2, Howard made 3 paintings. The first one consisted of both circular and vertical strokes, all smeared with horizontal markings. Blue was used on the left, red on the right. Howard's second painting consisted of yellow circles and verticals, both smeared. The third painting showed mostly yellow verticals, although a few yellow circles were present. The entire product was smeared. As in his painting of 1-2, Howard apparently was still ambivalent about the masculine-feminine role, with a slight trend now toward more acceptance of his masculine role. Although both forms were still smeared, the verticals became increasingly pronounced from the first to the last of this series of paintings.

On February 3, Howard did not paint. He spent most of the morning walking around with a doll blanket on his head  On February 6, Howard was able to express verbally the conflict seen in his paintings. His teacher reported: "Howard sought lots of physical attention, such as kissing me and throwing his arms around my neck. For the past two days he has said: 'My mother is going to buy me a dress and I'm going to get yellow curls and then I'll be a girl too.' He told his mother that he didn't want to go home any more. He wanted to go to his cousin Hope's to live. He brought a doll to me and said: 'This can be your little sister. Will you hug her?' " On the same date—February 6—Howard made 2 paintings. The first consisted of heavy swing scribbling, primarily in green, with a few strokes of red at the upper and lower margins. The second was also painted with green, in smeary strokes that had a circular trend.

From the time that Howard began to express himself at a verbal level, his interest in, and need for, painting diminished. The conflicting vertical and circular patterns were gone, as was the yellow trend, which ran through his period of more concentrated interest in painting. With verbalization concerning his conflict, there was a change not only in the painting situation but also in the pattern of his block constructions. His previously pronounced tendency toward closure disappeared, as did his interest in solitary activities and doll play. Active and co-operative play again characterized his behavior.

While Howard's paintings and behavior records do not yield a complete picture, it seems fairly evident that the vertical circular pattern and the recurrent yellow trend re-

[22] See pp. 19–21.

flected his concern over the baby, as well as his conflict over the boy-girl role. This latter had probably been somewhat stimulated by his close relationship with his cousin Hope and was brought to a focus by the arrival of his baby sister. It would seem that for Howard easel painting served as a valuable medium for expressing his problem while it was still at a non-verbal, unclarified level.

*Frank* is another boy who presents a parallel between the use of the circular-vertical pattern in easel painting and an apparent concern or conflict over his boy-girl and/or grown-up-infantile roles. Frank, at the time observations were started, had two sisters, one older and one younger than himself. The family, including Frank, spoke eagerly of the coming of a new baby and hoped it would be a boy. Frank was displaying much rivalry toward his sisters, particularly the younger one at this period. The following excerpts from daily records illustrate Frank's real concern about the coming baby:

10-15-37: Frank told of the coming baby in school that week. 11-19-37: Frank was building with blocks. He began to call out, "I'm going to have a new baby." Gilbert, whose family was also expecting a baby, followed suit. They were soon screaming back and forth at each other. 11-29-37: Frank came to school and said that mother and Judy (the younger sister) were both sick. He said his mother had a sick stomach. Later in the day he said they had a new baby brother and his name was Steven. He said the baby was nearly as big as Judy but that it did not look like Judy. (Actually the baby had not yet arrived.) 11-30-37: Frank said that his mother had gone to the hospital but that the baby had not yet come. 12-1-37: Frank said to the teacher in the bathroom: "Nanna says she's going to stay until my mommy comes back. You'll come and see me, won't you? You'll come and eat with me."

Frank had made four paintings during this period. All were characterized by full-page verticals smeared over with horizontal or diagonal swing scribbling and with left- and right-sided (parallel, paired, or two-mass) effects. No striking color usage was evident. (The smearing of verticals preceding the coming of the baby suggests resistance to the more assertive or grownup, mature role. The paired or parallel mass effects recall other children who used the paired-mass pattern when preoccupied with the mother-infant relationship.[23] Frank's overt behavior during this period—his conspicuous preference for young children, especially girls, and his lack of assertiveness in play—seems in keeping with the trends suggested by his smearing of verticals in easel painting.)

On 12-2-37 a baby sister was born. The nurse brought Frank to school that morning and commented: "Isn't it too bad—it was another girl." In the course of the morning, Frank several times claimed that the baby had not come. Teachers said they were uncertain whether Frank was denying the baby's arrival because it was not the wished-for boy or because it was not yet home from the hospital, or whether he was just not accepting the fact of the baby's arrival. Observers' notes state that all that morning Frank seemed preoccupied and that his play lacked spontaneity and enthusiasm.

On 12-8-37 Frank's block play reflected his preoccupation over the baby: He was building with blocks and remarked: "This is a fountain. It's a hospital. Mother is in the hospital, and here are the beds. I'm putting the sick people in the beds." Frank put little wooden figures in the "fountain" of his building. Several times while building he went through the motions of hitting children around him with a block. Actually, he never did so. He made a doorway and moved small wooden figures in and out. He took some blocks from Glen. He made beds, " 'Cause there are lots of people." Frank said: "We have to leave the building up until tomorrow." He put one figure on the bed. He seemed completely absorbed now in his building. When putting-away time came, he kept right on taking blocks and adding

[23] See p. 76.

to his building. A child asked: "What are you making?" Frank said: "A secret." The other child started to add blocks. Frank said: "Don't!" Then he added: "We're making a doctor's hospital. This is a chair." His next remark was "I went skating all by myself." The other child answered: "So did I." Frank continued with his earlier reverie: "It's a hospital. This is a window." He put another figure on the bed. He said: "The big fat woman should be here alone."

Frank became ill and was at home not only for the holidays but for a two-month period following Christmas. He returned to school on 2-25-38. On this day Frank sought the easel. He produced two paintings. Frank's first painting was begun with a red circle in the center of the page. This circle was almost completely obliterated with swing scribbling of yellow, green, and black. To the left of the obliterated circle he placed unsmeared verticals in green and black. The final effect was somber. Frank commented: "It's all dark" (see Pl. 84). The second painting consisted of full-page verticals in green, yellow, red, and black, with green predominant. It was unsmeared (see Pl. 85). (These last two paintings suggest a change from the submissive, i.e., circular, toward increased acceptance of the more assertive, more masculine, i.e., vertical, pattern. The daily records substantiate such an interpretation. The record of 2-25-38 stated: "Frank has been more aggressive than was usual before his long absence.")

On 3-1-38 Frank played with clay and talked, while doing so, of tiny babies. (The exact words either were not caught or were not recorded.) On the same date Frank also painted. (The order of his painting and clay experience was not recorded:) The painting consisted of a blue circle, roughly centered on the page, filled with red, then smeared over with blue. A black ovular mass was made above and to the left of the smeared circle. Black and green horizontals ran across the painting, and two long horizontals of red were placed above and below. We are reminded of Frank's previous paintings. The smearing of the circle again suggests a covering-over or repression of submissive feelings or desire to be the baby, while the unsmeared verticals hint of the return of Frank's earlier, more assertive, more masculine drives. The use of red for the unsmeared verticals suggests that these drives were emotionally charged.

Throughout March, Frank continued to be disturbed. The daily behavior record of 3-9 describes him as chewing everything—mittens, the neck of his suit, etc. At rest time during this period he frequently masturbated. On 3-4 Frank painted a smeared oval, predominantly green and black. On 3-15 he painted with short vertical strokes. The circular form had disappeared. Blue, green, and black predominated. On 3-16 Frank painted a product much like that of the previous day. The colors were predominantly blue, green, and black. In this painting, however, the short verticals were overshadowed by diagonals.

The paintings described suggest that Frank was working away from the conflict expressed in his circular vertical paintings. He was also verbalizing more freely. On March 23, he remarked: "Those two girls [Esther and Harriet—two smallish blondes] are babies. They look funny. But you [Freda and Fredrika—two husky brunettes] look all right. My sister's name is Freda, too. She's a baby." On March 25, he volunteered: "My baby is one year old. My sister is a year old, and she has a little bed." On this day Frank painted. His product again was away from the circular-vertical pattern, and there was no black in it. In this painting, yellow and green were used in intermingled horizontal and diagonal strokes, yellow predominant on the left, green on the right.

Frank made only one painting during the remainder of the school year. This (made on April 4) was of red and yellow swing scribblings. Frank made no further comments about the baby and was apparently no longer preoccupied with that subject. Progress records indicated that he was again playing happily with the children of his own age and that he had discontinued his aggressions on other children and their materials. His one crayon product of the year (made at the end of March) was named "Trucks and Cars" and further suggests that Frank had moved away from his emotionally disturbing preoccupations toward more objective interests.

In Frank's case, as in *Howard*'s, the analogy between painting pattern and personal conflict was most obvious before the period of verbalization. Once the problem reached a verbal level, painting seemed unnecessary as a medium for self-expression.

Other examples of an association between a contrasting use of circles and verticals in easel painting and conflicts involving submissive-assertive or masculine-feminine drives have been too numerous to describe in the detail given in the cases of Howard and Frank. The following section summarizes our more defined observations in this area and suggests, in general, that (*a*) persistent obliteration of verticals tends to be found in children who give other evidences—sometimes overt, sometimes indirect—of hostility toward the assertive or masculine role; (*b*) obliteration of circles tends to be found in children who give other evidences of reaction against infantile, submissive, or feminine roles; (*c*) alternating use of verticals and circles tends to occur in the work of children with distinctly ambivalent feelings in these areas.

Sometimes the conflict expressed in easel painting has seemed to be the reflection of ambivalent or contrasting aspects of the child's own nature. At other times the conflict expressed in the easel painting has seemed to make manifest a thoroughgoing obvious conflict with a rival of the opposite sex. Whether the conflict reflected in an easel painting is entirely localized within the individual or whether it reflects a partially externalized conflict cannot be judged from the paintings alone. As we have observed repeatedly before, sound interpretations must rest upon consideration of all available data.

#### SUMMARY OF CIRCULAR-VERTICAL PATTERNS USED TO EXPRESS CONFLICTS

1. *Unsmeared verticals.*—Some children whose paintings showed unsmeared verticals produced circular patterns when using crayons. The unsmeared verticals were done with paints, a medium more likely to reflect inner feelings. Observations suggested that the circular pattern done with crayons might be expected to accord with overt, adult expectancies and with the overt behavior of the children.[24]

Early in the year *Bee* painted well-defined verticals and horizontals, which resulted in decorative latticework patterns. In contrast to these, her crayon products were usually circular and pastel. In the group, Bee was self-contained and quite shy. She spent her time watching others. She seemed to withdraw from their advances. (Her overt behavior at this time was reflected in her crayon pattern). Toward the latter part of the year, however, Bee's behavior changed, and she revealed a preference for boyish activities and play with

[24] See pp. 131–33 for comparison of easel painting and crayoning.

boys. This change was reflected in her painting pattern, since her lines became heavier and her designs became less delicate and decorative.

*Hilda*, sister of *Bee*, entered the nursery school the year after Bee had gone on to kindergarten. She also showed a tendency toward vertical and horizontal strokes in painting and toward circular masses in crayoning. Hilda, like Bee, was self-contained and exceedingly shy in the group. (As with Bee, this was expressed in her crayon pattern). A strong passive resistance that characterized Hilda's behavior when with the group gave evidence of a strong assertive underlying drive which seemed to be expressed in her paintings, as she painted vertical strokes and smeared them.

*Ray's* recurrent theme in painting consisted of heavy vertical and horizontal strokes in deep colors, especially red. His crayon work contrasted with his paintings in that they were almost entirely circular scribbling or circles, filled. Ray, an only child, much loved and solicitously cared for by parents and grandparents, still retained his plump, happy, baby look. He played almost exclusively in a docile, dependent relationship with his cousin Stella. (The influence of this family-cultivated relationship was expressed in the circular crayon theme.) When Stella was not at school, Ray joined the boys, ran, jumped, climbed to heights, and showed marked activity quite in contrast to his more usual and adult-expected passive behavior. (Ray's basic feelings, we believe, were expressed in his painting pattern, while the the expected responses seemed evident in his crayon drawings.)

*Tess* characteristically painted vertical and horizontal strokes or angular forms, whereas her crayon drawings contained many circular forms. In school, Tess was quiet and inactive. She seemed to gain her satisfactions vicariously through watching others. (This submissive role is suggested by her crayon theme.) At home, Tess was favored by her father over her two older sisters and two younger brothers. Her father treated her like a boy. Her paintings, together with home observations, lead us to think that basically she felt herself in a dominant, assertive position while overtly in school she accepted the quiet behavior that she thought was expected of her and that she showed in her circular crayon patterns.

*Sara* characteristically used vertical and horizontal strokes when painting, and she used circles when crayoning. Sara, like *Ray*, had a deep underlying streak of determination and stubbornness that became exaggerated after the birth of her baby brother. She was basically an outgoing individual (expressed in her vertical-horizontal painting pattern). In her usual conduct at school, Sara accepted the family standards which expected her to be properly social, co-operative, and very much of a "little lady" (expressed in her crayon pattern).[25]

2. *Smeared verticals.*—The children who smeared verticals when painting seemed, for the most part, to be resisting their own assertive drives or to be expressing hostility toward an aggressive rival.

*Bert* and *Aldo* tended to smear verticals at the same time that they were covering over their assertive masculine drives. Both boys came from homes in which the mother-child relationship was unduly stressed, and both of them showed infantile, submissive, with-

[25] There were other children who, like Sara and Tess, tended to *paint verticals* and *crayon circles*, but, unlike Sara and Tess, they usually smeared their painting pattern (see, e.g., Ronny and Carol in subsequent discussion). Glen, whose vertical theme in both painting and crayoning belied his submissive overt behavior, is not here included, both because of his infrequent tendencies to smear and because he differed from these children in that his crayon and painting patterns were similar rather than dissimilar.

drawing behavior. They had had no chance to identify with their fathers. Bert revealed his underlying masculine drives toward the end of the year when his behavior became definitely assertive. Aldo revealed like underlying drives in his verbalizations of the free-association types. In their verbalizations both boys consistently evidenced masculine interests.

*Ronny* painted smeared verticals and crayoned smeared circles. The smearing of circles gradually lessened and then disappeared. At the time of these observations, Ronny was building block inclosures, which he carefully protected (the block inclosures suggest the crayon pattern), or towers, which he destroyed (the block towers suggest the painting pattern). Overtly, Ronny was extremely tense. He had a marked speech block which had begun during his mother's pregnancy a half-year before the period of observation. Constipation was reported as a home problem. He was dependent upon adults for attention and approval. His submissive behavior seems to be in accord with the unsmeared circular and the smeared vertical patterns.

*Frank, Howard, Jimmy,* and *Ronny* all smeared verticals preceding the arrival of new babies in their families.

3. *Cutoff verticals.*—The term "cutoff verticals" is used to describe a painting pattern in which strokes, usually horizontal, were drawn across the top of the vertical strokes. Cutoff verticals differed from the smeared verticals discussed previously in that the latter were indiscriminately covered with wavy, usually diagonal scribblings.

Cutoff verticals have been observed most markedly in children who were feeling strongly competitive and hostile concerning masculinity in someone of the opposite sex. Cutoff verticals seemed to express more clearly defined conflict situations than did smeared verticals.

*Loretta* used verticals cut off with horizontals in easel painting at a time when she was displaying much hostility and competition with her older brother.

*Esther* produced cutoff verticals during the fall of her second year in school, when her overt behavior was less sublimated than was usual for her and when rivalry feelings toward her younger brother first became apparent.

*Trixie* frequently cut off verticals with horizontals. She was at this time displaying a highly competitive attitude toward her siblings, particularly her older brother.

*Paula's* work showed the cutoff vertical pattern following the death of a seven-month-old brother and while awaiting the arrival of another baby.

4. *Crossed verticals.*—The crossing of verticals (resulting in the making of crosses), like the smearing and the cutting-off of verticals, seemed to express a definite desire to obliterate the vertical pattern. Children who consistently made crosses evidenced a parallel sex concern.

*Eric* made crosses, called adult attention to them, then overlaid them. At the same time that he expressed himself in this way in easel painting, he delighted in destroying his block structures. His usual overt behavior was overdocile and retiring. His detailed case records suggest a repressed interest in sex and clandestine sex play at home.

*Norman*[26] carried a crossed-vertical theme through his paintings. He masturbated a great deal. Both verbally and symbolically, he revealed a great concern about his penis.

*Perry* turned to crayoning and made 3 drawings showing the cross-pattern on the day after an older child had threatened to cut off his ears. He also had night terrors following this threat. He did not use the crayons at any other time during the year. Perry's choice of crayons rather than paints supports our observation that crayons are likely to be used under conditions of unusual and specific tension. The threat which apparently precipitated the crayon drawings and the nightmares is one which psychoanalysts have said may lead to castration fear. This interpretation accords with other observations we have noted on the crossed or otherwise obliterated vertical (Pls. 86–87).

*Jessica* obviously desired to be a boy. She not only wore boys' clothes but stood to urinate. Jessica turned from heavy, *unsmeared* verticals to crosses at a transition period when she was beginning to desire social approval and was attempting to conform to adult expectations concerning her female role (Pls. 88–89).

*Alan, David, Percy,* and *Will* each showed a period of crossed-vertical work that was paralleled in each one's history by one or more of the following factors: masturbation, exhibitionism, circumcision, and verbalization about sex organs that suggested heightened concern over sexuality.

5. *The smearing of structuralized patterns.*—The smearing of structuralized patterns—i.e., of patterns characterized by interrelation of straight lines or of angular forms—seems to have been frequent in children who were preoccupied with high standards. It was observed especially in girls who were overtly adopting a controlled pattern beyond their years. Such girls tended to come from homes in which pressure was indicated by such factors as "high expectancies by parents," "only child," "oldest child," "parents wanted a boy," "parents treated girl as a boy."[27]

*Carol* tended to smear structuralized patterns, to cover her block structures, and to destroy her clay work whenever she felt that she was being observed. Shy and withdrawing in a group of children and in the presence of adults, she was frequently dictatorial and bossy when with just a few children and when free from adults. One wonders whether the smearing, the covering, and the destroying of her products in the various media expressed symbolically her reaction against the high standards which she had overtly accepted or whether her gestures of destruction were attempts to cover or repress her self-assertive drives.

6. *Smeared circles.*—The smearing of circles has been a consistent painting pattern among children who seemed to be resisting either a submissive or a feminine role. Case data suggest that in some instances these children were resisting feelings localized within themselves and that at other times they

[26] Norman had been circumcised. According to some psychoanalysts, this might have heightened his sex concern. Our data are insufficient on this point to lend themselves to findings. Further investigation might be of value.

[27] Some of these background factors suggest that the problem of the child's sex role might have been significant. The smeared constructive pattern which incorporates the smeared vertical also suggests this possibility. As a matter of fact, however, no overt evidence of sex conflict occurred in the cases observed.

(boys and girls) were reacting against some individual (female) who was in a related and dominant role.

*Arline* tended to smear over circles *with strong verticals or wavy scribbles*. She was an only child, who was resistant to all adult expectancies. Overtly she was negativistic, aggressive, boyish, and defiant toward others of her own sex.

*Phoebe* smeared circles at a time when, like *Arline*, she was defiant of adult expectancies.

*Frank*, in crayoning, smeared circles with heavy verticals at a time when his paintings consisted of smeared circles and unsmeared verticals. These patterns, as we have seen, appeared when he was competing with the arrival of a baby sister in the home and at a time when Frank was swinging away from dependent, relatively infantile, and feminine interests toward more assertive and boyish behavior (Pls. 84–85).

*Joe*[28] smeared circles during a period when the home reported marked rivalry with an older sister.

*Harry* smeared circles with heavy verticals in both painting and crayoning and was in conflict with a thirteen-year-old sister, whom he bitterly resented and with whom, his parents reported, he was in continuous feud.

*Ardis*, characterized as "wanting authority but lacking in ideas and initiative," went through a period when she overlaid circles with vertical and horizontal strokes.

7. *Smeared verticals and unsmeared circles.*—The smearing of verticals along with the painting of unsmeared circles was observed in children who were in process of resisting the assertive or masculine, and of favoring the submissive or feminine, role.

*Howard*, as already described and illustrated (Pls. 80–83), produced the smeared vertical and the unsmeared circular pattern around the time of his sister's birth and at a time when his own verbalizations indicated a desire to be a girl.

*Brian* consistently used the smeared vertical and unsmeared circle pattern in painting during a period when he overtly sought feminine roles. He spent several weeks, for instance, completely living a "Lady Margaret" character. A Rorschach test given a year later evoked the response "Woman" to an ink-blot which usually elicited the response "Man."

*George* was noted to use smeared oblongs and unsmeared circles at a time when he was overtly attempting to follow the dependent, girlish pattern set by his older sister.

8. *Smeared circles and unsmeared verticals.*—Smearing of circles along with the painting of unsmeared verticals was observed in the products of children who were in the process of resisting or reacting against the feminine, and in favor of the assertive or masculine, role.

*Frank* (Pls. 84–85) worked with filled smeared circles and with unsmeared verticals over a two-month period following the birth of a sister. During this time he was becoming increasingly aggressive. Following the conversational line of the rest of the family, he had

---

[28] Joe and his sister shared a room, and Joe was at this time expressing fear of the dark and of being left alone. Possibility of sex play between the siblings was suggested by one adult who worked closely with Joe.

talked about expecting a baby brother. His painting pattern might to some degree have reflected his feelings against the baby sister who arrived, as well as against his own infantile, feminine drives which he was trying to master.

9. *Verticals and circles used differently on the left and right sides of the painting page.* —Some children were observed to use the two halves of their painting page quite differently to express their conflicting drives. While the trend is not so constant as some others that have been observed, it has seemed that many children used the side of the page corresponding to the dominant hand to express both their learned responses and those drives which were finding overt expression, while they used the side corresponding to the less dominant hand to express their more basic primitive drives and often their more repressed feelings. Such children tended to divide the painting page only during particular periods of stress when they were undergoing ambivalent pulls.[29]

*Neil*, left handed, went through a stage of painting circles on the left and verticals on the right. At this time he was overtly submissive. He played predominantly with girls who were markedly assertive and who took the lead. As Neil became more assertive and more boyish in behavior, his differentiated treatment of circles and verticals disappeared, and structuralized, straight-line, all-over-the-page patterns prevailed.

*Victor*, right handed, went through a period of painting circles on the left and verticals on the right. His crayon products were predominantly circles. At this time Victor was recorded to be "moody," and "not himself." A baby sister was born during the period of circular-vertical painting. In Victor's case the painting and crayon patterns suggest conflict undoubtedly set up by the birth of his sister. To be feminine was at this period, undoubtedly, to be desired. Victor in behavior, as well as in his painting pattern, gave evidence of his emotional disturbance and conflict. His behavior, however, like his painting, kept the pattern of masculine dominance throughout.

Parallel findings have, from time to time, been observed in the products of several other children, but the pattern of paintings and behavior have not shown the same consistency as was seen in Neil's and Victor's work.

*Bee*, right handed, painted a product different from her usual pattern (on 4-27). It had a vertical on the right and a circle on the left and was done just after the time that she had made the shift toward more aggressive play with boys.

*Edward*, right handed, painted verticals on the right and circles on the left (on 10-20) at a time when the feminine role interested him more than usual. In dramatic play, over a period of a month, he alternated feminine and masculine roles, sometimes playing father and sometimes mother. Once he protruded his abdomen, asserting "I have a baby here."

*Archie*, left handed and with a tendency toward submissiveness, frequently produced circles on the left and verticals on the right side of his easel paintings.

[29] Many children painted their designs as a whole, making no distinction between left- and right-hand sides of the page.

*Rita* (Pls. 47–50), right handed, tended in "left-right" paintings to produce clean constructive blue patterns on the left and smeary patterns on the right. This trend is not in keeping with our general observations, for Rita was overtly clean and precise and one would have expected the clean pattern to appear on the dominant or right side.

10. *Alternating emphasis on verticals and circles.*—The children whom we observed to show alternation in vertical and circular patterns also tended to show alternations in submissive and assertive feelings and behavior.

*Jessica* strikingly alternated between periods of strong, unsmeared verticals in warm colors and periods of circular work in cooler colors. Her crayon products paralleled her paintings. Jessica's overt behavior showed equally striking alternations, which paralleled the changes in her painting patterns. Her vertical paintings occurred at times of negativistic, aggressive behavior. Her circles accompanied periods when Jessica was trying to be accepted and when she was generally trying to be co-operative and agreeable.[30] (This parallelism between painting and crayon products, together with Jessica's intense drive to use the paints, gives support to the view that Jessica used these media to express her conflict.)

*Patty*'s typical paintings were full-page products with red and yellow verticals predominant. For brief periods during the year this pattern was replaced with circular forms often painted blue, with pastel and muddy effects. Patty was by nature a dominating child. Her assertive drives were probably heightened by the attitude of two older brothers who, to her great annoyance, treated her as an underling. Her natural desire for domination is in keeping with her usual vertical theme. Patty's periods of circular painting paralleled times when she was identifying herself more consistently with the girls in school and with their activities, e.g., she was entering into dramatic play, usually as mother, sometimes as sister or maid.[31]

*Jocelyn* characteristically painted verticals. This pattern was in contrast to her overtly shy and withdrawing behavior. Home evidence of jealousy toward a younger brother, also adopted, substantiated the impression given by her painting pattern, in that in painting she was actually expressing her repressed aggressions. During one two-week period, while her younger brother attended a nursery group located in an adjoining room, Jocelyn's easel paintings took on a circular pattern. Records of that period describe her as "giving herself up almost entirely to daydreaming." She also "cried a great deal," "clung to her mother," "was less active than usual," and "not at all herself." Her paintings during these two weeks reproduced the circular pattern through two recurrent masses, one orange and one blue, each maintaining its own position on a separate side of the painting page. Jocelyn's painting theme returned to the vertical pattern at the end of the two weeks when her brother was

[30] Jessica's assertive masculine drive seems to have been stimulated by the home situation and was usually heightened by stays at home. The circular theme, on the contrary, first appeared while the mother was on a vacation. It appeared a second time when the mother accepted the suggestion that Jessica be sent to school in a dress instead of her usual boyish garb.

[31] Patty's color usage is worth comment. Her circular patterns (in contrast to her verticals, painted in red and yellow) were done in cold colors. One would gather that they did not express Patty's basic emotional drives. Apparently being feminine (expressed in the circular theme), although it was constantly forced in the home, held no interest at this time for Patty.

withdrawn from school. Her behavior at the same time became less withdrawn and more as it had been in the earlier months.[32]

11. *Other variations of the circular and vertical themes.*—Three children with strongly ambivalent tendencies have revealed a painting pattern in which masculine and feminine symbols seemed embodied in a single pattern.

*Louis* over a period of time produced a highly persistent pattern of vertical masses. Each mass was separated from the other and was painted in a different, heavily applied color.[33] During the time of this pattern, Louis was overtly submissive. Typical of his reactions at this time was the following: When another boy rammed him with his wagon, his hurt expression quickly disappeared, he smiled and said: "I'll fix the wagon for you." His preferred play-companions were girls. As Louis turned to more active play with boys, his painting pattern changed.

*Edward* produced vertical ovals in crayoning at a time when he showed strongly ambivalent or composite feelings about his own masculine (versus feminine) role.

*Jessica* went through a stage of producing vertical masses made up by piling circular daubs one upon the other. At this time her overt behavior also reflected ambivalent feelings.

Still other individualized patterns which incorporated the vertical or circular pattern in ways that may be significant are the following:

*Stanley* worked consistently in *unclosed circles*. In the group he stood out as a child unwilling or unable to defend himself. We have observed persistent use of the closed circle to parallel an inward sense of restriction and a certain kind of immurement or self-protection. Stanley's case suggests that the unclosed circle may have reflected a sense of inadequacy in these areas.

*Brian* tended to produce verticals in black and blue and circular forms in orange. His closest and warmest contacts were with women and girls. His father was apparently not a figure in his life at this time, and he had no friends among the boys. The association between warm color and the feminine symbol, along with his use of colder colors for the masculine symbol, seem consonant with his experiences and interests.

*George* frequently used red vertically and blue in neat circles. This suggests his feeling of the masculine character as the more assertive, and the feminine as the more controlled, figure. Case data on George support the view that he was in conflict between these two drives. During his most free and happy school period, when he was outgoing and an undisputed and popular leader, he painted strong, warm-colored verticals. The home, however, put a premium upon the pattern of behavior set by George's older sister, who was delicate, somewhat handicapped physically, meek, submissive, and decidedly feminine. George's behavior periodically suggested that he was attempting to live the model of life as established by his sister. At these times he painted blue circular patterns.

*Jeff* used red for circles and green for verticals. He was functioning overtly at an immature, dependent, submissive level. The circles painted in the warmer color suggest that his

---

[32] It would seem that in her vertical paintings at school Jocelyn felt free to express her aggressive drives concerning her brother. During the period of circular patterns, she expressed, one surmises, her unhappy submission to her brother's intrusion at "her" school.

[33] The verticals suggest a masculine drive. The color-mass effects suggest an emotional, more feminine drive. His behavior pattern suggested similar ambivalent tendencies.

drive was for playing a submissive, dependent role at this time. That he actually had little emotional drive about maintaining himself as a male at this period is probably revealed in his use of green for painting the masculine symbol.

*Philip* used verticals of red on the left of his paintings, circles of various other colors on the right. Philip was overtly impulsive and uncontrolled. He was reacting strongly against the excessive demands for control placed upon him by the many feminine figures who were trying to "run his life"—mother, grandmother, sister, and nurse. The red verticals on the left suggest the basically assertive masculine drive.

This account has not included *Catherine, Dorothea*, and others who also seemed to use circles and verticals symbolically.

These brief reports, although roughly grouped to suggest general tendencies, are best regarded as but a systematized series of observations. As individual patterns they seemed to have a certain consistency and significance that justified including them. Further investigation is needed, however, if they are to be more than a set of highly suggestive observations. Our hope in including them is that others, by gathering more evidence than we were able to get, will substantiate or invalidate these, as well as some other of the less conclusive findings in this study.

### COMMON CONFLICTS IN YOUNG CHILDREN RECURRENTLY EXPRESSED IN THEIR PAINTINGS

The children described above not only give us some clues for further study of painting products but also point to factors that underlie certain common conflicts among young children. We have noted, for example, that the conflict over assertive-submissive or masculine-feminine roles is frequently precipitated (*a*) when there is the expectation or the recent arrival of a new baby in the family or (*b*) when there is a keenly felt rivalry with a sibling, particularly of the opposite sex.[34]

Factors in our case analyses that seem specifically to lead to the conflict between assertive and submissive drives in girls have been (*a*) the girl's status as only or eldest child (as *Bee* and *Arline*); (*b*) incidents preceding child's own birth, as when parents, having wanted a male child, subsequently treat the girl as a boy (e.g., *Jessica* and *Tess*).

Factors observed in case analyses which have seemed to lead boys into the assertive-submissive conflict have been: (*a*) lack of a father or of any strong masculine pattern (as with *Aldo, Bert, John*, and *Louis*); (*b*) too exclusive association with feminine personalities in the home (as with the

---

[34] Of the children included, Frank, Howard, Jimmy, Paula, and Victor all showed crystallization of the assertive-submissive or boy-girl conflict at the advent of a baby. In Howard the conflict seemed most sharply identified with the boy-girl roles. In Jimmy the conflict seemed more specifically focused on being dependent and infantile versus being mature and self-assertive. Of the children included, Carol, Eric, Harry, Jessica, Joe, Jocelyn, Loretta, Neil, and Patty all expressed this conflict in association with rivalries with a sibling of the opposite sex.

four boys just listed above, plus *Glen* and *Brian*); (*c*) so much satisfaction from the infantile, dependent role that there has not been sufficient incentive to develop from the infantile to the more assertive and mature role (e.g., *Ray*).

## SYMBOLISM

We have discussed children's frequent and seemingly unmistakable symbolic use of circles and verticals. When this study of children's usage of various media was initiated, the authors did not realize that generally recognized symbols would be extensively found in children's paintings and other creative products. Even a limited study of primitive art and an investigation of dreams reveal that the symbolism found in primitive art, the symbolism in dreams, and the symbolism used by young children appear to be all of a piece. The inner life of young children, the dream life of man, and the ideational life of primitive man apparently all draw directly from the stream of life that comes down through the ages and is transmitted with the germ of life from generation to generation.

While, at first glance or hearing, it may be difficult to accept the fact that certain patterns are utilized by children to express masculinity and others to represent femininity, due and careful consideration of their paintings leaves no doubt in our thinking that there is a specific association between masculine tendencies and vertical patterns and between feminine tendencies and circular patterns.

Verbalizations such as the following offer slight additional clues to be considered in connection with male and female symbolism as found in children's paintings and drawings:

*Louis* said, when the time came to put away the playthings: "I'm a big strong man—I'll pick up the straight blocks." *Kit* replied: "I'll pick up the round ones." *Louis* repeated: "I'll pick up the straight ones, Kit, don't forget."

*Jimmy* made his first vertical strokes in crayoning on 5-10, following a period of circular scribbling. For the first time he named his product. He called these first verticals, "Man."

*Sally* gave her first naming to a product that was a circular form. She called it "Girl."

In discussion with Dr. Edward Liss, New York City psychiatrist, the following incident was related: A child, confronted for the first time with the numeral 10 promptly identified the 1 (vertical) with Daddy and the 0 (circular) with Mommy.

### DIFFERENT SYMBOLS USED TO EXPRESS THE SAME CONFLICT

It is of interest to note that different children express the same conflict in various ways. Concern over the birth of a new baby in the family, for example, has recurrently been expressed and painted in four different forms: (*a*) blue-yellow overlay; (*b*) the container pattern, including concentric circles; (c) related or paired masses—usually one of the masses tends to be dark and the other light, one covering perhaps three-quarters, and the other one-quarter, of the page; (d) use of vertical-circular pattern.[35]

a) The use of blue-yellow overlay patterns in painting has already been discussed.[36] It would seem that the blue-yellow overlay pattern was sometimes used around the time of sibling birth by children not quite so advanced developmentally in painting as those who used the vertical-circular patterns. The container pattern, on the other hand, seems to have been used by children who had advanced beyond the vertical-circular pattern to an interest in relating forms.

b) Container patterns sometimes consisted of circles filled with smaller oval or circular forms.

Tony used the circle with smaller circles during the month preceding the birth of his sister. His painting pattern changed to vertical strokes after the sister's birth, and at the same time his behavior became happier and more outgoing.

Tess used the filled circular form preceding the birth of her brother and at a time when she was obviously concerned about the coming event.

Roberta, preceding the birth of her brother, used a circle as a container for smaller forms in both painting and crayoning. During the same period she emphasized enclosures in block building.

Timothy used the container theme toward the end of his nursery-school stay and at a time when the arrival of a new baby was imminent.

For these four children the parallel occurrence of concern over a new baby and use of the container theme seems to make clear a relationship between the two. For the following children the associations were even more explicit:

Angela's concern over a coming baby has been elsewhere discussed[37] Such concern as we have seen was variously expressed. At first it was through paired masses of color. Later on, when she was doing representative work, the container theme was recurrent with such diverse names as "Goldfish in a Bowl," "Boat," and "House." Finally, large and small connected figures emerged. Angela's concern was also expressed in dramatic play. The use of the container theme was but one phase in the cycle.

Paula worked in undifferentiated masses at the time a baby was expected in her home. The painting products themselves were not distinguishable from earlier or later work by color, form, or space usage. Paula did, however, seek the easel much more persistently just preceding the baby's birth than she did at earlier or later periods. Her recurrent name for her product, "Boat," suggested the container pattern and a possible tieup with the mother's condition.

Container patterns have sometimes been suggested by the tendency of a child around the sibling-birth period to border the painting page and to work within that border.

[35] See Pls. 80–83.

[36] See I, 28, 31.                    [37] See Pls. 22–23.

*Ralph* used the border pattern, together with a pronounced enclosure theme in blocks, only near the time that his mother was expecting a baby.

*Roberta* used the border to inclose her painting page, and she also used the circular container pattern during her mother's pregnancy.

*Elaine*'s paintings when a baby was expected in the family (fully discussed, pp. 38–40) tended to begin with bordering strokes and also showed the paired-mass effect.[38]

*c*) Paired effects, like container patterns, have been variously achieved.

*Howard* quite frequently used large and small circles on the same painting around the time of his sister's birth.[39]

*Edward*, during the time of his mother's pregnancy, persistently carried out patterns in which, according to his verbalized content, two objects were always related to each other: one was either inside the other, or one was attached to the other. Illustrative are his "Man in a House," "House with a Garage," "Bathtub with a Pipe," "Porch with a Driveway." It was at the time of these paintings that he protruded his abdomen one day and remarked: "I have a little baby here."

*Angela*, as previously indicated, very concretely worked out the mother-infant relationship through the paired-mass effect, as well as through paired realistic forms (also large and small, like the masses) and circles.[40]

*Alan* painted the paired-mass effect in the weeks just preceding his sister's birth. The larger mass covered about three-quarters of the page and the smaller mass about one-quarter.[41]

*d*) Use of the vertical-circular forms to express concern over the birth situation was discussed and seen in the cases of *Howard* (Pls. 80–83) and *Frank* (Pls. 84–85).

HORIZONTALS AND VERTICALS

Children who turned to straight-line strokes often tended to combine verticals and horizontals in easel painting. The two strokes are usually

---

[38] Because of the clear-cut symbolism, the container pattern, the large and small related forms, and the accompanying quite specific verbalism, we are including the reproduction of two sets of paintings: One by L. J. D. (not in the study, but one of the authors was present when this easel painting was spontaneously produced in the child's home). It makes explicit the seen, felt, and sometimes verbalized relationships we have been describing. The second series of paintings, by A. A. (also not in the study), was painted three days before his second little brother was born. A. A., ordinarily a happy, sturdy, outgoing little boy, was at this period quite upset. For more than a year he had drawn and painted a variety of subjects at an unusually high form level. These 3 were taken from a series of 6 painted in quick succession. Note the return to mass pattern to express his generalized emotion—also the container or inclosure pattern and the "self-portrait" of the crying boy, who also wants to be inclosed (Pls. 90–93).

[39] See Pl. 81.                     [40] See Pls. 22–23.

[41] See Alan's paintings (Pls. 64–67), Elaine's paintings (Pls. 68–74), and Angela's (Pl. 23) for similarity of pattern in terms of light and dark paired masses used apparently in each case to express concern over "mother–expected–baby" problem. Alan's paintings are distinguished from the others by a structuralized pattern derived doubtless from the great amount of block building that was his major interest. As previously noted, Alan's major interest in block building was reflected in the structuralized form that was part of his depiction of pregnancy (Pl. 67). Angela's overlay painting of 1-4-39 with a structure clearly visible also reflected her heightened activity with blocks (see discussion, p. 136).

combined in what we have termed "structuralized or constructive" painting patterns. Some children, however, have shown such a preponderant use of horizontals, as compared with verticals, in their paintings that it has been possible to make a comparative study of the two. Results of these comparisons suggest that emphasis on either or on both horizontals and verticals may be associated with assertive drives. They also suggest that, while horizontals and verticals may be used in basically similar ways, certain meaningful differentiations can be made:

Whereas verticals have frequently been used symbolically to indicate assertive or masculine drives, horizontals have not once been observed to be used in this way.[42]

Group comparisons between children with horizontal emphasis and those with vertical emphasis suggest that among children whose designs showed horizontal emphasis the pattern of behavior was likely to be more self-protective, more fearful, more overtly co-operative, and the children were more likely to come from homes where greater pressure was exerted.

The group differentiations described seem from our individual case analyses to be somewhat misleading and to represent an instance in which overt behavior cannot safely be assumed to reflect personal drives. Individual cases have revealed strong negativistic streaks in children who emphasized horizontals, which leads us to believe that it is with negativistic rather than with the co-operative drives that horizontals are basically associated. When horizontals do appear in easel painting paralleled by overtly co-operative behavior, it seems quite possible from the histories of the children that the painting pattern is a symbolically expressed reaction against the overt behavior pattern.[43]

A further differentiation in usage between verticals and horizontals has been suggested by Löwenfeld.[44] Running through children's representations, both pictorial and verbal, he found a tendency for the horizontal to be identified with movement, and the vertical, which is relatively fixed in space in relation to a base line, to be identified with stationary objects. We have noted the same trend. It has been particularly evident in the content

[42] Group findings suggest less adequate adjustments among children with vertical emphasis. Inasmuch as verticals are frequently used by children with assertive-submissive conflicts, this probably underlies the general findings.

[43] The records of Angela, Ardis, Betty, Irving, Ray, and Stella all support this interpretation. Of related interest, and perhaps worth considering, is the fact that many of us tend to use the horizontal movement to express negation and tend to shake our heads horizontally to indicate "No." We also frequently use a horizontal hand or arm gesture to indicate negation.

[44] *Op. cit.*, p. 7, n. 5.

of block structures. Children tended to give locomotor names to their horizontal structures and names of stationary objects (like "house" and "tower") to their vertical structures.

### OTHER ASPECTS OF LINE AND FORM

Verticals, circles, and horizontals represent only a few of the possible or
actual variations in treatment of line and form. They have perhaps been
given undue significance in this discussion because in our data they stood
out with the greatest frequency and persistence. Of all aspects of line and
form, they have seemed to be most identified with the expression and the
working-out of conflicts.

All the various aspects of line and form which will be described below
tended to appear as elements in given children's paintings. Usually they
were not the focal aspect. Their persistent recurrence marked them as associated with a particular characteristic of the given child. Only a few of
these patterns have occurred in sufficient children to justify statistical
analysis. But for those not handled quantitatively, parallel behavior tendencies have suggested possible relationships significant enough to note and
perhaps investigate.

Our observations have indicated that children whose work at given
times was characterized by *scattered, all-directional, unrelated strokes* tended
at parallel times to be scattered, impulsive, and aimless in their overt
behavior.

*Anita, Jeff,* and *Andy* (Andy, Pls. 94–95) each used scattered, all-directional, unrelated
lines in painting, at some stage of our observations, and each was at the corresponding period
scattered, impulsive, and aimless at play. A sketch of the footpaths made by these children
on a given morning, with shifts in color for each shift in activity, would not have been unlike the painting patterns which they produced.

A *back-and-forth diagonal swing* characterizes the earliest paintings or
drawings of children.[45] Its persistence beyond the earliest observed developmental stage has tended in our observations to be paralleled by a continued
pattern of impulsive, dependent, relatively infantile behavior.

*Single-directional strokes* have tended to occur in the patterns of children
who were more decisive in their attitudes than the group using the back-
and-forth swing. This is consonant with the developmental picture in which
the transition from scribbling to straight-line strokes is accompanied by
increasing self-control. Illustrative are *Archie* and *Tad,* who used single-

---

[45] See p. 107.

direction strokes and each of whom was a boy with a "single-track drive" and a decisive personality. *Phoebe* and *Jessica* also tended to work in a one-directional (down) stroke, and each stood out in her group for her negativistic attitudes.

*Zigzag lines* seemed, in the case of *Gregory*, to reflect his indecisive behavior. Gregory was outstanding for his hesitant reactions. He was unable to concentrate on a task and carry it through without many devious activities.

*Edgy, angular qualities* in paintings were pronounced in the work of *Arline* and *Dorothea*, each of whom stood out for her abrupt, determined, aggressive mannerisms.[46]

Children whose paintings seemed an *aggregate of tiny strokes or piecemeal additions* have tended to show this same piecemeal technique in their other activities. For example, *Phyllis* used the piecemeal technique in painting, and her special interests included puzzles and other activities which involved piecing things together. *Elaine, Bee, Hilda,* and *Carol* also followed a piecemeal technique in painting and an orderly, detailed, painstaking pattern in other activities.

*Concentration on broad outlines* would seem in keeping with concern for large outlines of projects rather than with working out details. *Eda* was a child who worked in broad outlines. She functioned on a highly intellectual level. Her verbal content expressed ambitions quite beyond her capacity for realistic representation. For her, realities were interwoven with flights of fancy. She was quite at a loss with such specific realistic materials as blocks.

Children who somewhat consistently began their paintings with a self-imposed, *restricted outline and then worked within it* tended to be among the more withdrawing, self-contained, insecure children. *Ann* and *Aileen* showed the tendency to work within such defined outlines. Children who started their painting at a relatively central point and worked outward tended to show corresponding outgoing drives and reactions. Suggestive of this way of working are *George* and *Albert*, both of whom shifted from working inward to working outward in painting as they changed from withdrawing to more outgoing overt behavior, and *Anita*, who tended to work in outreaching, borderless strokes. While suffering from a problem similar to Aileen's (that of inadequate sustained affection), Anita was trying to

---

[46] By way of contrast (pp. 55–56), as previously observed, children whose change of direction was characterized by curved strokes tended to be relatively unassertive, submissive, and adaptive in overt behavior.

solve her problem in quite the opposite fashion. The differences were reflected in the two children's paintings. Aileen, it will be remembered, almost always worked definitely within a self-imposed boundary or outline. Her behavior likewise was withdrawn, and she lived a life of strong emotions and fancy within herself. In contrast to this, Anita's dissatisfactions and hostilities were thrust outward in a series of all-directional aggressions that were reflected in her all-directional paintings.

The foregoing observations suggest that *filling in* of form might parallel self-oriented or inturned rather than outgoing emotional drives. Case analyses indicate that filling in of self-imposed outlines has been frequent among children like *Aileen* whose lives were full of strong emotional tensions. If we consider form-filling as a type of shading, our observations in certain individual cases are consonant with those of Löwenfeld[47] and of various Rorschach workers who have found shading indicative of intensified feelings.

Our group data, however, tend to raise rather than to clarify questions as to the possible significance of form-filling. Group data, in contrast to individual cases, indicate that filling of forms has tended to occur in children who as a group were evidencing controlled behavior and adapting well to their environment. In the individual cases already cited, form-filling was done by children tense with emotional anxieties. A more refined analysis of various types of form-filling evidently is needed. We have already noted certain basic differences between the children who filled self-imposed and self-created forms (like *Aileen*) and those who filled given forms (e.g., who bordered and then filled the painting page). Children who filled self-created forms showed considerably more initiative and self-determined behavior than did the children who bordered the page and then filled it. The latter group tended to be unimaginative. Further differentiation of this sort that distinguishes between self-created and given forms might resolve the apparent inconsistencies between our group trends and individual case findings.

The *force or intensity* of strokes is a characteristic that also needs to be considered in the interpretation of paintings. Heavy, tensely applied strokes have seemed to indicate (*a*) the energy and output level of the child and (*b*) the degree of emotional focus or tension under which the child was op-

---

[47] See Löwenfeld, *op. cit.*, pp. 25, 88, 105.

[48] Pressure is one of several elements described as a factor in "The Handwriting of Depressed Children" by H. J. Jacoby (published in *New Era* [London] [January, 1944]). To quote: "The

erating.[48] *Sadie, Archie, Richard*, and *Jessica* painted with heavy, forceful strokes. Each seemed to have high energy level. In Jessica and Archie, underlying emotional tensions probably intensified their energy output. It was observed that many children who neither revealed high energy level in overt behavior nor characteristically used heavy strokes, painted with heavy intense strokes at specific times when involved in strong emotions. *Sidney* ordinarily used light strokes. On a day of unusual rebellion and of temper outbursts he made two paintings with outstandingly heavy and broad strokes. *Anita* and *Edward* on certain specific days of emotional upset and of rebellion brushed so heavily that they scrubbed holes in their painting paper (see Pls. 35–36). In general, it has seemed that children whose paintings were considered most weighted emotionally (as judged by use of color-mass overlay techniques) tended to use heavy painting strokes.

In contrast to the foregoing, *light painting strokes* have tended to characterize the work of children like *Tess, Jocelyn*, and *Vivian*, who were inclined to be nervous, timid, and fearful. Lightly applied strokes have also been observed to characterize the painting of children like *Betty, Hope*, and *Wanda*, who were relatively dainty, demure, and "feminine." These children expressed only mild emotional drive. Children in a physically weakened condition, like *Rowena* and *Esther* during specific periods, also tended to use light painting strokes.

Group data show that children who worked with *long strokes* stood out for their more controlled behavior (which was seemingly often an unnatural characteristic, stimulated by overly high standards) and that children who worked primarily with short strokes showed more impulsive behavior (and seemingly happier adjustment at this particular age level) Individual analyses, however, point up the difficulty of attempting to base an interpretation on length of stroke alone. We have observed, for instance, that short strokes which were all-directional and scattered, as in the work of *Andy* and *Anita*, tended to parallel behavior which was impulsive and uncontrolled. Short strokes which were heavy and abrupt and frequently in a unified direction were noted in the work of children like *Sadie* and *Perry*, who had highly decisive, forthright personalities. Short strokes with thin, broken, irregular, or unrhythmic effects were observed in the

writing movements are under-sized; (2) various groups of characteristics, primarily the degree of pressure, speed and size are disproportionately constellated; and (3) the rhythm of movements and formations is disturbed, i.e. instances of sudden pressure or incalculable fluctuations of the writing angle or similar kinds of rhythmic disturbance occur." Other comments on size of letters and on feeble pressure are included, as well as an interesting Bibliography.

paintings of children like *Tess* and *Rachel*, who displayed such nervous tendencies as twisting of clothes and picking of nose, and during nervous, anxious periods appeared in the paintings of children like *Stanley*, *Will*, *Carol*, *Jessica*, *Edward*, *Esther*, and *Hilda*.

*Strokes which died out weakly* tended to occur in the work of children who evidenced little overt drive or capacity for seeing situations through to a sound finish. *Jeff* (Pls. 96–99), for instance, consistently showed a broken stroke with a weak finish. In overt behavior he tended to "walk away when another child took his toys," "leave tasks incomplete," and "run into a corner and whimper instead of protecting himself." *Virginia* also used strokes which died out weakly. She was described as a girl with "good ideas but no follow-through." She often would say "I want . . . . " and then, when given the object asked for, would make no use of it. Another of her habits was to attract attention with a boast. But having said, "I can . . . . ," she would fail to carry out the activity. *Bert* also illustrates this association between strokes which finish weakly and a personal lack of adequate follow-through.[49]

*Dots and daubs* were observed in the paintings of several children who in their overt behavior were outstanding for their extreme sense of order and cleanliness. For these children the painting experience seemed a medium for expressing their repressed desires to smear or soil. Many of the children already described as working out their conflict through painting, used colors symbolically associated with smearing, viz., brown, green, dirty orange. *Harriet* frequently made dots. Several times she called them "Tut-tuts." More often than not she ended by painting over them. This covering-over seems paralleled by her overt habits, which were neat and clean. *Gloria* used daubs and dots in painting at a time when giggling and pantomiming clearly revealed elimination content. *Edward* turned to painting dots and daubs at a time when he was showing an overt interest in scattering wet sand, which he called "wee wee."

Although we cannot objectively confirm the distinction, our observations have led us to feel that daubing may be a rather more direct expression of smearing interests, whereas dotting is done by children whose natural interest in elimination has been either more sublimated or repressed. Dotting was pronounced in children like *Betty* (Pls. 100–101) and *Jill*, whose high home standards would have forced, or at least directed, their natural habits and interests in elimination into "higher channels." These children

[49] Case analyses suggest that insecurity was often at the root of this tendency. This seemed particularly true of Bert, Jeff, and Virginia, also of Ronny and Angela during periods of conflict.

were inclined to express themselves through flights of fancy rather than in any direct form of activity or speech.

Group analyses have been made of the group of children who most frequently used dotting techniques in easel painting. The findings are, for the most part, in keeping with the foregoing discussion but do not give the coherent picture which certain individual cases suggested. Since there were only 25 children included in this group, it is not surprising that the generalizations are inadequate. A need for more intensive study is indicated.

Our observations indicate differences between children whose finished paintings looked *"clean"* and those whose finished products looked *"dirty."* [50]

*Dirty paintings* tended to occur among quite young children and among children who were overcontrolled, overadaptive, and too orderly. Accordingly, dirty painting would seem to have been the result of either one of two factors: (*a*) general immaturity, with consequent poor control and a natural delight in smearing or (*b*) need for release from a too controlled overt behavior pattern. The following extracts from case analyses reveal some of the more frequent associations which are in keeping with the foregoing observations:

*Henry*, who delighted in dirty and wet easel paintings and in water play, was overtly a very highly controlled child. His record indicated bowel control was established at three and one-half months and a strict cleanliness regime had been enforced throughout his life. *Esther* tended to produce dirty easel paintings and evidenced keen enjoyment of clay. She had been trained for bowel control at two months, was overtly neat and clean. *Walter* delighted in daubing dirty effects in painting. A parallel interest was in collecting such tiny things as dry beans and stems of green beans. He liked to play vegetable peddler. *Kit* made dirty paintings at a time when she was intensely interested in play with such other smeary materials as sand, dirt, mud, clay, finger paints, and water. She liberally spattered herself and the furniture whenever engaged in these activities.

*Ethel* produced drippy, dirty paintings at a time when she was displaying an absorbed interest in water, clay, and finger painting. *Edward* produced dirty paintings at a time when he was afraid to experiment with other materials, such as finger paints and clay, which might have soiled him; but, as he became freer, clay and finger painting became favorite activities. *Jill* achieved dirty effects in painting during a period when she was playing with sand. She was interested in collecting materials of one kind and another, including stones for use as "eggs." That dirty paintings were a form of release for Jill is suggested by the

[50] Illustrations (Pls. 61, 76) probably clarify distinction between "dirty" and "clean" paintings better than could our verbal definitions. Dirty effects usually have been produced by daubs and smears.

fact that her most aggressive day was one not of hitting or snatching but of *throwing dirt*. *Jocelyn* alternated between very clean and very dirty paintings. Overtly she showed a consistent aversion to dirt. Like Walter, she had a keen interest in collecting tiny objects, such as pebbles or kernels of corn.[51]

Our observations have made us wonder whether decorative effects might be another sublimated form of the desire to smear or soil. A tendency to decorative patterns has been found in children with a history of too rigid or too early cleanliness training, who had an overt pattern of neatness and orderliness, with a frequent tendency toward constipation and with a strong interest in collecting tiny objects. *Tilly*, whose painting and crayon products consisted of tight decorative scrolls, particularly exemplified this constellation.

*Clean paintings* have been observed most frequently among children who were controlled and adaptive in overt behavior and who seemed to have no strong conflicting feelings. These children seemed either to have accepted the adaptive pattern because of developmental readiness or to have found sufficient satisfaction in complying with external expectancies that they responded with apparent willingness to actual pressure. *Louise* is one of the few children who seemed to fit this latter description. Most children at the nursery-school level who were under pressure for control acquiesced less tranquilly than did Louise. They accepted standards overtly, but their conflicting desires continued to be strong, and they found an indirect "out" for them in painting. Many more children tended to get dirty rather than clean effects in their easel paintings.

Children who produced *wet or dripping paintings* have tended to fall into the same two types observed for children with dirty paintings: (*a*) either they have shown a generally immature pattern or reaction, or (*b*) they have found painting to be a release from their too controlled overt behavior.

Individual analyses suggest a parallelism between wet, dripping paintings and concern about elimination problems. *Edward, Jessica*, and *Susie* each reverted to an infantile habit, enuresis, at a time when they were producing wet and dripping easel paintings. *Gloria* produced wet, dripping products during a period when she was overtly expressing her interest in elimination functions. *Philip* stopped producing dripping easel paintings around the time that the home reported an end to bed-wetting.

---

[51] Among other children, not included above, who produced "dirty" paintings were Brian, Phyllis, and Violet.

Among the children who tended to *put the paint on sparsely* and with a dry brush, we particularly noted: (*a*) children with a general lack of confidence, and an attitude of aimlessness and disinterest; (*b*) children who were overtly assertive but miserly, i.e., they wanted much but gave back little—they made a little go a long way. *Arnold, Ardis, Jeff*, and *Veronica* all used dry strokes, and all were relatively aimless children, uninterested in school activities and, apparently, in all their present experiences. *Alice* and *Anita* used almost dry brushes and managed to dirty their painting pages with a few scattered daubs. Alice's whole behavior seemed one of marked withholding. Constipation was an extreme problem in her case. Anita messed up her painting page, just as she soiled upholstery, with a few well-directed daubs. Group data reveal several behavior tendencies in keeping with the characteristics described above; but, on the whole, the data associated with wet and dry emphasis have not been so telling as have the individual case analyses. Further investigation is indicated.

One further characteristic that has to do with line and form needs to be discussed briefly—namely, the *tendency to smear*. Observations suggest that smearing of paintings may have developmental, as well as general personality, implications. Some of the possible meanings are outlined below. They cannot be adequately evaluated without further, more refined investigations.[52] Individual case data suggest that smearing may result from at least three motivating factors: (*a*) Some children seemed to smear because of dissatisfaction with their products; in these situations, the developmental process seems to have been a factor. (*b*) Other children seemed to smear in order to conceal their basic feelings. (*c*) Still other children in the act of smearing seemed to express hostility against the pattern produced —and what it represented.

The first group of children mentioned above smeared their paintings during a brief period of time when their general development was showing change in other areas. They seemed to be striving toward a higher level of expression than they were able to produce. Dissatisfaction was evidenced by such incidents as the following:

For some time *George* had frequently smeared his painting products. Smearing was often accompanied by other signs of dissatisfaction with his work. Once he tore the product from his easel, crumpled it, and threw it

---

[52] In making a statistical approach to smearing or pattern overlay, distinctions should be made between (*a*) obvious overlay that covers the basic pattern; (*b*) smearing on the same page but not on top of the initial pattern, as in the case of Ruth; and (*c*) a few random marks scribbled over the basic pattern. In all cases, accompanying behavior and verbalizations should be considered.

into the wastebasket. He then proceeded to paint the same pattern over again—this time with improvements and without smearing. One day *Sally* made a grimace of displeasure after finishing a painting, smeared it, asked for another page, repainted an improved edition, and did not smear it. *Jay* frequently showed disapproval of his painting designs and proceeded to smear them. He showed like dissatisfaction with his block and clay products and often would approach a teacher with some such plaint as "Make me a car. I can't do it."

From our observations it has seemed that within the group who were smearing as part of their striving toward higher form level were a number of children who smeared as sheer release from tensions created by their sustained efforts toward control.

The second group of children tended to smear or cover over their basic patterns just as in actual life they tried to cover over their real feelings. They included children like *Carol*, *Glen*, and many others who were described in the various instances of conflict and overlay cited in chapter ii.

In the third group of children were those already described who in smearing their constructive patterns were apparently releasing feelings of hostility toward other people—frequently brothers or sisters. Among them were children like *Andy* and *Jeff*, whose covering of their structural designs paralleled their covering-over and resistance to every step of development, especially if control and responsibility seemed to be involved.

# CHAPTER IV

## SPACE USAGE AND SPATIAL PATTERN

THE limitations under which children worked at the easel warrant consideration. Under ordinary circumstances the children themselves were probably unaware of any limitations except such as have been noted when colors that were particularly desired were not immediately available or when easels were all in use.

In terms of colors offered, children were quite free to choose those they wished to use. In terms of line and form, they were entirely free to paint as they wished. But as regards space, children operated within definite limits. They were given paper with a circumscribed surface (17 × 22 inches). Each child's paintings defined and offered a permanent record of his reactions to the space offered. Our observations lead us to conclude that space usage and/or spatial pattern offer certain clear-cut indexes of children's responses to external conditions. ("Space usage" refers to amount of space used and placement of pattern, while "spatial pattern" refers to method used in painting the pattern.) Just as his use of line, form, and color in a variety of ways suggests clues to the child's inner life, so does his use of space suggest the pattern of his relationship with his environment.

The painting page may be considered as a sample of the child's surroundings. His use of it frequently corresponds to his use of his larger environment. Our observations have suggested that the following aspects of spatial usage and pattern may be significant.

I. *Extent of space utilized.*—(*a*) Painting beyond the border of the painting page, (*b*) painting spread all over the page, (*c*) painting within a restricted area, and (*d*) painting proportionate to page.

II. *Space usage with special concern for placement.*—(*a*) Emphasis at top of page, (*b*) emphasis at bottom of page, (*c*) emphasis on placement at right or left, (*d*) differential use of right and left, (*e*) centering, (*f*) balance of design.

III. *Method in space usage.*—(*a*) Scattered strokes, (*b*) work spread all over the page as a result either of controlled, deliberate stroking or of relatively uncontrolled stroking, (*c*) working over and over the same area, (*d*) small amount of retracing.

Certain related aspects of color, line, and form already described will, of necessity, be included in this discussion.

### I. EXTENT OF SPACE UTILIZED

*a*) A tendency to paint beyond the border of the painting page has been observed in children who have two somewhat different sets of characteristics but who have in common an unconcern or disregard for external expectations. Since provision of fixed space within which to work presents an implicit request to stay within a given boundary, it is not surprising that the children who disregarded the limits of this boundary tended likewise to disregard other requests or expectations.

One group of children who painted beyond the borders of the page showed immaturity in a variety of ways. They were still in the manipulative, large-muscle stage of development and were, in general, dependent in their physical routines. They likewise were inclined to be dependent in social situations, to lack confidence and initiative, and to show such infantile behavior as distributive attention and random attack on work. As a rule they played alone and were likely to be disregarded by the other children. Their limited physical and emotional control was evident. *Alvin, Arthur, Gregory,* and *Henry* were of this group.

Quite in contrast to these children who seemed to paint beyond the given limits because they lacked established controls were some other children who had progressed beyond the manipulative stage but seemed rather of some inner necessity to paint over more than the space provided. These children were, at the same time, showing overt defiance of authority and regulations in other areas. *Andy,* for instance, went off the painting page with scattered all-directional strokes just as he flaunted authority at home and at school by running away. He recognized no limits (see Pls. 94–95). *Anita,* like Andy, went out of bounds both in painting and in daily living (see Pl. 35). *Arline* and *Jessica* were others who frequently failed to stay within expected limits in painting as in other areas.

In this connection it is of interest to note that a large number of children who in their way of painting expressed need for more painting space than was given them were children regarded by the staff as having need for more love than they were getting. They were variously described as neglected and/or rejected in their homes.

*b*) Painting spread all over the page is painting which extended over all of the given space without necessarily filling the page and without going out of bounds. It likewise was observed in children with two different sets of characteristics.

Among some of the children, this painting pattern seemed a reflection of general immaturity and of large-muscle development. Illustrative behavior of this group included "lack of self-control," "dependent for help on adults," and "inclined to be negative, aggressive, and to have distributive attention." Included in this group for longer or shorter periods were *Alvin, Andy, Ardis, Arnold, Audrey, Chester, Irving, Jeff, Rachel, Thomas,* and *Veronica.* Other aspects of these children's paintings, such as scatter, all-directional work, wavy scribbling, no individualized theme or pattern in color, line, or form, also suggest the immaturity factor.

However, in those cases in which inadequate control can be eliminated as a factor, work all over the page seems to parallel and to reflect a relatively outgoing, assertive, self-reliant personality. This association was particularly apparent among children who changed during the course of observation from shy or repressed to outgoing behavior. In such instances, painting patterns repeatedly showed a parallel change from work in a restricted area to work all over the page.

*Benjy,* who on entrance to school was described as among the shyest of four-year-olds, changed within three months to the opposite extreme. Plates 78–79 indicate the parallel transition in his work from "painting in a restricted area" to "painting all over the page." *Albert* and *Ann,* each repressed even in speech, tended, at first, to paint in restricted, self-defined areas. With the advent of freer behavior and freer speech, their paintings and crayon drawings changed from restricted linear patterns to more open-mass effects. As Albert became freer, he began to paint full-page patterns. *Frank, Harry, Neil, Peter, Phyllis,* and *Polly* were all similarly observed to spread their work over the painting page as they became more outgoing in overt behavior.

*c*) Painting and crayoning done in isolated or restricted areas have in general—and specifically in the cases of *Aileen, Ann, Benjy, Harriet, Norman, Ralph,* and *Tilly*—paralleled withdrawing, emotionally dependent behavior tendencies. Just as these children restricted their use of allotted space on the painting page, so did they tend to circumscribe their other activities. It was not that they lacked ideas or potential initiative but rather that they seemed to feel that they must restrain their natural assertive, outgoing drives. They held themselves aloof or withdrew themselves from many activities.

That the restricted painting pattern and the circumscribed overt behavior in these children were not always in harmony with their basic drives is illustrated by an observation on *Louise:*

*Louise,* who ordinarily worked in restricted masses, was, by family intent, a model of orderly, polite, "proper" behavior. For purposes of observation, she was taken by herself to play in Dr. Hattwick's office. Louise first went to the easel where she painted her usual precise pattern with colors carefully kept separate. As she turned to leave the easel, she spied a block structure left by another child and said: "Don't want to step on the blocks. How can I get across? Oh, I see." She carefully skirted the block structure to get to the clay table.

After her clay experience, Louise was obviously freer. She said of the colors which she had used separately before: "I can mix these colors if I want to, can't I? I can come back tomorrow and finish, can't I? Maybe I'd better do it now." She returned to the easel and painted much more freely than before. Her final product consisted of intermingled colors, and it expanded over the painting page. When she had completed her painting, Louise left the easel. She was talking freely and continuously. She began to explore all the possibilities of the room. Finally, she walked toward the blocks which she had so carefully skirted before. She now kicked over the block structure and walked over the blocks with the remark, "Cause I don't like these blocks."

Not only have we observed that children turned toward more outgoing use of space as they became more outgoing in behavior, but we have noted that they turned toward more restricted use of space as they became more withdrawn in overt behavior. *George* had experienced a month of notably happy interplay and leadership paralleled by a tendency in painting to work all over the page. Through force of circumstance he was transferred to another nursery group, where he failed to establish himself and to gain acceptance. He soon "crawled into his shell," and at the same time his painting pattern changed to one of restricted masses. *Polly* and *Margaret* likewise produced paintings with restricted patterns during periods when they appeared to be isolated in their groups.

Even occasional daily experiences have been reflected in restricted painting patterns. *Archie,* isolated one day (4-3-38) for hitting and biting other children, painted a restricted mass which was in striking contrast to his usual pattern. *Alma* produced a restricted mass in painting, in contrast to her usual all-over-the-page work, on a day (3-2-38) when she was described as unhappy and unlike herself. On this day she appeared anxious and withdrawn and seemed fearful even of the pet rats which she usually fondled and cared for. *Aileen* has previously been described as reverting to her restricted painting pattern during the second year of observation on days of withdrawn, aloof, resistant, irritable behavior (see Pl. 5).

Our observations revealed other associations with work in a restricted area that seem worth noting and seem to merit further investigation. We observed that some children who worked in restricted areas achieved their effect through outlines or forms which they first made and then filled in.[1] Other children worked in a compact mass without making an initial outline. We have wondered whether there was an actual or significant difference between these two groups of children. An analysis of the children's records has led to the conjecture that the presence of the preliminary outlined form may differentiate the child who is consciously restricting his own drives toward initiative and full self-expression from the child who is more completely withdrawn and dependent at both conscious and feeling levels. Our observations suggest that the latter group of children may work directly in mass without preliminary outline form.[2]

We have observed that children who tended to make restricted forms or outlines, which they then filled in, worked in oval or circular more than in square or angular forms. This is rather to be expected, since both restricted mass and circular form suggest withdrawing tendencies. It was also noted that children who worked in restricted areas tended to use colors separately or to overlay them.[3] These three aspects of pattern—namely, restricted area, colors used quite separately, and colors overlaid—all reflect withholding, restrained, and/or highly controlled personality factors.

Our observations have also indicated that children who restricted their work in easel painting often made comparable patterns when working with other media. This was particularly evident in the tendency to use enclosure patterns in block building. *George*'s block building changed from tracks and towers to enclosures during the period when his painting changed from an outgoing pattern to work in a restricted area. *Ann* (see Pls. 51–55), *Neil*, and *Ralph* each persistently built enclosures with blocks at times that paralleled their painting of restricted patterns.

*d*) Children described as painting proportionately to page (i.e., who apparently painted freely, yet whose strokes were so adapted to the size of the page that they neither ran over nor seemed cramped)[4] tended to stand out as a group for their adaptive behavior. These children were generally well adjusted, had easy relations with children and adults, shared readily and

---

[1] Of 30 children who consistently worked in restricted areas, 18 achieved their effect through first making outlines and then filling them; illustrative are Aileen, Benjy, Harriet, Norman, Sally, and Tilly.

[2] Group comparisons on form-filling (particularly of form-filling and page-filling) suggest this possibility. We are quite tentative on this point.

[3] Illustrative of separate color placement in restricted areas is the work of Louise (Pl. 76); illustrative of overlay in a restricted area is Ann's work (Pls. 51–55).

[4] For illustration of painting proportionate to page see Pl. 38.

worked purposively, and were sought after and popular. At one period or another of our observations, *Angela, Catherine, Edith, Esther, Gertrude, Hope, Shirley,* and *Thelma* illustrated this tendency.

## II. SPACE USAGE, WITH SPECIAL CONCERN FOR PLACEMENT

There were not enough children in our study who conspicuously and consistently placed their painting patterns on one particular part of the page to warrant statistical analyses of these tendencies. Individual observations, however, suggest various associations that seem worth recording:

a) Some children observed have shown a pronounced tendency to concentrate most of their painting at the top of the page. In many of these cases such factors as physical stature and high personal standards or aspirations have seemed involved. *Sidney* and *Victor*, both relatively tall boys, seemed, on the basis of height alone, to find it easier to work toward the top of the painting page.

Curiously enough, there was a tendency for some of the most undersized children also to focus their paintings toward the top of the page. *Sadie*, one of the smallest children in her group, was accustomed to emphasize the top of the page, even though she had to climb on a chair to achieve her purpose. *Archie's* small stature and his strong drive to be big have already been illustrated and discussed (Pls. 13–17). Archie's kindergarten paintings and drawings almost invariably showed one or more indications of being weighted toward the top, e.g., flag flying in the sky, smokestacks and smoke streaming across the sky. *Will*, the smallest child in his group, characteristically painted at the top of the page. One day he said to a child painting near him: "I paint here [upper half], you paint here [lower half]." *Walter*, a show-off, tended to emphasize the top of his painting page, much as he called attention to the top of his head by carrying blocks on it and asking people to look at him.

Among some other children, emphasis on the top of the painting page tended to parallel and perhaps reflect high standards and high aspirations in other than physical areas. *Barbara, Carol, Elinor, Freda, Peter, Rita, Ronny, Sally, Sandy*, and *Thelma* were motivated by high standards, and each showed a tendency to emphasize the top of the painting page.

b) Only four children were observed who painted pronouncedly at the bottom of the page. Two of them, and a third who used a base line in crayoning, were distinguished by the fact that they were among the most stable, most "firmly rooted" children observed. A conjecture as to the possible relatedness between these factors is offered as a possibility for future exploration. *Ross* characteristically emphasized the bottom of the page. He was outstanding in his group for his highly stable, constructive tendencies. *Stella* characteristically worked from the bottom up. She likewise stood out for her stable, calm, placid disposition. Emphasis on the bottom of the page was also observed in the paintings of *Rowena* and *Henry*. For neither of them do the foregoing associations exist, nor are there any other associations which clarify this tendency in these particular children.

*c*) Of particular interest are the possible associations between aspects of personality and the differential use of left and right sides of the painting page. The part which actual handedness has in the tendency to emphasize the one or the other side of the page is not clear. *Harvey*, *Neil*, and *Steven*, all left handed at the easel, tended to emphasize the left half of the painting page. But *Jill* and *Mac*, who also were inclined to emphasize the left half of the painting page, painted with their right hands.

In some children the side of the page emphasized has seemed to depend on the side of the easel first approached on the given day. Shyness seemed a factor in these instances.

*Phyllis* usually started painting from whichever side she approached the easel, and her final products showed an emphasis on the side on which she had started to paint. Phyllis was overtly shy. Her hesitancy in making a proportionate use of all the page suggested a reserve in usage of space which paralleled her reserve in other experiences. *Louise*, like Phyllis, tended to take a one-sided stance at the easel and to emphasize the side on which she stood. Like Phyllis, Louise was at this time overtly shy in the group. For example, although interested in the costumes, she did not dare approach the costume chest until the other children were playing elsewhere in the room.

*d*) Our observations suggest that it is probably less the side of the page emphasized than it is the differential treatment of the left and right sides of the painting page which holds valuable clues for study of personality.

The work of many children suggests that the left- and right-hand sides of the painting page may be used differently to reflect a conflict between basic personal drives and overt behavior. Some children apparently use differential treatment of the two sides of the paper as other children use color overlay. One hypothesis which seemed to warrant exploring was that children tended to use the side of the painting page corresponding to the dominant hand to reflect overt behavior, while they used the opposite side to reflect their repressed feelings. (With some interest one recalls the old maxim, "Don't let your right hand know what your left hand is doing.")

*Elinor* did not use the left- and right-hand sides of her page differentially, but she did use the left and right hands for different techniques in ways that accord with the foregoing hypothesis. Elinor was left handed. She tended to use her left hand to draw at a high-representative level. Drawing for Elinor was a learned response, taught by her mother. Elinor consistently used her right hand to erase or smear her representations. Elinor's history reveals an overtly controlled child with repressed desires to play with boys and to participate in other activities not in keeping with her mother's plan of life for Elinor. A follow-up Rorschach described Elinor as "not overtly destructive but has an underlying destructive tendency."

*Ronny*, a left-handed child, produced paintings in which the left half—his dominant side —was characterized by clean blue strokes in keeping with his overt behavior, while the right half—his subordinate side—was characterized by dirty-brown strokes in keeping with his more repressed interests.

*Barry* has already been described in relation to his tendency to overlay blue on top of warmer colors, paralleled by a conscious drive toward control (I, 25–26). In his differentiated left-right pictures, it will be remembered that Barry used blue on the right—his dominant side—red on the left. Similar relationships were noted in kindergarten products of *Esther* and *Aileen* at periods when they were overtly striving for control.

*Andy*, *Jeff*, and *Phoebe* have already been described as children who were still functioning at an impulsive level that was below their age and their true ability. These children tended to overlay their structuralized, higher-level painting. They also were likely to make differentiations between mass (expressive of impulsive reactions and their overt behavior pattern) and line (expressive of controlled, channelized tendencies). Jeff and Phoebe, both right handed, placed mass on the dominant right side, in keeping with their overt impulsive reactions. Andy, left handed, placed mass on his dominant left side—also in keeping with his impulsive overt behavior.

Several children previously described in our summary of verticals and circles used the vertical and circular themes in differentiated left-right patterns that paralleled other indexes of boy-girl or of assertive-submissive conflicts.

Our observations have further suggested, as in the case of *Rita*, that on these differentiated left-right patterns the pattern corresponding to the dominant hand is not always the pattern which reflects overt behavior. Here, as in every aspect of children's paintings, our generalizations meet with many exceptions, variations, and modifications.

*e*) Centering on the painting page has been observed in sufficient children to make possible group comparisons. Comparisons have indicated that the children who centered their designs were likely to be more self-directed, more self-centered, but, withal, to show more affectionate and more adaptive behavior than the children who placed their designs off center.

*Alma*, quiet, self-reliant, extraordinarily well established in her relations to others as well as to herself, showed a persistent centering of her painting pattern, which was paralleled by balance and proportion in all areas of her living.

*Gloria* showed marked tendency toward centered painting during a period when her dramatic play quite consistently showed a self-centered theme (she was the sick baby). At this time she modeled "Little house, me inside," with clay; and with crayons she produced concentric circles representing the family constellation with herself in the center. Centeredness and self-centeredness were observable in all areas at the same time.

*Ann* and *Arline* each characteristically centered her painting pattern. By force of circumstances each of the children had become self-centered and to a considerable degree self-directed. Neither one, however, could have been described as having made a satisfactory adaptation to children, adults, or environment. These exceptions accentuate the danger of generalizing from a single aspect of painting.

*f)* Balance has seemed the outstanding quality in the painting of some children. Often these children have been observed to make a stroke on one portion of the page, to stand back, survey their work, and then make a balancing stroke on the opposite side of the page.

Balance of design has been observed in the work of several well-balanced children who seemed to be making thoroughly adequate adjustments, as, for example, *Alma* and *Kit*. But it has also been observed and has seemed to be a more consciously worked-for characteristic in the paintings and other creative media of some of the children who were least well adjusted but who were striving for adjustment, balance, and acceptance.

*Kenneth* was the least-liked boy in his group. He was pathetically eager for social contacts, but a spastic condition caused so much bungling and such frequent hurting or annoying of other children in his efforts to establish contacts that the children avoided him and even ganged up against him. Their attitude seemed only to heighten Kenneth's desire to play with them. In crayoning, in block work, and in painting, Kenneth showed an extraordinary will to create balance in design and building (Pl. 102). This strong desire for balance seems to have been a compensatory drive that expressed his will to have balance despite the lack of it in his own physical makeup. His drive for balance and harmony in human relationships seemed comparable to his drive for balance through material media.

*Floyd* was another poorly co-ordinated child, who was likewise eager for social relationships and relatively unsuccessful in establishing them. Like *Kenneth*, Floyd showed keen concern for balance in his painting, crayoning, and other creative work. Striking in his products was the occurrence of drawings in which one half was the mirror-image of the other half.

*Ann*, with no obvious physical defect, had strikingly poor social relationships despite her strong desire for contacts with other children. She showed much concern with balance and was frequently observed to appraise her painting and then to add balancing strokes to what she had previously painted.

*Sally*, one of the moodiest, most ambivalent children observed, so far as social relations were concerned, showed a pronounced focus on need for balance. This emphasis decreased during intervals when Sally's social relationships were most improved.

*Jessica*, when she first expressed a friendly, rather than an aggressive or hostile, attitude toward others, showed a marked interest in attaining balance both in her painting and on the large outdoor play apparatus. This concern for balance was especially pronounced during the period when Jessica was revealing her desire for social give-and-take with the query, "Will you play with me?"

*Sandy,* another rather moody girl, showed a strong interest in achieving balance on the painting page, on walking and incline boards, and in "weighing the right and wrong of things." At the time when all this was particularly noticeable, Sandy was obviously striving for social and emotional equilibrium.

The foregoing would seem to indicate that striving for balance in creative media often parallels striving for personal adjustment. This accords with Murray's statement that "bodily and emotional coordination are probably related to some degree." [5] Such relationship is suggested not only by the examples cited but also by our previous observations on line and form. [6]

### III. METHOD IN SPACE USAGE

Space usage has been discussed in terms of color, line, form, and placement of design. Various other aspects that have to do with method of stroking, such as (*a*) scattered strokes, (*b*) filling a page, (*c*) working over and over the same area, and (*d*) small amount of retracing seem to merit consideration.

*a*) Scattered strokes usually occurred in the paintings of children who stood out as a group for their less controlled, less mature, more assertive, and frequently tense behavior. While the uncontrolled, immature reactions of some of these children suggest a developmental factor, the assertive tense drives of others suggest that personality rather than developmental factors led to the painting patterns.

Scattered strokes characterized the paintings of *Andy, Audrey, Irving, Jeff, Thomas,* and *Veronica* while they were in the stage of involuntary muscular control and seemed a reflection of their lack of co-ordination and integration in all activities and areas. [7]

Less persistent and extreme use of scattered strokes characterized the paintings of several children as they made the transition from back-and-forth swing strokes to controlled and directed use of line. Scattered strokes in these cases seemed to reflect a stage of development as children experimented and teased out their first separate controlled lines.

Scattered lines that were apparently deliberately made were also observed in the work of several other children. In these cases they often were paralleled by deliberate aggressions in overt behavior: *Anita* and *Bruce* each used deliberately scattered strokes in painting at the times that they were making aggressive attacks on other people and on their pos-

[5] See Henry A. Murray *et al., Explorations in Personality* (New York: Oxford University Press, 1938), pp. 732–35.

[6] See chap. iii.

[7] See pp. 108–10 and Pls. 94–99.

sessions. Relatively deliberate scatter has been observed in the work of some children who were overtly repressing desires to dab and smear and who were finding an outlet for their feelings in easel painting (illustrative is *Rita's* painting, Pls. 47–50).

In several children, parallel tendencies to scatter and dot were observed. As already noted, dotting as well as scatter may reflect overtly expressed desires to smear.

*b*) As with various other aspects of space usage, our observations suggest that if full-page painting is to be correctly understood and interpreted, we must know to what extent the factors of control and/or deliberate intent entered into the making of the final product.[8']

Consideration of our quantitative data indicates the need to distinguish between children whose all-over-the-page work seemed the result of relatively uncontrolled putting-on of strokes and children whose all-over-the-page work seemed the result of deliberate, controlled action.

For the children whose painting all over the page seemed a by-product of inadequate control, the whole behavior pattern was one of immaturity. They evidenced such tendencies as aggressiveness, attention-seeking, asking for unnecessary help, and were likely to be dependent in routines and to lack self-control. The children who filled the page with deliberate, controlled stroking showed none of this immature behavior but stood out as a group for their outgoing, self-reliant, assertive actions and their highly adaptive behavior.

For many of the children who were inclined to fill the page, page-filling seemed but a secondary interest. *Loretta, Patty, Ruby, Sara,* and *Stella* tended to produce full-page paintings, but their major interest seemed to be in experimenting with and in intermingling colors. The paintings of these children were often characterized by multicolored effects and showed no rigidity in pattern and no set form. These children tended overtly to be self-assertive and to show warmth of personality. Both in painting and in overt behavior they seemed to be expressing freely their personal desires to cope with their environment. *Robert* filled his pages with long, deliberately placed verticals. His way of painting suggested an aggression against given circum-

---

[8] Such consideration has not been necessary in the discussion of color, line, and form, for children's treatment of each of these tended in itself to be an index of degree of control. However, without supplementary evidence, many aspects of space usage do not indicate degree of control or deliberate intent.

stances. In overt behavior, particularly in dramatic-play activities, he like-wise tended to make bold attacks upon the very objects of which he was most fearful. *Glen* filled his pages with strong, red, vertical strokes and seemed, like Robert, to be expressing aggressions. Glen, however, as already related, did not carry this aggressive attack over into overt behavior.

*Arline, Carol, Erwin, Jessica,* and *Percy* and several other children who did not ordinarily do so were noted on occasions to produce full-page paintings when their painting activity was accompanied by social interplay and when interest in the painting itself was apparently secondary. The fact that *Albert* and *Ann* turned to full-page painting during periods of freer and more as-sertive overt reactions further suggests, as do the foregoing examples, that there may be a parallelism between full-page tendencies and outgoing drives or behavior.

In contrast to the children described above are those whose primary and deliberate intent, when painting, seemed to be to fill the painting page. It was among these children that the painting pattern was frequently paralleled by highly adaptive tendencies in other areas. *Bee, Carol, Elaine,*[9] and *Hilda* are illustrative of the tendency to paint with a definite concern about filling the page. These children approached their page-filling in a methodical, sys-tematic way. Production of latticework, which was then filled in—or border-ing the edge of the page before filling in—was a frequent tendency. These children were inclined to be unassertive so far as expressing their personal desires was concerned. They seemed to have identified themselves with the standards and expectancies given or imposed on them—standards and ex-pectancies which, in general, were above their level of readiness and under-standing. While these children may have had self-assertive drives, such drives often appeared to be blocked off or overlaid by a greater desire to conform. Accordingly, overt behavior was characterized either by lack of imagination and initiative or by bossy, dictatorial attempts to get other children to live up to the adult-imposed patterns.[10]

Our observations have revealed several painting tendencies which seem to be more frequently associated with page-filling than are others. Page-filling was done, for the most part, with vertical and horizontal strokes or

[9] While Elaine's paintings seem to differ from those of the other children in that they ex-pressed more emotional content, they fit the general description of pages methodically filled by deliberate intent and paralleled by a strong tendency toward adaptive behavior.

[10] Page-filling by children who lacked imagination was sufficiently striking so that we tried to imagine ourselves in the given child's place. We wondered whether the child guided by over-high external standards approached the painting pages feeling that he must make the most of the allotted space, and he accordingly filled it; or was it that the youngster accustomed to being told just what to do could think of nothing more imaginative than to fill the given space?

with diagonal or wavy swing strokes.[11] No tendency for page-fillers to work in circular strokes was observed. Since verticals and horizontals, like page-filling, tend to reflect high standards and assertive outgoing drives, perhaps it was to be expected that pages would be filled with these rather than with circular strokes.

Some children, and particularly *Bee*, were observed changing from page-filling to an interest in abstract, all-over-the-page designs.[12] Full-page paintings were also characteristic of *Stella*, who showed a strong parallel interest in design with other media. She spent much time making designs with color cubes and also with hammer, nails, and wooden pegs. Stella's mother made beautiful embroidered pieces. Her father was a tailor. Was Stella's interest in design perhaps a by-product of their way of life?

Another curious association with page-fillers is the fact that the most pronounced page-fillers were among the heaviest, stockiest children observed.[13] We note this fact but have no comments to make on it.

*c*) Working over and over the same area, another method of using space, was likely to parallel strong emotional focus. Children who worked in this way as a group tended to be self-controlled, repressed, withdrawing, fearful, and emotionally dependent.[14]

Working over and over the same area may be thought of as shading, a tendency which Löwenfeld[15] and others have related to muscular tensions and intensified feelings. Children, according to these authors, shade the parts of their paintings that are to them important and/or emotionally weighted. Working over and over the same area in young children's paintings seems to have the same connotations. *Ann*, *Aileen*, *Edward*, *Elaine*, and *Norman*, all of them expressing emotional problems through easel painting, tended at those times when they were most disturbed to work over and over the same area as one feature of their persistent painting patterns. All showed a parallel tendency in overt behavior to cling to certain given activities for long periods, performing related actions over and over as though they could never become sufficiently satisfied, or at least satisfied enough to leave what they were doing.

[11] Ann, Alan, Carol, Jill, and Ruby achieved full-page results with vertical and horizontal strokes.

[12] See particularly Bee, Pls. 117–20.

[13] Illustrative of this trend are Carol, Elaine, Hilda, Ruby, and Stella.

[14] Of the 66 children who consistently worked over and over the same area: 22 also showed a restricted mass technique, 26 showed a strong repetitive pattern, 32 showed form-filling, 56 showed smearing, 58 showed heavy strokes, and 52 showed overlay.

[15] Viktor Löwenfeld, *The Nature of Creative Activity* (New York: Harcourt, Brace & Co., 1939), pp. 25, 88, 105.

*d*) In contrast to the foregoing, the children who did little retracing showed relatively self-confident, outgoing, adaptive behavior. They were inclined to be friendly with adults and children, to show initiative in play, to have many interests, and to be sought after and popular.

As we consider our discussion of space usage, we realize that we perhaps have raised more questions than we have answered adequately. Our evidence on certain aspects of space usage has yielded only a group of observations that seemed to have some coherence. We have put them in the record with the hope that they may stimulate further investigation. In any proper treatment of the subject, each aspect of space should be considered in association with each of the aspects of color, line, and form previously discussed. It is only as all aspects are analyzed—first separately and then as part of the total pattern—that they can assume their proportionate significance.

# CHAPTER V

## TRENDS IN YOUNG CHILDREN'S PAINTINGS PRESENTED AGAINST A BACKGROUND OF CHILD DEVELOPMENT

IF WE are to get a true picture of the significance of children's paintings, we must view them in relation to the paintings of other children of the same age. In the course of our discussion of color, line, and form we have interpolated known facts on child development as well as certain observations that have been made in connection with this study. At this point we should like to offer a somewhat more systematic presentation of painting trends against a background of child development, because we believe that it will clarify the total picture which we are attempting to give.

The small number of children at each age level prevents our offering normative material. We believe, however, that the consistency of trends and the coherence of the picture which the data present justify the interpretations that we offer and that, notwithstanding gaps and limitations, future normative studies will be facilitated by the findings here presented.

We wish to stress the fact that it is trends more than specific figures with which the discussion in this chapter will concern itself. Our material may differ from usual age data and our trends may be placed at somewhat higher age levels than are ordinarily given, but it should be kept in mind that we are dealing with characteristic patterns rather than with the actual dates of first appearance of any given tendencies.

In keeping with the age limits of the present study, this discussion will deal primarily with developmental trends between eighteen months and five years of age. Only such other data from earlier and later years as will add perspective to the nursery-school years will be incorporated.

### GENERAL DEVELOPMENTAL PICTURE BETWEEN TWO AND FIVE YEARS OF AGE

During the span of their lives between eighteen months and five years children are in the process of making a striking transition both in their inner drives and in their overt behavior.

At eighteen months children primarily do the things they *feel* like doing, regardless of what other people wish or think. They are likely to be continuously active, impulsive, and self-centered. In contrast, the four- or five-year-old is beginning to do those things which other people approve and expect; he is attempting to control his impulses in order to behave in socially acceptable ways.

While children are in the process of making the swing from impulsive toward reasoned responses and behavior, they are making a parallel shift from purely subjective self-centered interests to relatively objective concern for people and the world about them.

These changes take place gradually throughout the nursery-school years. During this period, as throughout life, dominance of interest shifts continuously from subjective to objective and back again. In the early years, as later on, there is frequent overlap between subjective and objective interests and attitudes.

At two the child is but a shade removed from the impulsive, self-centered being he was at eighteen months. At three he still tends to be impulsive and self-expressive rather than controlled and adaptive. Around three, children are likely to be more naturally self-expressive than at either earlier or later periods of their lives. By the time they are three they have mastered certain basic motor processes so that focus on process is no longer necessary, and they have, accordingly, more energy with which to give vent to the many active impulses that drive for expression. In addition to their having more energy automatically freed for a variety of uses, a majority of three-year-olds are relatively unimpeded by the outward forms which are bound to curtail responses later in life.

The present study was oriented and initiated around this hypothesis as to the general developmental trends between two and five years of age. The following data on age and characteristic responses, particularly as these are related to usage of paints and other media, accord with the generalized picture given above.

#### DEVELOPMENTAL TRENDS IN PREFERENCE FOR MATERIALS

Our age data on preference have indicated that easel paints were preferred beyond all other materials studied at the age of three and three and a half. Easel paints were a close second to dramatic play for children at the age of four and four and a half. Blocks and crayons exceeded easel paints as a preference at the age of five.[1]

These findings indicate that easel paints—the medium most directly as-

[1] In our nursery schools we also found that the easel was preferred by the three-year-old groups more than by the four-year-old groups. Preference for the easel after the age of four tended to be associated with factors other than development, such as a lack of previous opportunities to paint or need for expression of feelings not finding an adequate outlet in more overt behavior. See Dorothy Van Alstyne, *Play Behavior and Choice of Play Materials of Preschool Children* (Chicago: University of Chicago Press, 1932). This study grew out of an exploratory study made by Rose H. Alschuler.

sociated with expression of feelings[2]—were preferred at the age when children tend most freely to be expressing themselves. Blocks and crayons— media more closely allied to reasoned, controlled behavior and to a realistic interest in the outside world[3]—gained in preference as children moved toward a more controlled, externalized, and/or objective phase of their development.

### DEVELOPMENTAL TRENDS IN USE OF COLOR VERSUS FORM

Our data have shown that *color* was emphasized far more than *form* throughout the nursery-school years. Since color is the medium through which feelings are predominantly expressed,[4] we should expect it to be favored during children's most highly impulsive, self-expressive period of development. Similarly, we should expect form, the medium of expression more closely allied with controlled and reasoned responses, to receive increasing emphasis as children move toward more controlled and adaptive ways of operating.

Our age data have shown a pronounced increase in color interest between the ages of three and three and a half. It is during this period that most children, having pretty well mastered the elementary processes of handling materials, find that focus on the mere process of painting (i.e., the back-and-forth swing of the brush across the painting page) no longer satisfies them. For many children the great urge to express their varieties of feeling then begins to find ready outlet through use of color. Color usage as a form of self-expression takes a definite upswing during this period.[5]

Form emphasis in our data has shown the greatest increase between the ages of four and four and a half. It is during this period that the influence of the environment is becoming more defined; that realistic, constructive interests are showing increased vitality; and that, at the same time, form usage (the clearest index that we have of reasoned and controlled drives) may be considered as coming into its own as one aspect of the whole developmental trend toward control.

Our age data have shown that color tended to be more often emphasized by girls than by boys. Since girls tend toward more free expression of emotions than do boys,[6] their greater focus on color is not surprising.

---

[2] See chap. vi.

[3] See pp. 129 ff. and 134 ff.          [4] See chap. ii.

[5] Data also revealed a second increase in color emphasis between four and four and a half. Case analyses suggest that previous lack of opportunity to paint, plus need for expression of feelings not permissible in more overt behavior, are probably more significant factors in this trend than is age per se.

[6] See p. 15, n. 2.

### DEVELOPMENTAL TRENDS IN COLOR PREFERENCE

Children's color preferences undergo a definite change between two and five years of age. Change in preference is particularly marked in so far as red and blue are concerned. While our data do not show a consistent trend at each half-year level studied between ages three and five, they do show a decreased preference for red and an increased preference for blue at four and a half and five as compared with three years of age. They likewise show a decrease in the use of warm colors in general and an increase in emphasis on cold colors in general between the ages of three and five. The period of greatest transition from warm to cold emphasis tends to be between three and three and a half—a period already described as nodal in the transition from emotional to controlled behavior.

As extensive study by Staples[7] is in keeping with these trends. Among the one hundred and eighteen children ranging in age from five and a half to twenty-four months who were given the task of reaching for colored disks, red was the outstanding preference, with yellow second and blue and green next in order. Among fifty nursery-school children, ages two and a half to five years, red was still preferred, but the difference between red, green, and blue was slight. In Staples' study, as in ours, a transition was indicated. Among one hundred grade children, ages seven to twelve years, Staples found that blue was the preferred color. Among one hundred college students blue was likewise preferred, with other colors ranging in the following order: green, red, and yellow. Staples emphasized the fact that the two colors most liked by adults—blue and green—were those least liked by infants.

These trends are in keeping with our color findings as previously outlined. Free emphasis on red was found, in general, to parallel such strong outgoing emotions as characterize the early years, a period already described as the primarily impulsive stage of development. In contrast to the use of red, emphasis on blue was found to parallel just such attempts at control as tend to occur repeatedly during the latter part of the nursery years.

The findings which we have described for blue also held in our data, in general, for green. Children showed an increased interest in green with increase in age.[8]

---

[7] Ruth Staples, "The Responses of Infants to Color," *Journal of Experimental Psychology*, XV (1932), 119–41; also *Psychological Bulletin*, XXVIII, No. 4 (April, 1931), 297–308.

[8] Green makes its sharpest increase in emphasis between four and a half and five, and red makes its greatest drop at the same time. Since these two colors are complementary in a physical sense as well as in terms of feeling quality, the parallel changes in opposite directions accord with expectancies. Just why the change occurred at four and a half instead of at three and a half or four is a matter of conjecture. It should not be interpreted without consideration of the fact that our

Our findings for yellow do not indicate a like parallelism with red. Yellow tended to show its greatest emphasis around the age of three and a half, the nodal period, when blue also showed a temporary peak.

Personality data give a clue to the possible significance of this peak in the use of yellow and blue. Blue usage often expresses or symbolizes the learned responses, whereas yellow is used frequently when the more infantile drives continue to be present. The nodal period (when blue and yellow are most used) is one of marked ambivalence and of frequent conflict between the desire to be grown up and the strong inclination to remain infantile. The peak usage of blue and yellow during this period would seem to reflect this conflict.

Interest in mixing colors or in using a variety of colors has been observed to increase with age. Such increased interest in complexity of color usage would seem an expected complement of the increased differentiations in intellectual concepts and in the emotional and visual experiences that come with age.

### DEVELOPMENTAL TRENDS IN COLOR PLACEMENT

If, on the basis of preceding generalizations, one were to speculate on children's placement of color, one might expect children's responses to be about as they are:

*a*) In the impulsive stage of unbounded interest in self-expression, children are more concerned with sheer use of color than with any particular placement of it, especially as careful or conscious placement implies a degree of control not ordinarily found during this period. Use of single colors or indiscriminate mixing and mingling of colors may be expected to predominate during the impulsive stage of development.

*b*) In the transition period from impulsive to controlled behavior an increasing interest in color placement may be expected. Some exaggerated attempts at control, as, for example, an occasional tendency toward careful separate placement of color, may be expected to appear at this time.

*c*) Controlled behavior having to a large extent been attained, the rather rigid attempts to express control as suggested by separate placement are now often replaced by freer usage, as seen in intermingling or purposive mixing of colors.

Although our data are indecisive in regard to indiscriminate mixing, they

age data deal with persistent tendencies and not initial occurrences. Specific age listings may be misleading, inasmuch as all developmental changes involve a range of time and not an invariable fixed point. Most of our age data give fairly clear-cut contrasts between the ages of three and five, with considerable variability between these ages. They suggest that transition is continuous throughout the period.

do indicate a period of emphasis on separate placement around four and a half years of age, followed by a period of emphasis on intermingling at four and a half and five. The data bring out an additional tendency not suggested above—a high incidence of overlay prior to five years of age.

Observations, already documented, have indicated that overlay tends to reflect repression and inadequate adjustment. The relatively high incidence of overlay in our data among children under five years of age seems to indicate that many of the children were not making an easy transition from impulsive to adaptive, reasoned behavior. Environmental pressures undoubtedly played a role. Perhaps such conflicts during the transition from impulsive to reasoned behavior are altogether usual and inevitable.

Pressure toward control—a tendency quite frequent in the homes of the children whom we studied (39 per cent of the children came from homes that offered evidence of overhigh demands)—might be considered one external factor which would contribute to overlay, but our statistics do not bear out this possibility. The conflicts reflected by consistent overlay have apparently been too highly individual and too varied to have been caught in our statistical analyses. [9]

DEVELOPMENTAL TRENDS IN CHILDREN'S USE OF LINE AND FORM

Development in use of line and form may perhaps be most readily thought of as progression through the following stages:

a) The stage of *scribbling*. This occurs during the period generally identified as one of manipulation.

b) The stage of *first experimentation with line and form*. This stage may be identified with the first faint beginning of form and/or pattern such as may be observed to characterize children's handling of many of their experiences and materials at this period.

c) The stage of *representation*. This stage is characterized by deliberate attempts at reproduction. Recognizable forms are produced. This period parallels increased capacity for organization of ideas and activities in all areas.

Fuller discussion of these trends follows (for illustration see Pls. 103–9).·

SCRIBBLING

Scribbling is the first reaction of the infant when he is able to apply a drawing pencil, crayon, or brush to paper. Eng[10] reports it as occurring in her niece at five months of age. It remains the most frequent mode of expression in the drawing or painting medium up to the age of two.[11]

---

[9] General tendencies associated with overlay are described in chap. ii.

[10] Hilda Eng, *The Psychology of Children's Drawings: From the First Stroke to the Colored Drawing* (London: Kegan Paul, Trench, Trubner, 1931).

[11] Barbara Biber, *From Lines to Drawing* (New York: 69 Banks Street, 1930).

Krötsch has defined scribbling as the stage before causal connection can be deliberately established between the impulse to movement and the line that follows.[12] Eng seems to have extended the term to include more conscious experimentation with line and form. She said:

> Wavy scribbling is in the first period the fundamental form of a child's drawing. Circular scribbling shows a higher form of development . . . . , then zig-zag lines, angles, crosses, straight lines and other single lines and forms. . . . . This latter kind of scribble requires shorter, more differentiated and better adapted movements, a greater capacity of understanding, distinguishing and separating lines and forms, more numerous mental pictures, better memory, greater combination of will impulse. . . . .[13]

Krötsch, like Eng, seems to have applied the term "scribbling" to experimental, as well as to involuntary, strokes. According to Krötsch,[14] the first strokes are rhythmical movements, which are in a sense undifferentiated and uncontrolled. Gradually the child begins to appreciate that there is a relation between the conscious experience of muscular movement and the strokes on the paper. After that he continues to go through the process more and more consciously until, having observed the relationship over and over again, he discovers the causal interdependence of movement and effect. It is now, according to Krötsch, that scribbling proper begins. The movement which at first involved "broad and simple impulses" becomes more differentiated with "shorter and multiple impulses . . . . forms are at first made in almost straight lines and finally, in spirals."

We have found it desirable to limit the term "scribbling" to that stage of relatively involuntary movement when one cannot establish a causal connection between impulse and line. We have observed, like Eng, that this earliest scribbling seems, at least in nursery-school groups in which easels are used, to take the form of a rhythmic back-and-forth swing resulting in a single mass. In this stage we have noted that even the direction tends to be predictable. If the arm is horizontal to the page (as is usual in the standing position at the easel), the swing tends to be in a diagonal, slightly curved direction.[15] When produced by the left hand, the swing is from lower right to upper left. When produced by the right hand, the swing is from lower left to upper right. When the arm rests on the paper (as when the child sits

---

[12] W. Krötsch, *Rhythmus und Form in der freien Kinderziehung* (Leipzig: A. Haase, 1917). Reported by Viktor Löwenfeld in *The Nature of Creative Activity* (New York: Harcourt, Brace & Co., 1939), pp. 17–19, 134; also by Eng, *op. cit.*

[13] Eng, *op. cit.*, pp. 4 and 104–5.      [14] Krötsch, *op. cit.*

[15] Throughout development, we have found that curves preceded straight strokes. Harms has reported an interesting case in which a child with eye strain, who was apparently slipping back to a less differentiated stage of vision, got the impression that objects had circular rather than angular form (see Ernst Harms, "Child Art as an Aid in the Diagnosis of Juvenile Neuroses," *American Journal of Orthopsychiatry*, XI, No. 2 [April, 1941], 191–209).

at a table and sometimes when he sits at the easel), the swing tends to take a horizontal rather than a diagonal direction (Pls. 103–5).

We have noticed one deviation from this rhythmic back-and-forth swing in the early stage of drawing that may represent a stage earlier than the rhythmic swing but one which ordinarily appears so early in the normal developmental scale that it has not been generally recognized as a usual first trend in human development. This deviation has consisted of short, broken, scattered strokes which seemed the result of uncontrolled movements and which apparently had quite different implications from the short, broken lines of the child who is working with more conscious or deliberate intent.[16]

Eight children in our study produced short, broken, scattered lines during the stage of involuntary control[17] when most children are producing the rhythmic back-and-forth swing described above. Each of these children tested below average level at the time that the observations were taken. Each showed inadequate development and adjustment in other more overt aspects of behavior, particularly in social relationships.

Gesell has supplied data which suggest that linear marks may be a developmental preliminary to the curved or wavy scribble, as shown in the accompanying tabulation.[18]

| SPONTANEOUS BEHAVIOR | PERCENTAGE DISPLAYING BEHAVIOR AT: | | | | | | |
|---|---|---|---|---|---|---|---|
| | 52 Weeks | 56 Weeks | 80 Weeks | 2 Years | 3 Years | 4 Years | 5 Years |
| N. | 48 | 28 | 37 | 34 | 31 | 22 | 57 |
| No combination of paper and crayon. | 0.46 | 0.26 | 0.05 | 0.06 | 0.03 | ........ | ........ |
| Bang on paper. | .31 | .32 | .35 | .03 | .03 | ........ | ........ |
| Linear marks. | .10 | .74 | .65 | ........ | ........ | ........ | ........ |
| Scribble. | 0.00 | 0.00 | 0.57 | 0.62 | 0.39 | 0.09 | 0.16 |

These linear marks are characteristic of children far below the age of nursery-school attendance (according to Gesell, they may be expected of children around fourteen months of age). Their persistence in a nursery-school child would seem an indication of retarded and/or disturbed de-

[16] See illustration of the two types of linear strokes (Pls. 94, 106–7) and discussion of more deliberately broken strokes (pp. 78 ff.).

[17] These children included Audrey, Charlotte, Chester, Irving, Norman, Rowena, Thomas, and Will (see also Pls. 106–7).

[18] Arnold Gesell and Others, *The First Five Years of Life: A Guide to the Study of the Preschool Child* (New York: Harper & Bros., 1940), chap. vii.

velopment and perhaps of low mentality. Stated in other words: The rhythmic back-and-forth swing, resulting in a single mass, may, around the age of two, be indicative of an integrated, properly functioning organism, while the broken, scattered strokes made without conscious control may, if persistent or characteristic beyond the ages of one and a half or two, be a reflection of a poorly integrated individual, that is, of an individual who has a poorly integrated neuromuscular system.

Observations in our study support these findings. If they are substantiated by further experimentation, they may provide a valuable diagnostic clue to the neuromuscular organization and to the operating level of children at an age or stage of development when standardized testing is difficult.

Several children were observed whose work approximated the scattered all-directional, uncontrolled pattern described above but was less extreme and stereotyped. This second group of children was one capable of performing at a controlled level. Their strokes were, for the most part, not so short, not so few, and not so stereotyped as those of the children previously described. This group of children on test did not reveal subnormal intelligence, but they did exhibit several other characteristics in common with the other group.

*Andy, Anita,* and *Jeff* have provided the most clear-cut examples of children capable of some degree of control, who had a tendency toward scattered, all-directional strokes of the less stereotyped kind. These three children had several characteristics in common. All of them tested lower than the average for the particular group to which they belonged, and all seemingly tested at a level below their true capacity, as judged by occasional, sporadic performance.

These children tended to be disorganized, distractible, and scattered in all their interests and activities. They flitted from one activity to another. In painting, each was likely to try a little of each color, as well as work in every direction. As suggested before, a drawing of the footpaths of each of these children on the playground in a given morning, particularly if made with a different color for each change in activity, would have shown a pattern somewhat similar to the paintings produced by each of these children (see Pls. 94–99).

On investigating the dynamics of these three children, we learned that not one of the three had any incentive to do well, to attempt self-control, or to "grow up." Each of these children came from a home in which there was clear-cut evidence of rejection by one or both parents.

Although capable of performing at a constructive, and at least an average, level, these children did not progress but remained too long in the impulsive, undirected stage of development. The difficulty was not lack of inherent quality or capacity but lay rather in the environmental conditions, which did not offer ordinary incentives for development. As is well known, young children's basic stimulus toward exercising controls derives from desire to please some adult—usually one or both parents. The child who is not wanted or appreciated by his parents has not sufficient incentive to exert controls or to develop in usual fashion. The paintings of children growing up under these circumstances may be found to be characterized by the broken, unrhythmic, unrelated strokes indicative of low developmental level.

Conscious experimentation with line and form, outlined as the second stage in the use of line and form, seems to depend for its appearance upon actual drives toward control on the part of the child himself. As the previous examples suggest, environmental forces may play a large part in the appearance of these drives and in the seemingly parallel interest in line and form.

Among the more frequent trends and deviations which we have noticed in relation to this phase of development are the following:

1. Retarded appearance of conscious experimentation, paralleled by a generally retarded pattern of development. This may be the result of limited congenital endowment or of inadequate environmental stimuli toward development (as illustrated above).

2. Increased emphasis on color, with work in mass technique rather than in line and form and with a strongly repetitive painting pattern usually present. This trend has been observed in emotionally disturbed children who were more preoccupied with their emotional problems than with making the swing toward controlled and adaptive behavior. Some of these children persisted in the color-mass technique throughout the nursery-school years and even beyond this period. One child persisted in his color-mass pattern in kindergarten whenever he had an opportunity to paint or crayon during free play. He followed the group tendency toward representative work during regular art periods. Many children who made the transition from color and mass to line and form reverted to the color-mass form of expression when faced and disturbed by an emotional problem.[19]

3. Premature appearance of line and form, paralleled by an overt pattern of relatively controlled, reasoned overt behavior. Children who turned prematurely to line and form were likely to work in abstract, nonrepresentative, nonrecognizable patterns and to persist in making these abstractions after other children at their stage of development had made the normal shift to representative form. The children who most markedly showed this tendency were those who were attempting to avoid unpleasant emotional experience by a complete denial of expressed emotion. These children were likely to use color emphasis or mass or scribbling techniques as their general adjustments improved.

4. A steady progression from (a) scribbling through (b) experimentation

[19] Exemplified by Angela, occasionally by Aileen and others.

Children tend in the early years to paint themselves as they feel from within.

## AILEEN: 4 years, 9 months

PLATE 1

Like the early representations of many other children, this was a self-portrait. Both the crying eyes and the open mouth were true to life.

## BRIAN: 4 years, 2 months

PLATE 2

Conscious of a slightly defective foot, Brian emphasized legs through a number of extra appendages. He gave extra weighting to the side corresponding to his own defect.

PLATE 3

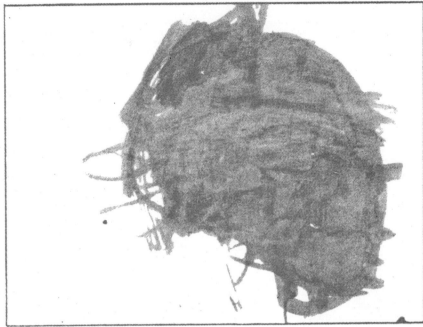

*10-11-37.* This ovular red mass pattern characterized 133 of the 187 paintings Aileen made during the first year of observation. Through repeated verbalizations and other data we learned that this form meant "home" to Aileen.

PLATE 4

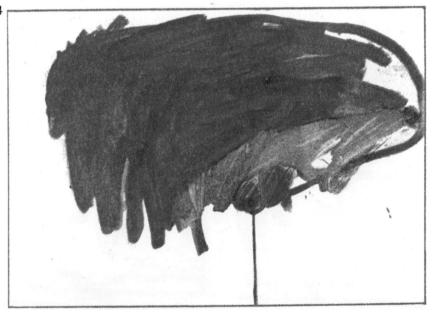

*2-25-38.* The same form persists, but here the ovular outline is cut across with firm multi-colored strokes. Both in variety of colors used and in firm quality and extent of stroking, Aileen went beyond her usual self-restricted pattern. This outgoing painting was paralleled by a period of lessened tension and expressed happiness over her mother's remarriage, which occurred at this time.

* Age given indicates child's age on date of painting that immediately follows, e.g., Aileen was 3 years, 6 months on 10-11-37. When Pl. 12 was painted, she was 6 years older.

PLATE 5

*12-5-38.* This painting is much like Plate 3 painted one year earlier. Aileen periodically reverted to this pattern over a number of years. Continued use of the small restricted, isolated mass suggests Aileen's withdrawn position in the group. Repeated emphasis on red paralleled her strong drive and known need for consistent affectional relationships.

PLATE 6

*1-20-39.* This painting was similar to that used by Aileen in her first human representations. It was more rectangular and more like a house or structure than like the rounded human representations of most children. Aileen's subsequent history indicated her constant preoccupation with house or home. Like many children anxious to communicate with others, she frequently painted her initials on her pictures.

P<small>LATE</small> 7

*1-20-39*. On the same date as she painted Plate 6, she outlined her first human figure. It has extraordinary symmetry in design, balance, and color:

P<small>LATE</small> 8

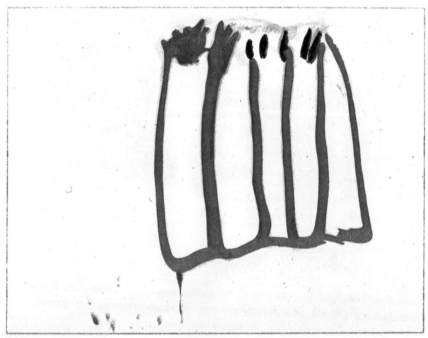

*3-13-39*. With slight reference to objective reality, Aileen records her impression of a zebra.

PLATE 9

*3-29-40*. This was painted two and a half years after Plate 3. We note the earlier form now conventionalized in lower left corner. In center, abstract self-portrait—Aileen on a pedestal. Her name printed clockwise lends support to this interpretation.

PLATE 10

*4-2-40*. This left-right pattern with red oval on left and blue form on right suggests that Aileen was trying to push her emotional problems away from awareness and was trying to accept educational standards. (Implications on color usage and left-right pattern analyzed in later chapters.)

PLATE 11

*Spring, 1940.* On noting that Esther was building a hen coop, Aileen announced that she, too, would build one. Hers became the fanciful, pedestaled structure at left, with chickens perched on top. In blocks, clay, paint, and dramatic play, Aileen's pedestal-like projections expressed her self-centered feeling of being apart and aloof from life around her.

PLATE 12

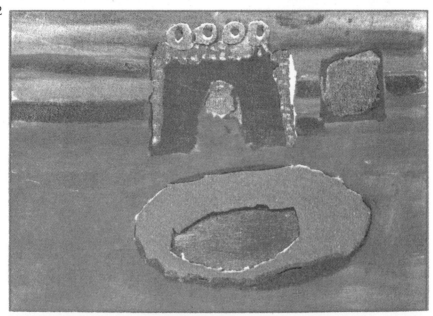

*Spring, 1943.* Throughout the third grade, Aileen had a particularly happy experience because the teacher capitalized on Aileen's concern about home. A pioneer cabin (a home) was built and decorated in the schoolroom. Aileen incorporated her earlier red ovular form in the hearth rug and the four plates which she designed for this home. Although the inside of the cabin was dark, Aileen spent much time playing and studying there.

PLATE 13

*3-25-38.* In his early swing scribblings, Archie always managed to finish his paintings with a large swing to the top of the page. His unusually small stature made this a real effort. In extending himself figuratively and literally, he was asserting his frequently expressed desire to be a big man.

PLATE 14

*2-27-39.* Self-portrait. At this period Archie was biting other children.

PLATE 15

*5-19-39.* In his abstract paintings, Archie as a rule focused toward the top of the page. The title given was "String on a Star."

PLATE 16

*Spring, 1939.* Archie stands on a chair to give height to his block structure. His block structures, like his paintings and drawings, projected his drive to be tall (see biographical summary).

PLATE 17

*Spring, 1940.* Note that the man is taller than the house. At this age, self seems more important than environment and is often depicted accordingly. Height is here accentuated by a hat. In school Archie often insisted on wearing a hat, which gave him added stature. Children with high aspirations were more likely than other children to picture skies and sky lines.

PLATE 18

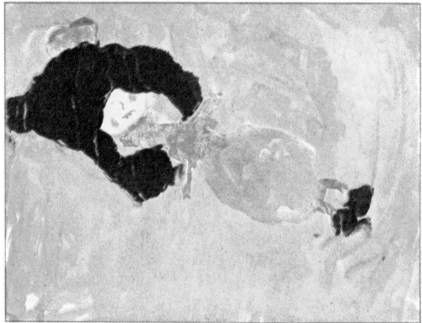

*4-6-38.* Elinor, long awaited and much desired, was born and bred with the feeling that she was the "Princess." Observers noted that at various times she preened before the mirror and remarked on her resemblance to Snow White. She entitled this painting "Snow White Asleep."

PLATE 19

*4-7-38.* A self-portrait. Like most little girls with curls, she accentuated hair.

PLATE 20

*Spring, 1941.* One of a number of similar drawings done in first grade. The Princess receives homage. Hair continues to be an important factor.

PLATE 21

*1943—third grade.* A more sophisticated version of the same theme which, as we see, continued to dominate her life (see biographical summary).

PLATE 22

*2-10-38.* Crayon of this date and painting of 3-11-38 are similar in color and space usage. Angela, like some other children preoccupied with a particular problem, used crayons and paints in approximately the same way.

PLATE 23

*3-11-38.* At three different times when her mother was pregnant, Angela reverted from a higher form level to this general type of all-over mass painting. Each of the three times her palette and her pattern were somewhat similar. Each time she tended to overlay warm colors with colder ones.

PLATE 24

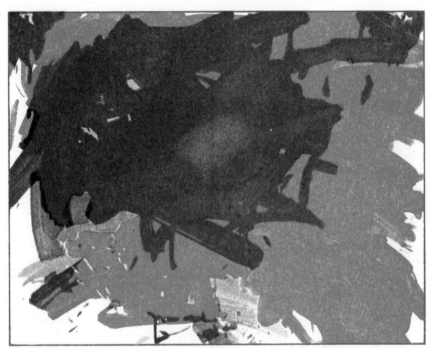

*3-17-38.* Angela remarked: "I make a hook, I make a circle. . . . . I'm going to make. . . . Look this is a fire. I made three pictures" (actually she had made only one).

Records indicate that her mother had a miscarriage later in the month. Throughout this period, whether Angela worked with clay, crayons, or paints, she showed considerable tension in posture and movement. Tongue-rolling was evident. At the same time she carried toys around in a blanket (often done by children whose mothers are pregnant). For three weeks there were many difficulties in nursery school. During this period there was no painting, and a sudden dislike was evidenced for music and rhythms, which she had formerly enjoyed.

PLATE 25

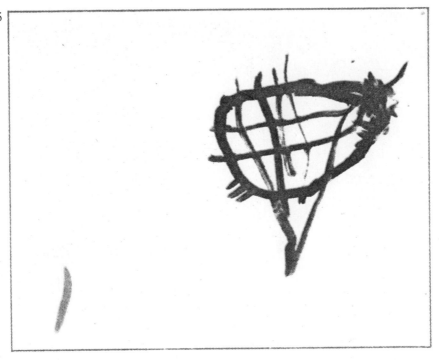

5-20-38. She was again interested in music and painting. Teacher's report at this time reads: "Well adjusted—very co-operative most of the time now." On this date she made 3 blue crayons and 2 blue paintings. Note higher form levels and choice of blue for both crayon and paintings. Many children change, as Angela did, from mass to form and from warmer to colder colors as their difficulties clear. Blue often was used to express their more controlled responses. (End of school year.)

10-13-38. On this date the record of Angela's dramatic play reads: "I'll be the bad mother. We've got a new baby. It came at the hospital." She then played baby was sick. (Her mother was again pregnant, and, as before, Angela was informed of the coming event early in her mother's pregnancy.)

10-18-38. Record reads: "Angela is very excitable. Her mother is in the hospital."

10-24-38. Mother returns home after miscarriage.

PLATE 26

*10-28-38.* Angela reverts to mass paintings to express her generalized emotional disturbance. Palette is somewhat similar to that of 3-17-38. This time black is used instead of blue. Use of orange and red or pink continues. Angela again was carrying a blanket, rubbing it against her lips when tired. Her continued preoccupation concerning the baby was obvious.

PLATE 27

*1-4-39.* Angela first painted a structuralized pattern with orange and red, then she heavily overpainted it with colder colors—blue and green. That her old problem was still bothering her was evident not only in her painting but also in her dramatic play. She was alternately taking the roles of sick little girl, mother, and dead baby.

PLATE 28

*1-21-39.* During play interview, alone in the office with Dr. Hattwick, Angela remarked as she moved all the dolls out of the structure she had built: "The family is moving away from the mama because she is not a good mommy." Note the mother left lying on the bed.

PLATE 29

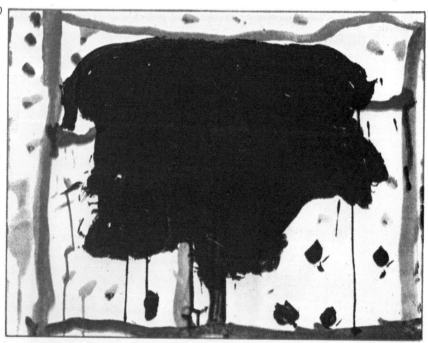

*2-9-39.* This large decorative frame and spots had begun as a figure with large head. It was heavily overpainted and called a "witch." Simultaneously, she was playing witch in dramatic play. As she began to talk about and dramatize her problem, it seemed to clear. Form soon again emerged in her painting.

PLATE 30

*3-3-39.* Four human figures, two large and two small, connected by arms coming from the heads. Angela used red very little at this time. As we observe her use of yellow and green, we remember that yellow is associated with infancy and green frequently connotes emotional dearth. *

PLATE 31

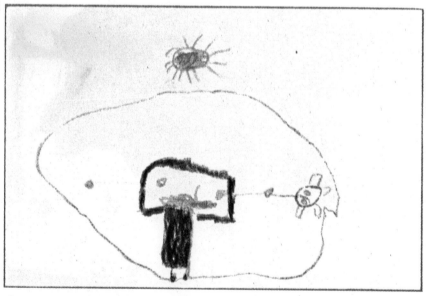

*4-17-39.* Crayon corresponding to Plate 30 shows mother and child connected. Purple, orange, and pink are predominantly used. The mother was pregnant again. This time, although the pregnancy was still an anxiety to Angela, she was less tense. She again began to play the "sick little girl."

* Figures not unlike these are found in petroglyphs (see Julian H. Steward, *Petroglyphs of California and Adjoining States* [Berkeley: University of California Press, 1929], Pls. 23E and 59E).

PLATE 32

*5-5-39.* This picture Angela called "A Man and a Rabbit." The old pattern was given a new name. The impulse which stimulated the picture was probably quite different from that which stimulated the title. Note long legs, which were also characteristic of Angela.

PLATE 33

*5-5-39.* Increased release and disturbance are seen in this second painting of the same date. We note return to mass painting. This pattern, with two-thirds of the paper dark and one-third lighter with a dark blob in the lighter portion, seems somewhat comparable in pattern and space usage to Angela's earlier mass paintings, as well as to the paired-mass paintings of Alan, Elaine, and several other children whose mothers were pregnant. During this pregnancy, Angela was more able to handle her problem and feelings. By 5-11 and thereafter, she painted constructive patterns without overpainting them, and she used both warm and cold colors as children not preoccupied with problems are likely to do. On 5-14, she said to the teacher: "I'm going to have a baby, you know." She now could talk about it directly and no longer had to repress or act it out symbolically.

PLATE 34

*11-1-38.* It would seem more than coincidence that Sally used red, in heavy scribbling, as she exclaimed: "Dick ran into my leg, and I am mad at him!"

PLATE 35

*11-29-38.* In contrast to Aileen's restricted masses, which symbolized her shut-in, unsatisfied emotional life, is this painting of Anita's. It is typical of a period in which red was smeared and daubed on in heavily incrusted fashion, with lines going in all directions all over the page and sometimes beyond. The impression is of a wild and messy painting. During this time Anita was expressing her hostile emotions in an amazing variety of aggressive episodes (see biographical summary).

PLATE 36

*10-26-37.* Controlled anxiety evident in school was reflected here, as Edward covered his isolated red mass with blue. His strokes were put on with such tension that the paper tore in the center.

PLATE 37

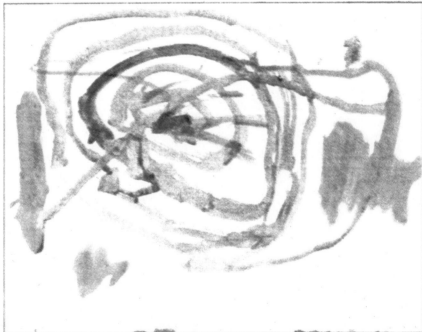

*4-10-38.* This painting shows a contrasting form and color usage that reflects Edward's improved adjustment. He called it "Spider Web on the Grass."

Plate 38

Plate 39

*12-15-37.* Entitled "Dog Chasing Kitty," these two paintings reflect Esther's dramatic play of that period, as well as her high-quality aesthetic reactions and her keen motor ability. They give an extraordinary impression of movement, probably due to Esther's unusually good co-ordinations and excellent physical development.

PLATE 40

*2-23-38.* This was the first time Esther overpainted. A number of like products character-ized this period, during which Esther frequently had night terrors and wet her panties.

PLATE 41

*11-23-38.* The following fall she was quite aggressive toward other children. There was con-siderable tiger and bear play. This period was paralleled by wet, messy, more outgoing, wild-patterned red and orange paintings.

PLATE 42

*Kindergarten, 1940.* Esther was again conforming in painting and behavior to the description of one teacher, viz., "the most sublimated four-year-old I've ever known."

PLATE 43

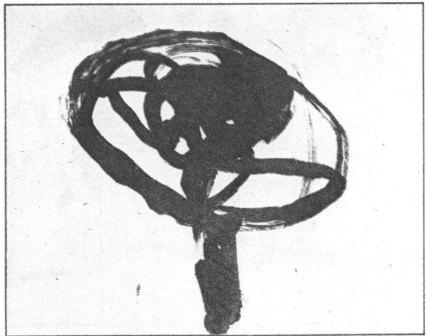

*1-19-38.* A typical "anxiety-blue" picture in self-restricted form. Danny was overtly tense. The family showed overconcern and pressure because of his persistent failure in defecation control.

PLATE 44

PLATE 45

*1-21-38; 1-24-38.* When his parents left town for a month, Danny's tensions were released, and he painted these pictures. Both are typical "dirty," smeary pictures such as are frequently painted by children preoccupied with problems of elimination. Regardless of colors used, greenish-brown or brownish-green palettes often characterized the paintings of children absorbed by elimination problems.

PLATE 46

*1-26-38.* As Danny began to come to school by himself, he became more overtly self-assured and soon had voluntarily established defecation control. As this problem cleared, he developed structuralized patterns, painted with clearer colors and cleaner effects.

PLATE 47

*2-2-39*. In her first two pattern paintings, Rita expressed her desire to smear (*at right*) along with her usual controlled pattern (*at left*). The teacher recorded that "she was happier today than she has ever been in school."

PLATE 48

*3-16-39*. After a month's absence, Rita returned to school and again painted a two-pattern picture. To the left the clearly outlined face shows ears and mouth shaded with blue. The blue-covered apertures seemed to express her mother-controlled responses. The smeary mass on the right offers a striking contrast.

PLATE 49

*4-18-39.* On entrance to school, Rita went immediately to the easel, carefully outlined the house with black, and remarked: "Mother told me to make a house. This is the house for my mother." After laying down her brush, she picked it up and smeared the upper half of the house. Although done for her mother, she did not take this painting home.* That (1) she painted the house with black paint, (2) smeared the upper half of it, and (3) did not take the picture home, although expressly made for her mother, all indicate her reactions against the home situation.

PLATE 50

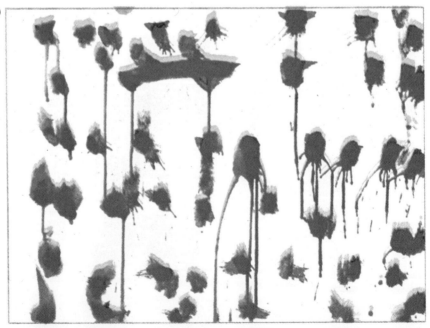

*4-19-38.* Rita carefully spaced precise blue dots over the entire painting page. With considerable vehemence she covered each one over with a dripping dab of orange. On that day, as on others, when she had comparable experiences, teachers and observers noted that, following painting, Rita seemed more at ease and more ready to relax at rest time.

* For significance of pictures taken home see pp. 154-55.

PLATE 51

*2-10-38.* Ann persistently overlaid yellow with blue and green, when using both crayons and paints. In follow-up observations made several years later, the same palette was still evident, although the form level was higher and there was less overlaying.

PLATE 52

*4-26-38.* Same palette as in Plate 51. The painting is more spread out and the overlay is more lightly put on. This suggests that Ann was less tense than in the period represented by Plate 53. Actually, after six months of persistent silence in school, Ann had at this time begun to say an occasional word when alone with a teacher or with a few children.

PLATE 53

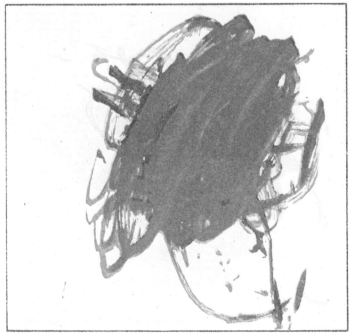

*5-12-38.* Greater isolation, as well as more aggression, are reflected in this more heavily painted and more restricted form. At this time Ann was beginning to be aggressive in attacking others, destroying their structures, etc.

PLATE 54

*6-8-38.* On this day Ann brought her much-loved cat to school. This evidently gave her a feeling of confidence and belongingness. After speaking practically not at all at school, she became overtly aggressive in talking both to children and to adults. On the day following, *6-9-38*, she did this yellow painting. She was now talking and behaving in accordance with her basic feelings. There was no further need for covering over.

PLATE 55

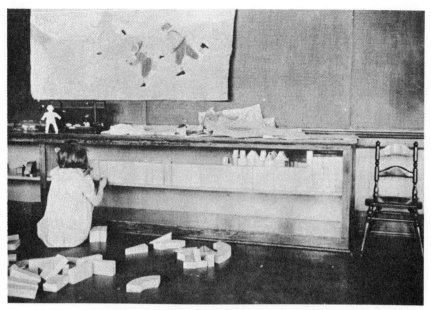

Just as Ann had concealed her thoughts by not speaking and had covered over her natural basic color, yellow, so she often covered her block structures with her skirts while theoretically busy putting the blocks away. Note how Ann built and concealed a structure back of the other blocks in the right-hand corner of the upper shelf.

PLATE 56

*1-11-38*. Fredrika was one of a number of children whose messy greenish palette for a time paralleled an interest in excrement. This picture was entitled "Man Looking through a Window That Has Been Rained on and That Has Not Been Washed All Day." The greenish palette over blue was done with considerable energy.

PLATE 57

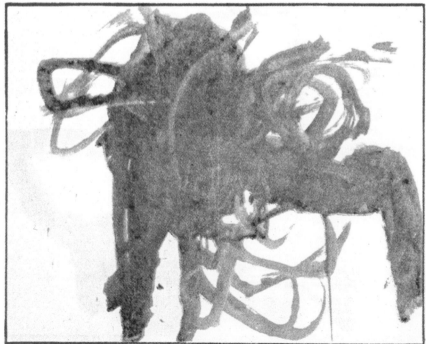

*1-11-38*. This painting, done on the same date as Plate 56, shows the same palette, but looks even dirtier. It was entitled "Incinerator with Garbage in It."

PLATE 58

*2-21-38.* Her placement of colors here, with more intermingling and less overlaying, indicates her decreasing concern with elimination and her increasing interest in other areas. About two-thirds of this picture, "Rainstorm Which Made Everything Muddy," was overpainted with black.

PLATE 59

*2-23-38.* As her concern for elimination cleared, her use of color became clearer, and her paintings showed a more constructive pattern. This was paralleled by less interest in smearing with clay and more constructive block play with boys. The title "Train" for this picture points to her locomotor play with boys.

Dots and dabs characterized the work of several children whose overt behavior showed an extreme sense of order and cleanliness. These children came from homes in which cleanliness was stressed and emphasis was put on being "nice little girls."

## JILL: 4 years, 2 months

PLATE 60

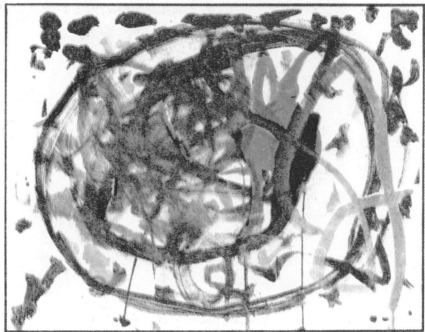

*1-10-39*. At the overt level, Jill was too controlled, neat, and precise. Painting apparently served as an outlet for her desire to smear, and no matter what colors she used, Jill was likely to achieve a greenish palette. Even she recognized this, for one day she remarked: "Lots of my pictures are green."

Several other children's paintings, like Jill's, have suggested that color effects or palettes may be more revelatory of unconscious drives than the basic colors used. In these cases, as in Jill's, painting served as an outlet for smeary drives not permitted in overt behavior.

PLATE 61

*1-11-39.* "Dirty" dabs, such as these, are frequently found in the paintings of children concerned with defecation. Their interest seems to find an outlet in easel painting.

PLATE 62

*5-15-39.* By this time the problem had been somewhat worked out, and we find a less direct and more sublimated expression of the desire to smear and dab. Energy by this time had been channeled into more socially accepted forms.

PLATE 63

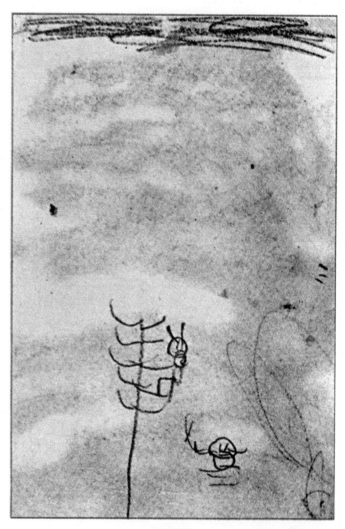

*4-1-40*. Black was chosen by Edward to suit his anxious mood. Of this picture he said: "He's climbing a tree to get away from his father. His father wants to take him in the house. He's done something bad." And then he added: "He got himself all wet. His father wants to talk to him about it. He's afraid he's going to spank him."

Linear abstractions are often typical of the child who is trying to escape strong emotions.

ALAN: 3 years, 7 months

PLATE 64

A

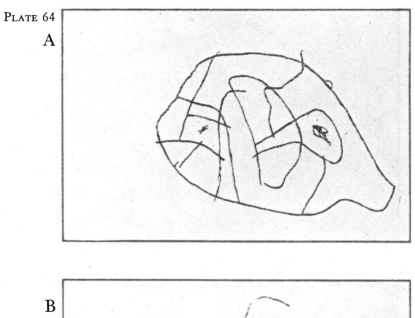

B

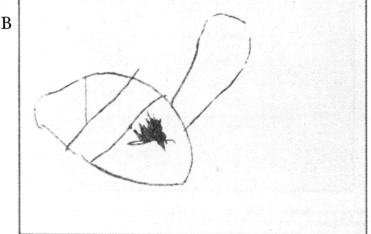

*2-18-37.* (*a*) This purple form enclosing a structuralized pattern was named "Apple" by Alan. (*b*) On the same day this form with projection was entitled "Airplane."

PLATE 65

*11-22-37*. Alan crayoned but did not paint during his first year at nursery school. Characteristic of his crayons were mass swing scribblings, with yellow and orange underneath and purple on top. Alan and many other children used purple as they did black to overlay warmer colors, just as in actual living they seemed to overlay or repress their affectional emotions. When not scribbling, Alan typically worked in linear abstractions (as in Pl. 64).

PLATE 66

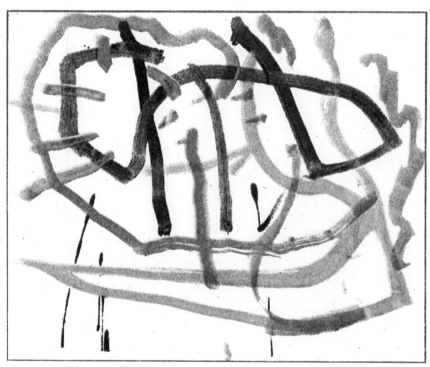

*1-27-39*. After a year and a half in school, Alan produced his first painting during a controlled observation when alone with Dr. Hattwick in her office. His first painting in the group followed the next day. In his predominant selection of cold colors and in his immediate turning to line and form, his early paintings suggest that he was trying to avoid expression of his emotions. His keen interest and experience with blocks is reflected in his use of space and in the structuralized pattern of his painting and crayon designs.

PLATE 67

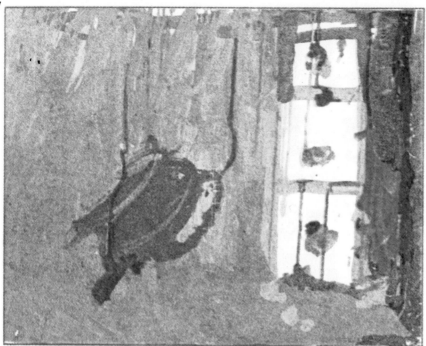

*7-24-39.* Painted just a few weeks before the new baby was born, this picture with (1) its use of dark and light paired masses, (2) its more solid effect to the left, and (3) its use of inclosed blobs recalls paintings done by Angela, Elaine, and others who were also aware of and disturbed by the mother's pregnancy. The lattice design reflects Alan's high block usage.

PLATE 68

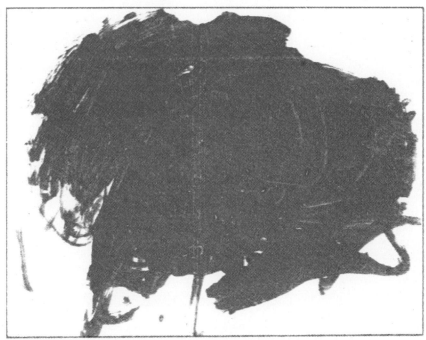

*1-14-38.* This blue restricted mass, put on with heavy, tense strokes, was similar to paintings of other anxious, too controlled children. As we saw paint put on in this way and analyzed the accompanying behavior, we found that the term "controlled anxiety" characterized both paintings and behavior.

PLATE 69

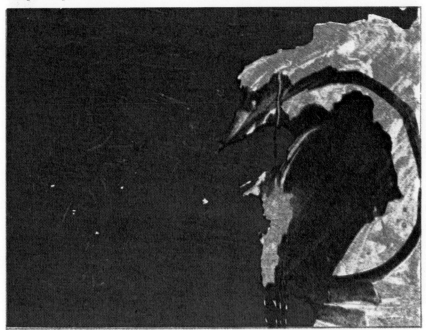

*2-23-38.* Elaine again chose blue for painting, then said: "Have to have a little black, too." Note paired masses with two-thirds of page overpainted with blue, one-third lighter color. Circular form with dark blob in middle probably expressed child's concept or feeling of mother carrying child within her. Elaine had been told of mother's pregnancy. As observed before, this pattern is somewhat like those of Angela and Alan, painted under the same circumstances at quite different times.

PLATE 70

*3-30-38*. This painting began with an edging and the ragged angular mass of blue, then a mass of green and one of yellow. She then covered the page with orange. "That's a scribbly," said Glen. "It's a wall, like that," exclaimed Elaine, pointing to the "blue wall." Three weeks earlier Elaine had made a clay wall (see pp. 38–40, for significance).

PLATE 71

*4-6-38*. Back at school after two days' illness at home. A series of black paintings had been initiated on 3-22-38. For a considerable time after this date, black was persistently asked for and used. A solid black mass painted all over the page was the predominant pattern. At times there was an underlay of warm colors. Paintings were sometimes called "night" and were paralleled by night terrors, by frequent getting out of bed to go to the toilet, and frequent enuresis during the day. Painting pattern of this date suggests continued preoccupation with pregnancy. It was on 4-7-38 that Elaine learned that "Blackie," the school rabbit, had been eaten by a dog.

PLATE 72

*4-22-38*. On this date Elaine made *her first overt comment* about the baby, stating that it had come. On this day, too, she broke away from her solid black series. She painted only edging of blue, yellow, and orange, and used no black. During the next ten days she reverted to all-over black paintings, asking for black when it was not there. Enuresis was frequent.

PLATE 73

*5-9-38*. In dramatic play with Gilbert in the doll corner, she said: "The parents went to bed." She then covered the baby (doll), head and all, saying: "So that the flies won't get the baby." She immediately thereafter went to the bathroom but was already wet. Paint, less heavily put on than earlier in the series, suggests lessening tension.

PLATE 74

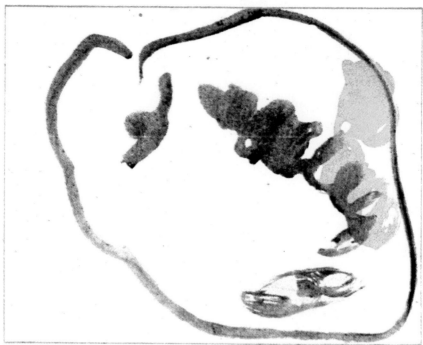

*5-23-38.* After ten days' absence, Elaine returned to school and had much doll play with Gilbert, who had a young baby in his family. She and Gilbert talked about their babies. After hearing the story of Baby Ann read aloud, she said: "If the baby is a boy, I'll call him Blackie [the name of the school rabbit eaten by the dog]. If it's a girl, I'll call her Snow White." After this outspoken hostility, in which she identified the baby with the dead rabbit, Elaine again painted in outline form, with blobs enclosed. On both occasions when she spoke of the baby she used outline instead of mass. Like Dan, Angela, and others, as Elaine began to express her problem in words, her acute anxieties and her need to paint seemed to subside. In the only two other paintings made before school closed, Elaine ceased to overlay warm with cold colors and moved from mass toward use of line and colder colors.

PLATE 75

A

B

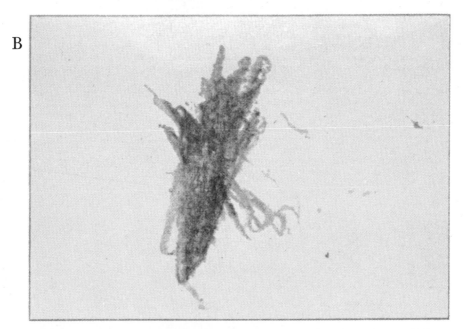

Regardless of colors used, Margaret's palette, like Alan's and that of several other children, usually gave the impression of being muddied green or brown. Both crayons and paintings reflected the melancholy outlook of these children who, for various reasons, felt unloved. Twice Margaret labeled her products "A Fraidy."

PLATE 76

*1-5-38.* Among children of this age (4 to 4 years, 6 months), the tendency to place colors so carefully that they did not touch one another usually indicated that children were being pushed into too rigid conformance with environmental molds. As these children achieved better balance in living, they began to intermingle colors.

LORETTA: 4 years, 5 months

PLATE 77

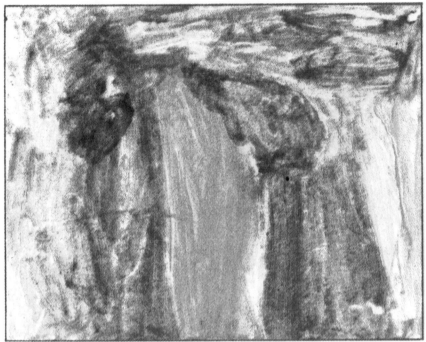

*4-17-39.* Free intermingling of colors without either careful separation or overlay character-ized the paintings of Loretta and others who were expressing themselves freely and in a variety of ways. All these children operated without much evidence of strain or emotional tension.

BENJY: 4 years, 2 months

PLATE 78

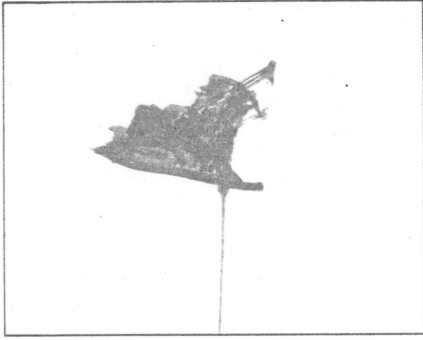

Within three months, as Benjy changed from a shy to an aggressive four-year-old, his painting pattern showed parallel change. Note transition from small restricted form filled with cold color (2-16-38) to freer form using more of page. General effect is smeary.

PLATE 79

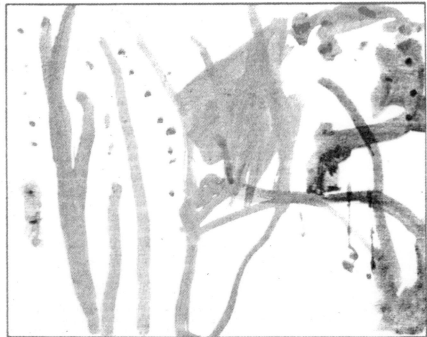

*5-27-38.* Here much greater freedom is evidenced. The strokes are more widely spread out on the page, and the colors are warmer and more varied.

PLATE 80

Most of Howard's painting and crayon products were made during a period of considerable tension that preceded and followed his sister's birth.

*1-4-39.* The crossed-out verticals suggest denial of the assertive or masculine role. His use of red suggests a strong emotional factor. Both observations are corroborated by his records.

PLATE 81

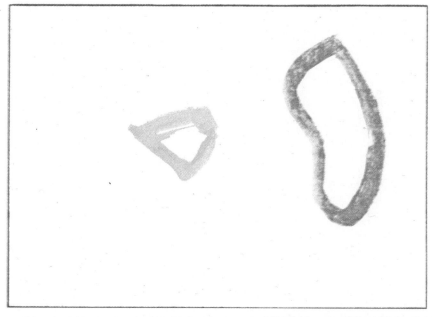

*1-16-39.* The shift from verticals to circles suggests an inner conflict concerning the baby to be born shortly. Large and small circles painted in juxtaposition were found in a number of cases in the paintings of children preoccupied with the mother-infant relationship. Yellow used for the small circle (baby) and blue for the larger circle accords with discussion in chapter ii.

PLATE 82

A

B

*1-27-39.* A sister was born on 1-17. Note yellow verticals smeared on left, red verticals on right. On the second painting of same date, yellow verticals on left were crossed out. Clear, unsmeared red circles on right remained.

PLATE 83

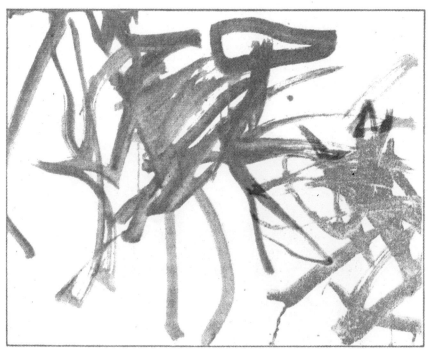

*2-1-39.* Both vertical and circular strokes were smeared, indicating a continuing inner conflict. For Howard, easel painting was a valuable medium for expressing his problem while it remained unclarified and at the nonverbal level. Shortly after this date, Howard became verbal about his conflict, his painting ceased, and his overt behavior again became easy and outgoing, as it had been earlier in the year.

Frank also presented a parallel between use of circular-vertical pattern in easel painting and concern or conflict over his sexual role. In a family with three sisters, a new baby was expected and another boy greatly desired. Paintings made preceding sister's arrival were characterized by circular strokes and full-page mass effects. Behavior records at this time indicate that Frank was unusually unassertive. Frank was ill after the baby's birth and out of school for two months.

PLATE 84

*2-25-38.* On this date, Frank's first day back at school, he produced two paintings. In the first, a weakly painted, red ovular form is almost obliterated by aggressively painted diagonal and vertical strokes.

PLATE 85

*2-25-38.* On the second painting of the same date, green and yellow verticals are unsmeared. The red and black ones on the right are slightly smeared. These two paintings suggest a shift from earlier circular pattern and submissive role to increased acceptance of assertive masculine role, now expressed in almost clear verticals. Observations on this date record that Frank was "more aggressive than was usual before his illness."

PLATE 86

*11-7-38*. Perry showed almost no interest in clay or painting. Three of the only four crayon products he made were done on the day following an older child's threat that the doctor would cut off his ears. The threat, which apparently precipitated nightmares at home and the crayon drawings at school, is one which psychoanalysts have said may lead to castration fear. Their interpretation corresponds to our observations and interpretation in this situation. Note clear-cut stretch of verticals across page, many of them accentuated at beginning by heavy dot. The verticals are smeared with diagnoal and circular structures.

PLATE 87

*11-7-38*. Clear verticals, each introduced by heavy dot and smeared with horizontal strokes. There was no subsequent evidence of difficulty.

Jessica, an assertive girl who obviously desired to be a boy, wore boy's clothes, and stood to urinate.

PLATE 88

*10-28-38.* A characteristic painting of this period, when entire focus was on verticals.

PLATE 89

*3-13-39.* As she began to desire social acceptance and to meet adult expectancies, she began to smear her verticals. Verticals then became fewer, shorter, and less firmly painted. Like various other children who showed alternation between vertical and circular patterns, she tended to show corresponding alternation between assertive and submissive behavior.

PLATE 90

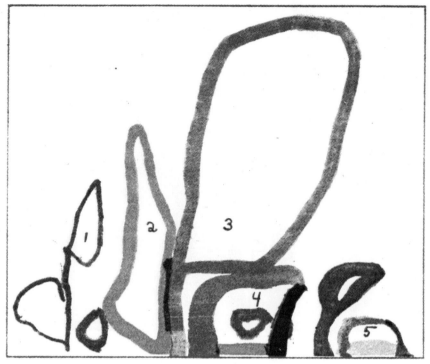

This painting was made 3 months after baby brother was born. Asked by one of the authors, present when it was painted: "Would you like to tell me about your painting?" L. J. D. pointed from right to left and said (5) "me," (4) "my mother with my brother inside her," (3) "my mother with my brother inside her," (2) "my father," (1) "my brother." Note the elongated, more vertical designs of father and brother; the large, round mother, who has just been pregnant; the related sizes, colors, and forms with rounded corners to represent mother and daughter—also concentric forms entitled "my mother with my brother inside her."

* L.J.D. 5 years, 6 months, and A.A., 5 years, 4 months, whose paintings follow, were not observed as part of the study, but both children were well known to the authors. These particular paintings (Pls. 90–93) seemed to warrant inclusion.

A. A.

Plate 91

A. A. had been doing paintings and crayon drawings for over a year at a very high representative level. Products previously seen included buildings and streets in perspective, auto-
mobiles, etc. This retrogression to mass technique, painted three days before his brother
was born, is accordingly of marked interest. As in the paintings of Alan, Angela, Elaine,
and others, we find a dark blob enclosed in lighter mass. (These are 3 of a series of 6 easel
paintings done in quick succession. This was the first.)

PLATE 92

Container pattern parallels paintings of Tess, Tony, and others (p. 75).

PLATE 93

This "crying child enclosed" doubtless depicted himself as he felt—unhappy, and in that desirable, enclosed position occupied by the coming baby. This is another form of "container theme."

PLATE 94

*5-3-38*. Scattered, all-directional strokes were characteristic of a number of children who had distributive attention and were consistently impulsive and uncontrolled.

PLATE 95

*12-2-39*. Painting and behavior nineteen months later are still below level of real ability. Spatial usage and form derive from Andy's large block usage and train play.

PLATE 96

*12-15-37.* Like Andy's and Anita's paintings, Jeff's were made up of short, all-directional strokes. All three children, because of their home situations, lacked incentive to grow up. Jeff's strokes ended weakly, as did his behavior. When other children took his toys, he usually whimpered and walked away. Jeff was ambidextrous. He started this painting with his left hand and finished it with his right.

PLATE 97

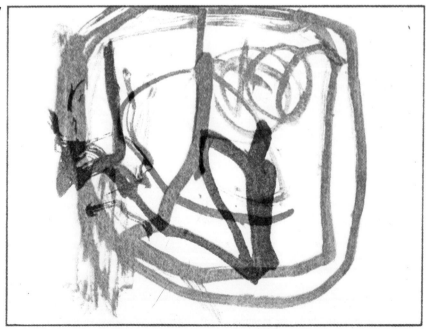

*4-25-38.* Jeff came to school and said: "My sister died." This was not true, but for the moment he wanted to believe it. On that day he more nearly approximated his real ability than on any other day during that period.

PLATE 98

*5-8-38*. Jeff again reverted to mass painting and low form level.

PLATE 99

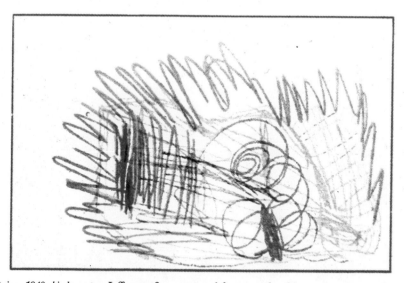

*Spring, 1940, kindergarten*. Jeff, now five years and four months old, continued to work at a relatively low level. Current use of mass techniques with both crayons and paints suggests that he was still emotionally disturbed.

PLATE 100

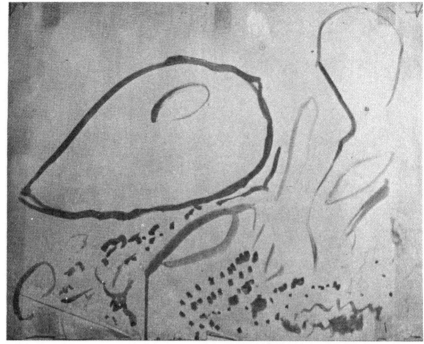

*10-11-38*. This was Betty's characteristic pattern when she first entered school. Observations suggest that her dotting stems from drives similar to those suggested for Jill (Pl. 62).

PLATE 101

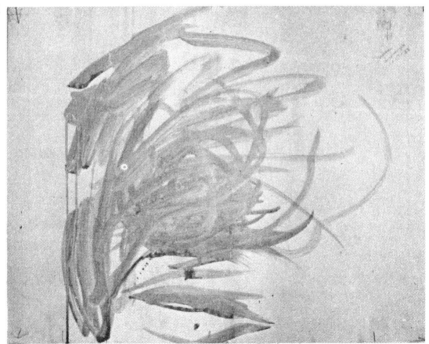

*11-11-39*. The pattern changed abruptly after dismissal of nurse. Reversion to mass techniques often seems to accompany emotional upsets such as Betty experienced at her nurse's departure.

PLATE 102

A

*Spring, 1939.* Kenneth, suffering from a spastic condition of the left arm, showed extraordinary will to obtain balance in painting, crayoning, and block building.

B

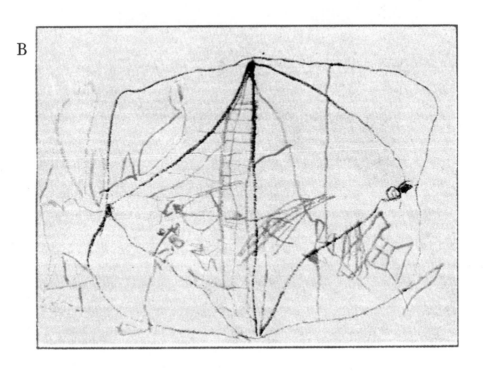

PLATE 102

C

As we note small block inserted near top, we realize that great effort must have been made to secure balance for the blocks above.

Rhythmic back-and-forth swing is usual among two-year-olds standing at an easel.

PLATE 103

Two right-handed children paint typical diagonal swing. The rhythmic back-and-forth strokes go from lower left to upper right.

PLATE 104

A left-handed child swings his strokes from lower right to upper left.

PLATE 105

Two-year-old children sitting at a table are more likely to draw horizontal masses of wavy, scribbling lines.

Children whose development is atypical are likely to express themselves in characteristic ways.

IRVING: 2 years, 3 months, to 3 years, 3 months—I.Q. 70, left-handed

PLATE 106

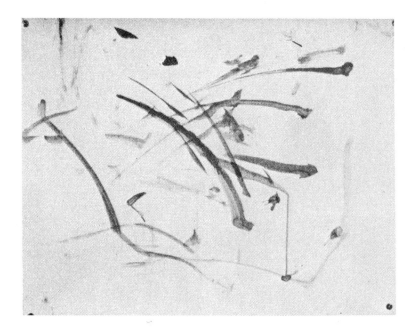

*5-17-38.* Dabs and short scattered, all-directional, dying-out strokes characterized Irving's paintings. All his products were so much alike that any one of them could represent his paintings for the year.

PLATE 107

Charlotte, another deviate, rated subnormal on tests of intelligence. She co-ordinated poorly and lacked vitality. Painting was one of her few spontaneous interests. Like Irving, she
had a stereotyped pattern. It was the only one she produced during her four months' attendance.

PLATE 108

The *vertical* is one of the earliest differentiations from the curved strokes that make up wavy scribbling. The horizontal is likely to appear later than the vertical.

PLATE 109

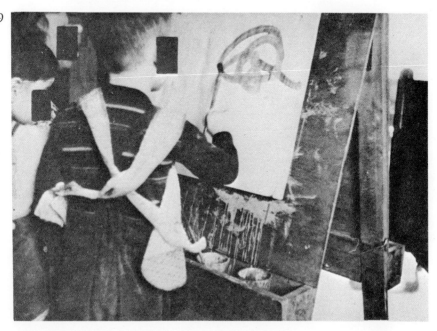

*Controlled circular* patterns appear as children experiment with line and form. The oval or circular form, as a rule, precedes square or rectangular forms (just as curved lines precede straight ones).

PLATE 110

In realistic representations of human forms, children are likely to paint those parts of the body which they have experienced most keenly. Head and feet are usually depicted first, and, as inner awareness develops, other parts of the body are added. (Same as Pl. 7.)

PLATE 111

*1-19-40.* A realistic representation entitled "Camera and Lady." The fact that the feet of the tripod rest in space makes it no less realistic. Five- and six-year-olds, left to themselves, still tend toward individualistic rather than realistic representations of human forms. As the importance of environment increases, the importance of self gradually decreases.

Titles and other verbalization sometimes are revealing because they come from within the child. At other times, stimulus comes from the immediate environment.

ELINOR: 4 years, 6 months—left-handed

*4-8-38.* Said Peter: "What's that?" Elinor answered: "It's supposed to be Blackie" [the school rabbit eaten by the dog]. Dick came along and asked: "Is that Floppie?" [Elinor's dog]. Elinor said: "I think it is." Billy D. said: "It looks like a rabbit. Rabbits have long ears." Elinor replied: "Know what this is? It's Floppie going to bed."

A few minutes later while group of children watched: "This is our wallpaper. It's Floppie going to bed."

Gilbert, ordinarily a happy, outgoing little boy, absorbed in block play, showed a brief, keen interest in using crayons and paints just before and after his baby brother was born.

PLATE 113

*11-22-37.* Family constellation drawn and named by Gilbert. His two sisters to the left, himself in the middle, Daddy (elongated, heavier black lines), Mommy (multicolored, more rounded forms).

PLATE 114

*11-23-37.* Gilbert painted some green-bluish circles and loops and volunteered: "This is Mommy." A baby brother was born within the week.

PLATE 115

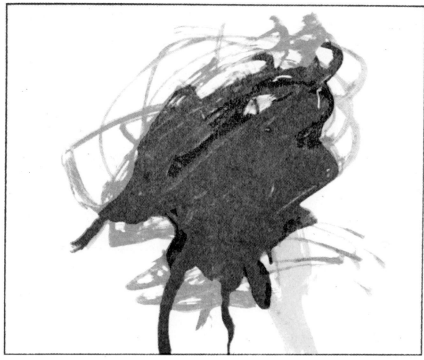

*12-2-37.* The color combination, yellow overlaid with blue, was frequent among children who were in conflict over their desire to remain the baby (often in competition with new baby) and to grow up (see pp. 30–32). After this date, Gilbert did not paint for several months. Gilbert's major interest was in blocks. His subsequent returns to painting, both in nursery school and in kindergarten, usually coincided with periods of emotional disturbance.

Some children used crayons and paints in contrasting ways. With crayons they expressed their overt behavior; with paints, their more basic drives. Bee and several other little girls ordinarily used themselves and their crayons very much as did other girls of their age. Occasionally, however, when using paints they expressed their conflicting drive toward more assertive, boyish behavior.

PLATE 116

*1-28-38.* Later design, as well as conflict in behavior, are foreshadowed in this crayon. On right, rectangular forms in pastel colors foreshadow the later, freer painting designs. On left, circular more feminine forms. *Only with crayons* did Bee use circular pattern. On back of this picture was a vertical swing done mostly in red. At times the two sides of the painting and crayon pages are used in quite distinctive ways and connote conflict in the same way as does the left-right pattern (see pp. 65, 131–32).

Plate 117

*3-25-38.* This full-page, heavily stroked painting was typical of many easel paintings done by Bee as she became more overtly assertive. It foreshadowed lattice design.

Plate 118

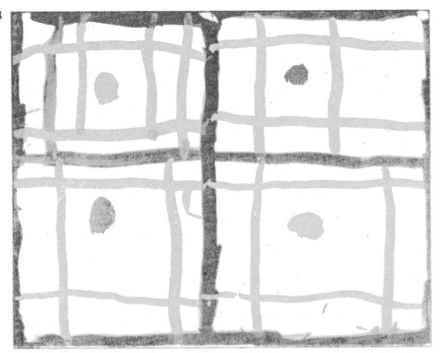

*5-17-38.* This unusually symmetrical, carefully painted decorative design was the first of 4 paintings done on this date. As Bee painted on that day, she became more released, and her paintings became increasingly wild and smeary.

PLATE 119

*5-19-38.* Decorative pattern accords with overt girlish behavior. Dots dabbed on, in contrast to carefully painted dots in preceding plates, as well as smeared brown lattice lines, suggest sublimated interest in defecation.

PLATE 120

*6-10-38.* As Bee played more freely with blocks and boys, the lines in her structuralized painting patterns appeared to be less purely decorative and sublimated and became more outgoing and aggressive.

with line and form to (c) representative work—within the age limits suggested below. This progression has characterized the work of children
whose daily living expressed healthy adjustment and development, children
who had made a relatively easy transition toward realistically oriented behavior, who were eager to adapt to the external world and to communicate
with others. Follow-up evidence on these children has suggested that they
tended to turn rather readily to those skills which facilitate communication
with others, namely, reading and writing.

Of the tendencies outlined, the steady progression from scribbling
through experimentation with line and form to representative work seems
to be the one most consonant with sound, unhampered development. Age
data connected with this developmental pattern are of interest.

Biber's findings have indicated that children who were developing in the
manner just described (4 above) tended to move from scribbling to conscious experimentation between the ages of two and three.[20] The small number of children under three in our investigation, as well as our technique
of scoring characteristic rather than first appearances, precludes a report
on the transition from scribbling to conscious experimentation. Our findings that unrelated lines were most pronounced at three and three and a
half, however, is in keeping with the age trends reported by Biber.

As we observe children who are moving from scribbling to conscious experimentation, we find them first focused on making lines with no thought
of relating or organizing these lines. The strokes are often laboriously made,
short, and jerky (Pl. 108). Ability both to direct the line and to break the
line when so desired must apparently be developed through practice. The
strokes which children make during this period may often be distinguished
from the short-line effects of the involuntary undirected stage by (a) greater
pressure, (b) more abrupt ending of the stroke, (c) repeated attempts to produce a line in a given direction, and (d) greater variety and increasing
dexterity and complexity from one product to another. When these children are being observed over a span of time, overt signs of increased concentration and self-direction also give evidence of the greater degree of effort
and control which are entering into their work.

The realization that lines may be used to block out or organize space and
thus the realization that lines may be used to create forms probably come
to children in the process of their early experimentation with line. As children gradually become fluent in the use of line, they begin to favor strokes
that take a particular direction or form a certain shape. At this stage, the
child's treatment of line and form reflects increasingly the status of his developmental level, as well as his particular personality factors.

[20] Biber, *op. cit.*

Particularly outstanding in the early differentiations concerning lines are the trends in straight lines versus curvilinear strokes. We have already considered personality factors in this area. Chronological age and developmental level as factors will now be discussed.

All available evidence, with the exception of the eight cases cited above and Gesell's figures (p. 108), suggest that the curved movement is used at an earlier period from a developmental standpoint than is the straight line. If we generalize from the time when integrated movement first appeared (i.e., the wavy, scribbling stage), the case for first appearance of the curve is clear cut. We know that wavy scribbling precedes the vertical or straight-line stroke. We know that the circle comes before the square or other angular form. Eng has observed that the curved line can be followed more naturally and easily by eye than can the straight line. Harms reported the tendency noted before for a subject with eye strain to begin to see things as curved rather than as angular. [21]

The vertical is one of the first specific differentiations from the wavy scribble. In one of his summaries of development, Gesell gives the following data: [22]

| Age (In Months) | Task | Age (In Months) | Task |
|---|---|---|---|
| 15 | Scribble | 42 | Trace diamond |
| 18 | Imitate vertical | 48 | Copy cross |
| 24 | Imitate circle | 54 | Trace cross |
| 30 | Imitate vertical and horizontal; mark two times for cross | 60 | Copy diamond |
| | | 66 | Print letters |
| 36 | Copy circle, imitate cross | 77 | Copy diamond |

Gesell omits the square from this summary because he has found that the age of performance varies greatly and is dependent upon the method which the child hits upon to produce the angular corners.

An integration of Gesell's age data on the vertical, circle, and square is presented in the table on the facing page. [23]

Gesell found the vertical appearing in spontaneous drawings of children at eighteen months of age. Our data suggest another point of swing toward the vertical between the ages of three and three and a half.

Our case analyses have suggested that the vertical is associated with assertive behavior tendencies. From this standpoint, the foregoing age findings take on new significance, for it is around eighteen months of age and again

[21] *Op. cit.*

[22] See Gesell and others, *op. cit.*, chap. vii.

[23] The number of cases on which percentages are based in this table varies with each performance and age group listed and can best be found by turning to the original reference (*ibid.*)

around three and three and a half years of age that children make new or increased steps toward self-assertion.[24]

The increased emphasis on verticals around the age of three may also be a reflection of sex differentiations which are occurring at this time. At two, boys and girls tend to be much alike in play interests and in emotional dependence. By four, the boys tend to have taken on a more masculine pattern.[25] When emphasis on verticals was broken down in terms of sex, we found a more pronounced tendency toward the vertical stroke in boys than in girls at three and three and a half, a partial swing in favor of the girls at four and four and a half, and a return to more frequent emphasis on verti-

| PERFORMANCE | PERCENTAGE OF GIVEN AGE GROUP SHOWING CHARACTERISTIC (GESELL) | | | | | |
|---|---|---|---|---|---|---|
| | 1½ Years | 2 Years | 3 Years | 4 Years | 5 Years | 6 Years |
| *Spontaneous work, controlled observation:* | | | | | | |
| Vertical.......................... | 0.16 | 0.18 | ........ | ........ | ........ | ........ |
| Circle........................... | .03 | .15 | ........ | ........ | ........ | ........ |
| Square........................... | ........ | ........ | ........ | ........ | ........ | ........ |
| *Drawing from imitation:* | | | | | | |
| Vertical.......................... | .47 | .79 | 1.00 | ........ | ........ | ........ |
| Circle........................... | 0.32 | 0.59 | 0.86 | ........ | ........ | ........ |
| Square........................... | ........ | ........ | ........ | ........ | ........ | ........ |
| *Drawing from pattern (copying):* | | | | | | |
| Vertical.......................... | ........ | ........ | ........ | ........ | ........ | ........ |
| Circle (well-rounded)............. | ........ | ........ | 0.09 | 0.08 | 0.21 | 0.72 |
| Square (four well-defined corners).... | ........ | ........ | ........ | 0.10 | 0.38 | 0.83 |

cals by the boys at five years of age. These trends suggest the need for further investigation of the possibilities just described. Our own sex data are shown in the tabulation giving age and sex comparisons.

Developmental trends with the circle and with square or angular forms indicate the appearance of the circle before the square.[26] In our data, circles tended to decrease in frequency of occurrence between three and five years of age, while angular forms tended to increase in occurrence during the same age period. The decrease in circular forms was most pronounced between four and four and a half years of age, and the increase in the square

[24] For references on relation of self-assertion to age, see David M. Levy and Simon H. Tulchin, "The Resistance of Infants and Children during Mental Tests," *Journal of Experimental Psychology,* VI (1923), 304–22; Ruth Kennedy Caille, *Resistant Behavior of Preschool Children* ("Child Development Monographs," No. 11 [New York: Teachers College, Columbia University Press, 1933]), p. 142; George D. Stoddard and Beth L. Wellman, *Child Psychology* (New York: Macmillan Co., 1934), pp. 359–62.

[25] Observation confirmed by Lois Murphy in her play interviews and reported through correspondence with authors.

[26] See Gesell data, *op. cit.*

or angular form was particularly pronounced between the ages of four and a half and five.

The age findings just described fit generalizations previously made, i.e., that the circle tends to be associated with the more emotional reactions and the square or angular forms with the more externalized, adaptive, reasoned behavior. The decrease in circular forms and the increase in angular forms occur at the stage when children are moving from emotional toward controlled behavior, [27] at the stage when sex differentiations are becoming clear cut. [28]

While these parallelisms in development seem warranted as working hypotheses, we must remember that other factors than development per se may contribute to the emphasis on circles, verticals, squares, or rectangles

AGE-SEX COMPARISONS IN USE OF VERTICALS IN
EASEL PAINTING AT NURSERY SCHOOL LEVEL

| Age Group (Years) | Number of Cases | | | Percentage Emphasizing Verticals | | | Percentage Showing Increased Use of Verticals | | |
|---|---|---|---|---|---|---|---|---|---|
| | Boys | Girls | All | Boys | Girls | All | Boys | Girls | All |
| 3......... | 10 | 8 | 18 | 0.50* | 0.38 | 0.44 | 0.10 | 0.00 | 0.06 |
| 3½........ | 18 | 30 | 48 | .72 | .67 | .69 | .28 | .27 | .27 |
| 4......... | 25 | 17 | 42 | .48 | .82 | .62 | .20 | .29 | .24 |
| 4½........ | 17 | 18 | 35 | .53 | .72 | .63 | .24 | .28 | .26 |
| 5......... | 15 | 8 | 23 | 0.87 | 0.75 | 0.84 | 0.33 | 0.25 | 0.30 |
| Total.... | 85 | 81 | 166 | 0.61 | 0.69 | 0.65 | 0.23 | 0.25 | 0.24 |

* Italics indicate sex with predominant trend at each age level.

in any given child's painting. Circles and verticals, in particular, may take on symbolic meaning in the expression of emotional conflicts and, in so doing, may lose their purely developmental implications.

Another stroke which is frequently used and which has not yet been discussed is the horizontal. Age data suggest that the horizontal is likely to appear later than is the vertical line.

Gesell found that 42 per cent of children observed could imitate the horizontal at the age of two, and 95 per cent could imitate the horizontal at three. (In contrast, 79 per cent could imitate the vertical and 59 per cent the circular stroke at the age of two, and 100 per cent could imitate the vertical and circular strokes at three.) In his study of block building, Gesell has noted similarly that the building of a tower is an earlier development than the making of a horizontal row. [29]

In our data there is a lag of the horizontal behind the vertical similar to

[27] See pp. 101–2.          [28] See p. 113.          [29] Gesell and others, *op. cit.*

the lag which Gesell has found. Our data give no added insights into the possible significance of the horizontal stroke. Löwenfeld's observations, however, raise 'the question as to whether there may be a developmental parallelism between the sensations of standing upright and the vertical, and between the subsequent sensations of moving upright through space, i.e., of walking, and the horizontal. Löwenfeld has described in this regard a drawing in which a child made several strokes that were vertical and one that was horizontal, with the explanation: "You see they [the verticals] stand. I [the horizontal] am riding."[30] He goes on to state: "We can now clearly understand the difference between a vertical line which is bound to a base and is finite and the floating, infinite horizontal line."

Like Löwenfeld, we have noted that the names which children give to vertical and horizontal structures both in drawing and in block work suggest differentiated feelings about the two. Verticals are frequently referred to as stationary objects: smoke stacks, towers, etc. Horizontals are more often referred to as movable objects: trains, cars, locomotives in general.

### DEVELOPMENTAL TRENDS IN REPRESENTATION

Representation of a realistic, recognizable type becomes a possibility for most children between the ages of four and five, although the work of the majority of children observed by us did not tend to be characterized by recognizable and realistic painting patterns.[31]

As children near the stage of representative work, the following possible trends have been observed: (1) There are children who follow the conventional, usually accepted patterns of representation; their work may be described as "realistic." (2) There are children who follow highly individualized schemes of representation, who tend to depict the feel of things rather than the look of them; their products may or may not be recognizable to us, and their work may be described as fanciful or symbolic representation. (3) There are children who persist in repetitive themes characterized by color and mass techniques rather than by form. (4) There are children who persist in an increasingly complex structuralized, seemingly abstract pattern.

Further consideration of these trends suggests the following:

1. The children who have turned readily to conventional, realistic representation have seemed from our observations to be those who had made rather straightforward progression through the preceding stages of de-

---

[30] Löwenfeld, op. cit., p. 53.

[31] Children frequently turn to recognizable representation in crayon work before painting, another possible bit of evidence that they are probably able to do representative work with the easel paints before they feel quite ready to adopt this mode of expression.

velopment. Their recognizable representations tended to follow a period of constructive work with interrelated verticals and horizontals or squares and rectangles. They were apt to be objectively oriented to the world around them and to be interested in communicating with others. More often than not their first representations were of human beings. Follow-up observations have shown that these children are making a relatively ready transition to academic school programs (Pls. 110–11).

2. It has seemed from our observations that the children who were more internalized and preoccupied with self were the ones who tended to turn toward fanciful rather than realistic representations. Many times the products of these children would have been quite meaningless to us without their accompanying comments. Once a child had verbalized about his paintings, however, we were frequently able to get the feel of the associations which apparently motivated his work.

*Edward*, for instance, described a painting of scattered, unrecognizable forms as a room of furniture and proceeded to name the items. The bulkiest form, which far overshadowed the rest in size and position on the page, Edward called a "piano." At this time a piano figured prominently in Edward's home life. His parents, who previously had been accustomed to a piano and had frequently expressed their longing for one, had finally achieved their wish. Edward, who had already been receiving training in music from his mother, now began practicing with enthusiasm. He played frequently and sang for visitors in the home. The mother reported that the piano had seemed to bring them together as a family. The piano was evidently the center of activities in the home, just as it was the important feature of the easel painting.

*Aileen* is another example of an emotional, self-centered child who tended toward the felt rather than the realistic type of representation. Particularly striking in this connection is her "zebra," a product which lacked all the conventional form which we tend to associate with zebras, yet which is strikingly recognizable through both color and line effects. The "portrait" of herself on a pedestal is another example of Aileen's attempt to represent how ·she fancied herself rather than her actual appearance (see Pls. 3–12).

It is of interest to note that circles rather than squares or other angular forms have tended to characterize these more fanciful representations. Particularly have we observed this in representations of houses. The circular form with the label of "house" almost invariably reflects a self-centered child. The constructive house of straight-line and angular construction is more likely to be the product of a realistically oriented child.

Löwenfeld's study has also revealed a distinction between the child who paints what he sees and the child who paints what he feels. He has used the term "visual" and the term "haptic" to distinguish these two types of children. The visual type starts from his environment and produces an impressionistic type of work. The haptic child begins with bodily sensations and tactual space and gives us an expressionistic form of work.

Realistic and felt elements are not necessarily confined to separate prod-ucts. They may be found together in a single painting or drawing. In such a case we may be fairly sure that the less apparently realistic element is the one about which the child feels most deeply. That is the aspect of the paint-ing which is most likely to lead us to the internal dynamics of the child.[32]

3. Children who, at the usual stage of interest in representation, have continued to work in individualized repetitive patterns with a color-mass technique, have already been described.[33] These are the children who have tended to be too absorbed in their emotional problems to make an objective or externalized adjustment to the world around them. Their themes or patterns are repetitive until their problems are, to some extent at least, resolved.

4. Children who have persisted in increasingly complex structuralized patterns of an *abstract* nature at the stage of usual interest in representation have in some instances (*a*) seemed to have special abilities along structural, mechanical, abstract lines and/or, in other instances, (*b*) seemed for some personal reason to be using this type of expression as an escape from more personalized or socialized activities.[34] These children tended, in general, to be more interested in materials than in people. Some of them developed very interesting abilities in design. When recognizable representations were produced by these children, they were more often of inanimate than of human or other living beings.

### TRENDS IN REPRESENTATION BEYOND THE NURSERY-SCHOOL YEARS

The description which Löwenfeld gives of the developmental trends in painting or drawing between the nursery-school years and adolescence is so helpful in extending our understanding of drawing and painting and so clearly represents a continuation of the trends which we have described as beginning in the nursery-school years that it seems valuable to summarize it for the increased perspective it throws on the early years.

Löwenfeld has observed[35] that children at five and six still tend more toward an individualistic or felt, rather than a realistic or externalized, type of representation when depicting human beings. This was so even though they use conventionalized, schematic patterns for inanimate objects, such as trees. He has observed that between the ages of six and ten, human repre-sentations increasingly follow a conventional scheme, whereas portrayal of external objects, such as trees, become individually and increasingly differ-entiated and varied. These trends he interprets as evidence of the fact that the importance of self is now decreasing and the importance of the environ-ment is increasing.

[32] See also pp. 10–11.
[33] See p. 16.
[34] See, e.g., Neil (p. 53) and Alan (p. 54).
[35] *Op. cit.*

By the age of nine or ten, Löwenfeld reports, the child's confidence in his own creative power tends to be shaken by the increased significance of the environment. He is so guided by how things ought to look that he loses faith in his products when they do not meet this criterion. At nine, for instance, the child who had previously felt able to express motion, such as reaching, now feels at a loss about introducing such action into his work. Forty-four per cent of nine-year-olds and 43 per cent of ten-year-olds showed this loss in ability to relate what they had previously been able to express.

But the emphasis on environment does not stop at nine. It continues to grow, so Löwenfeld has observed, until it reaches a peak around the age of twelve. By this age the environment has become so much more important than the self that the inanimate object, as, for example, the tree, may overshadow the entire drawing and the human representation may be scarcely visible if present.

Although Löwenfeld's investigation goes no further along these lines, general knowledge of development suggests that during adolescence emotions again focus on self. A comparative study on expression of emotion would probably reveal more parallelism between nursery-school and adolescent years than between nursery-school years and any intervening period.

#### DEVELOPMENTAL TRENDS IN SPACE USAGE

In decided contrast to our findings in the case of color, line, and form, our data have revealed almost no age differentiations in the use of space. Three of the tendencies toward relationship that have appeared—increase in number of strokes proportionate to size of page, decrease in scattered work, and decrease in work all over the page—would seem largely to parallel the better co-ordination and balance that come with increased age and development. The fourth—increase in filling the page—may be a reflection (*a*) of increased awareness of external expectancies and/or (*b*) of an increasingly externalized orientation of behavior.

The dearth of relationships between space usage and developmental changes may be in keeping with our observation that space usage seems to reflect external stimuli and relationships rather than the inner life of the child.

# CHAPTER VI

## SIGNIFICANCE OF EASEL PAINTING AS COMPARED WITH OTHER MEDIA

ALTHOUGH this book is devoted primarily to a study of children's paintings, it is clear that our insight into the nature and meaning of easel painting can be enriched if we compare children's use of paints with their use of other creative media. In this chapter, accordingly, we shall review our observations of easel painting in relation to crayoning, to clay and block activities, and to dramatic play.

Within the framework of our observations it was found that, as a means of self-expression, easel paints were used more often than any of the other materials. In addition, of the media under consideration, easel paintings provided the most diverse aspects, the most subtle variations, and could be most readily preserved for further analysis.

As is generally known, some children choose and show preference for paints. Others choose and find equal satisfaction in blocks, while still others apparently find gratification in clay, in crayons, or in dramatic play. It seemed important to investigate the source of these differences in choice of materials and also to note children's behavior while using them. We wanted, furthermore, to ascertain, if we could, the degree of tension and release during and after usage, as well as whatever else we could find out about other significant aspects that inhered in the related activities of young children.

In weighing the values of the different media, due allowance had to be made for variations that existed within different situations. Inasmuch as opportunity, choice, and usage at home are often quite in contrast to those at school, records from the home seemed important and were obtained. In the course of some months we also learned that when a single child was alone in a room with a friendly adult who had invited him in to play, his choice and usage of materials were frequently quite dissimilar from his reactions in the group situation.[1] With these widely varying factors in mind, we gathered as many potentially meaningful observations as possible. Such findings as have to do with easel paintings as compared to other media are here presented.

[1] See, e.g., Alan, p. 130, and Louise, p. 90.

SOME CHARACTERISTICS OF CHILDREN WHO PREFER PAINTING, ALONG
WITH SUGGESTED IMPLICATIONS AS TO THE SIGNIFICANCE
OF THEIR CHOICE

Children who predominantly sought easel paints were found, as a group,
to be more concerned with self or internal problems than were other
nursery-school children. They tended to fit into one of the following descriptive categories: (1) to be among the youngest and least mature children
in the nursery groups; (2) to come from homes which exerted too much control in various areas of the child's life; and (3) to be involved in strong emotional conflicts and to be more preoccupied with resolving these conflicts
than with reacting objectively or wholeheartedly to people and situations.
For children in all three of the suggested categories, painting apparently
served as an outlet for impulsive or emotional drives.

### 1. YOUNGEST AND LEAST MATURE CHILDREN

The youngest and least mature children in the nursery schools frequently
preferred easel paints. Examination of two sets of data, in addition to those
referred to above, bear out the association suggested between easel painting
and age.

Comparison of three groups of children, in which grouping had been determined on a maturity, as well as a chronological age, basis, indicated that
children in the nursery unit primarily made up of three-year-olds were preponderantly more interested in easel paints than were the children in the
other two groups, which were made up primarily of four-year-olds.

A study of preference for creative media in different chronological age
groups (groups built around the age levels of two and a half, three, three and
a half, four, four and a half, and five) indicates a steady decrease of preference for easel paints between the ages of three and five.

Developmentally, these are the years when children are swinging from
impulsive sensing and manipulating of everything around them toward
more-controlled and directed responses. Activities naturally follow developmental changes, and so we find focus of interest, as a rule, shifting from the
use of paints, which are fluid and easily manipulated toward blocks and
other concretely organized materials, which readily lend themselves to a
more organized, constructive type of play.[2]

[2] See chap. v; also Dorothy Van Alstyne, *Play Behavior and Choice of Play Materials of Preschool
Children* (Chicago: University of Chicago Press, 1932); and Arnold Gesell and others, *The First Five
Years of Life: A Guide to the Study of the Preschool Child* (New York: Harper & Bros., 1940).

Additional support for the belief that easel painting is a preferred and relatively good medium for self-expression among immature children was found in examination of the preferences of eight children whose development was retarded. Six of the children observed—*Charlotte, Irving, Norman, Rowena, Thomas,* and *Will*—at the time of this study tested at or below an I.Q. of 80. Two other children—*Chester,* a highly distractible, near-blind child, too inattentive to yield a test score, and *Audrey,* a postencephalitic with an I.Q. of 88, were, in their volatile interest and deviate behavior, more like the six retarded children just described than like the rest of the group.

Six of these eight children showed a major interest in easel paints; the seventh, *Norman,* had a strong interest in painting; and the eighth, *Thomas,* displayed no strong interest of any sort. Four of these eight children— *Audrey, Charlotte, Chester,* and Norman—also showed a major interest in crayons. None showed a major interest in blocks. Only Chester showed a major interest in clay. *Will* and *Rowena* showed a major interest in dramatic play of a purely imitative type. Of the five media studied, easel painting clearly had the greatest appeal to these children, who were functioning at a relatively low level and who had few constructive outlets for their energies.[3]

Several other children who likewise functioned at a rather low level were also particularly interested in painting. These children apparently did not have adequate incentives to make them want to develop their abilities. In this group were *Anita, Andy,* and *Jeff.* Rejection on the part of one or both parents was indicated in the backgrounds of all three of these children. All seemed unaffected in the school situation by what adults thought of them. They were not responsive to suggestion or criticism. They seemed more interested in remaining infantile than in growing up. Anita said on one occasion, "I want to suck my thumb until I'm big like Mother." Jeff was a teaching problem because of his extreme dependence and his refusal to adapt to the expectancies of his age level, as, for example, standing to urinate.

In the nursery school, all these children reacted as they felt, relatively impervious to outside stimuli. All three showed a major interest in easel paints

---

[3] These children's characteristic paintings had features which distinguished them from the rest of the group.

and/or clay. None of the three became interested in crayons, blocks, or dramatic play. All of them tested at low average while in nursery school. Sporadic performance during the year of daily observation, however, and tests taken in subsequent years revealed that each child had potentially higher ability than he was able to use at that period.

These children probably got more satisfaction out of paints than out of other materials for a variety of reasons. Paints were readily adapted not only to their infantile interest in manipulation but also to their short attention span, their distributive attention, and their social attitude expressed, in part at least, by lack of concern with other children's activities. Painting during these early years can be done with no conscious attention to the task, and it yields satisfaction in the process without concern for the product. The product is finished whenever the child feels like putting down his brush, and the "finished product" need not be seen in relationship to what others are doing or have done. The implication in these findings is not that painting is primarily the activity of retarded children but rather that, when most children go on to other and more varied activities, disturbed and retarded children continue to find high satisfaction in easel painting.

### 2. CHILDREN FROM HOMES WITH TOO MUCH CONTROL

Children coming from homes which exerted too much control of various kinds comprised another group of children who were especially interested in painting. These children, in contrast to the group described above, came from families that were overconcerned about maintaining high standards. At first glance, it seems strange that this group of children, too, should have evidenced a preference for easel paints.[4]

In various ways these children showed that too much and too early pressure had been exerted upon them. They tended to be overcautious in entering new activities and to be constantly aware of what adults might be thinking. Most of them were inclined to be critical of themselves and of other children.

Remarks such as these of *Carol*'s were typical: "We can't leave this mess for the teachers." "Your mother wouldn't like it this way." These children often seemed too concerned about cleanliness. Frequently they behaved like miniature adults. They apparently found it difficult to accept and enter into the ordinary activities of children of their age. When they

---

[4] The children in this particular grouping showed an outstanding interest in both easel paints and crayons, but they tended to use the two media in contrasting ways and apparently for contrasting purposes. This point is discussed in more detail on pp. 131–33. Outstandingly illustrative of this group were: Ardis, Barbara, Betty, Carol, Dora, Elinor, Esther, Harriet, Henry, Jean, Jill, Jocelyn, Kit, Louise, Paula, Peter, Phyllis, Philip, Polly, Rachel, Rita, Ruth, Ruby, Sadie, Sally, Tess, Tilda, Trixie, Una, and Wanda. Several children, namely, Elaine, Edward, Jocelyn, Phoebe, and Sally, tended to fall into both this group and the group next described (pp. 124–28).

thought that they were out of range of the adults, however, they were likely to assume domineering, bossy, or otherwise assertive roles that were not displayed when they knew that any member of the teaching staff was near by. When fully absorbed in painting, these children tended to show free, assertive, impulsive behavior not apparent in their more guarded moments.

For several of these too controlled children, including *Carol*, the easel was a preferred occupation, which seemingly afforded a shelter from other children's activities in which they were not quite ready to participate. At the same time it offered a vantage point from which to watch the group.[5] In this group of children interest in easel painting at various times coincided with their lack or loss of security feeling. Examples of this were: (*a*) painting was a major interest for Carol, but her interest became perceptibly intensified when her particular school companion, another large, self-conscious child, was withdrawn from the group; (*b*) the days on which *Elinor* painted and those on which she did not paint were markedly parallel to her days of solitary and friendly interplay; (*c*) *George*, at ease and popular in one group, usually played with blocks and participated with children in dramatic play. Transferred to another group, in which he felt unhappy and socially ill at ease, his interest changed to easel painting.

While these children often seemed to seek the easel as a retreat from the social situation, it seemed obvious that the painting in itself gave the children real outlet and satisfaction.

A further reason why these too controlled children, like those who were immature, probably found satisfaction in painting is that products in this medium are less susceptible to adult standards than are products in other media. Supporting this statement from the point of view of the children who consciously or unconsciously wished to be free from adult standards are the following facts:

*a*) On entrance to nursery school, most children have had no experience with easel paints. They have not been conditioned to their usage and so feel relatively free to express themselves without reference to adult standards.

*b*) The fluidity of the paints is conducive to experimentation and free expression and is not conducive to concern over form and representation, characteristics usually emphasized by adults. (We have previously noted that adults on looking at children's drawings are prone to make such remarks as, "If you'd do it this way, it would look more like a tree," etc.)

*c*) Other children's paintings in the nursery situation give the same impression of formless mass, and so there can be little self-consciousness created by comparison with the work of others.

[5] The conditions under which the easel paints were available in the nursery-school setting introduced significant factors.

A further reason why easel painting may provide an easy first step toward self-expression for these children is that it provides a release which in no way violates their established controls.

Easel paints are applied with a brush, which makes it unnecessary for children to get messed up or "dirty." The too highly controlled children often shy away from clay and/or finger paints because of their concern over cleanliness. They so much fear to get their fingers dirty that not only will they avoid these smeary materials if they can but, once they have touched them, they will frequently be too concerned with getting clean to enjoy the experience.

Our observations suggest that when some children break abruptly from highly controlled behavior and indulge in random smearing, they develop a sense of transgression and tend, in consequence, to revert to even more rigid control. *Carol* and other children, at first, were inclined to become tense and upset during their periods of smeary paintings. Case data suggest that feelings of guilt were basic to their reactions.

Inasmuch as easel painting, which is a relatively clean medium, can and does occasionally arouse a sense of transgression as described, it is obvious that play with those "smeary," "messy" materials—clay and finger paints— may be even more conducive to such feelings and therefore be less desirable as first steps in freeing overcontrolled children. Case data suggest that some chidren naturally find easel painting the first step toward freer behavior. Once they have become somewhat freed through painting experiences, children can then turn to clay and like media without being overcome by feelings of dislike and guilt. It is not only the presence of an intermediary tool, the brush, but also the wide possibilities for symbolic expression that may make easel painting a more readily acceptable outlet than clay or finger paints.

*Fredrika* illustrates the relatively more sublimated form which easel painting can take as compared to clay and finger painting. Working in the two latter media, *Fredrika* expressed her interest in the eliminative function by identifying her products with excrement. In easel paintings she expressed, or rather disguised, her interest and feelings through her symbolical color choice and placement ("dirty" colors put on to make dirty-looking paintings) and through her verbal associations, which at the same time involved the element of something dirty—not excrement, but "garbage," "dirty windows," "mud," and the like.[6]

### 3. CHILDREN ABSORBED IN THEIR OWN CONFLICTS

Children absorbed in their own emotional conflicts tended to prefer easel paints. This third group of children who showed preference for easel paints

[6] See Pls. 56–59; for discussion of "dirty" paintings see p. 83.

were those who had, for the most part, passed the impulsive phase of development but were involved in conflict situations which still held them in a state of emotional absorption. They were children who tended to be repressed and unadaptive in overt behavior. They were too concerned with their personal problems to be able to react wholeheartedly to the world about them. Evidence suggests that these children, like the immature, the retarded, and the overcontrolled children (discussed in a and b above) were also expressing with paints the feelings which they could not put into words and which they were not yet ready to express in any other more overt fashion.

The striking parallelism between onset or duration of conflicts and onset or duration of painting interest points to the fact that painting meets a real need among emotionally disturbed children. Several children observed in the course of this study were preoccupied with their emotional problems during their entire stay in nursery school. These children include *Ann*, *Aileen*, *Elaine*, *Jessica*, *Norman*, *Ruth*, *Sally*, *Tilly*, and *Virginia*. All these children showed persistent interest in easel painting.

Other children were observed who went through emotional conflicts during specific periods of time. Observers recorded the behavior of these children before, during, and after the periods of conflict. The children tended to show a definitely greater interest in painting while preoccupied with their conflict than they showed (a) before the conflict appeared, (b) after they could verbalize their conflict, and (c) after the conflict was resolved.

For several children, painting seemed to be a means of raising their problems to a level where they could talk about them. They painted persistently until they were ready to talk of their problems. This sometimes happened while they painted; sometimes it happened afterward. Once able to verbalize their difficulties, they often worked them out more directly in other media. Some of these children seemed able to resolve their conflicts by merely raising them to the verbal level. Once they could talk about what was bothering them, they sloughed off their troubled, preoccupied mood and returned to their customary friendly and easy behavior.[7]

*Gilbert* ordinarily was a happy, easygoing little boy. But around the time of his brother's birth he "painted out" and expressed with crayons his concern over the family situation. Through follow-up observations in subsequent years we learned that Gilbert returned to easel painting on the infrequent occasions when he got into emotional jams (see Pls. 113–15).

*Paula* went through an upset period during the third month of her mother's pregnancy. At this time she readily gave way to tears and other emotional outbursts. She avidly sought the easel and refused to participate

[7] See pp. 136, 153.

in other activities. If the opportunity to paint was withheld too long, she gave way to tantrums. Paula's entire history, as well as her behavior while painting, suggest that painting was a real release for her.

As already indicated, *Howard* (Pls. 80–83) showed interest in painting only around the time of his sister's birth, when it became for him a compelling occupation. Neither *Vera* nor *Jocelyn* had showed particular interest in painting until their younger brothers attended nursery school. Then each of them overtly revealed jealousy, was emotionally disturbed, and spontaneously sought the easel. *Eric* and *Joe* were preoccupied with personal problems following long stays at home. These boys, too, turned to easel painting for short periods of time on their return to school. *Hugh* became emotionally disturbed while his mother was out of town and he sought paints at this time.

That children who are having inner conflicts may find emotional release in easel painting is suggested not only by parallelism between their obviously disturbed state and their painting interest but also by the behavior of these emotionally disturbed children while painting.

Children who were usually self-contained about their problems have been observed to become talkative and to reveal otherwise unexpressed hostilities and aggressions during their painting experiences. *Paula* sang out with obvious glee while painting: "I gotta nurse sick in bed, she caught it in a car, and she hurt her ear and she had to go to the hospital!"

*Aileen*, who ordinarily gave in too easily and withdrew from conflict in the group, voiced a defiant mood at times while painting: To Alma: "I'm making a lot. You can't paint." To Priscilla: "No, I'll paint all day so you can never have a turn." To the group at large: "I won't let you paint." To Angela, about Priscilla, while screwing up her face: "We won't make presents for her. We don't like her." To the group at large, in defiance of the teacher's suggestion that it was time to go in: "We won't go in, will we?"

*Margaret*, who, like Aileen, withdrew from conflicts in the group, gave in too easily, and was frequently teased by children because she cried on the slightest provocation, displayed her only observed aggressions while at the easel. On November 4, Margaret made two paintings with heavy, vertical masses. She kept interrupting her painting to turn and talk to whomever was near and then spit at them. She alternated strokes on her painting page with dabs at the sidewalk on which the easel stood. Sometimes she dipped her brush in the dirt. At times she hit the rack which held the jars of paint. She did this so vehemently that the paint splashed out onto her paper. On November 21, Margaret sought the easel and painted two products, both composed of vertical masses of many colors. She painted with concentration and stroked vigorously. After painting—for no apparent reason—she began to slap at and tease the assistant teacher. She stopped this abruptly when the children were called together for rest.

The most frequent and recurrent responses of children to painting, as revealed in situational diary records,[8] suggest that the painting experience is highly charged with emotional or feeling factors:

[8] "Situational diary records" were observations limited to a single experience, as with paints, crayons, clay, or the like. For example, see p. 21.

## MOST FREQUENT AND RECURRENT BEHAVIOR TENDENCIES FOUND IN "SITUATIONAL DIARY RECORDS" OF CHILDREN AT EASEL PAINTING

1. Behavior suggestive of felt need for and satisfaction from paints
   a) Actively sought easel and waited for it in face of obstacles
   b) Expressed satisfaction and apparent insatiability through such comments as, "I won't be through till morning," or "I'm going to paint all day"
   c) Produced large numbers of paintings in a single painting experience
   d) Smiled or sang at easel
   e) Was more outgoing in speech and in friendly overtures at easel than in other observed behavior in the group
2. Behavior suggestive of social desires and needs
   a) Stood at easel watching others (seemed as much or more interested in others than in the painting)
   b) Showed obvious tendency to avoid attention
   c) Showed strong tendency (usually stronger than in other observed situations) to seek attention
   d) Showed ambivalence in seeking and avoiding attention
   e) Voiced desire for social contacts while painting
   f) More outgoing in social behavior at easel than otherwise
3. Behavior suggestive of aggressive drives
   a) Spit while at easel
   b) Smeared while at easel
   c) Hit easel hard, teeth clenched
   d) Smeared work with obvious intent to destroy and took pleasure in the process (sometimes a child gestured over a page as though to smear it, but did not touch the page—an evidence of inhibited aggression)
   e) Attacked others verbally or in more obvious ways while painting or directly thereafter
   f) First self-defense at school occurred at easel
4. Behavior suggestive of cleanliness concern or of satisfaction with opportunity to smear
   a) Interest in wetness of paint
   b) Obvious expression of satisfaction while smearing
   c) Took great care to avoid smeared product
   d) Expressed concern over need to wash hands or to keep self clean
   e) Recurrent tendency to go directly to toilet after painting experience
5. Behavior suggestive of oral tensions
   a) Sucked brush at easel
   b) Sucked fingers or thumb while painting
   c) Sucked lip
   d) Rolled tongue while painting
   e) Whistled while painting

Particularly impressive to observers, though relatively lost in the itemization of the foregoing outline, were the repeated evidences of intense craving for the easel which accompanied both the onset and the continued interest of many children in this medium. Waiting, begging, crying, and tantrums, such as were earlier noted in the case of *Paula*, were typical of a number of children during the period of their most intense concern with painting.

Also impressive to observers were children's verbal expressions of satisfaction while painting. Such spontaneous remarks as "I want to paint all day" (*Catherine* and *Danny*); "I'll paint all morning" (*Don*); "I won't be through for a long time" (*Arlene, Archie, Paul*); "I feel like painting" (Danny); "When my mother comes, I'll still be painting" (*Angela*); and "I'm never going to be through" (*Aileen*) were relatively common in the painting situation. Such expressions were less frequently noted during activities with clay and not at all with the other media observed.

In keeping with such expressions as the foregoing were the tendencies of children who were emotionally involved to paint for long periods of time and often to produce large numbers of paintings during a single painting period.[9] Griffiths likewise observed that children absorbed in problems or periods of emotional stress tend to produce more material than children whose energy is expended in more objective ways.[10]

The preceding incidents are all suggestive of insatiability and may be clues to children's felt, but undefined and unmet, emotional needs. They indicate that easel painting was sought by children involved in their own emotional pressures and conflicts.

Why the emotionally involved children sought the easel in preference to other creative media in the group has been partially indicated: (*a*) The relatively solitary position of the easel in the nursery-school room fosters withdrawing from the group and also self-expression; (*b*) the fluidity of the paints and the variety of the colors are conducive to an infinite variety of expressive possibilities and encourage freedom from boundaries of line and form; (*c*) a lack of associations between the painting medium and adult standards makes the easel a relatively easy medium for self-expressive emotional responses. All these factors undoubtedly help to make easel painting a popular medium among children involved in their emotional adjustments and suggest reasons for the value of easel painting as a diagnostic medium in the group situation.

### EASEL PAINTING COMPARED TO OTHER MEDIA

Our insight into the significance of easel painting increases as we compare children who prefer easel paints with those who prefer (1) crayons, (2) blocks, (3) clay, and (4) dramatic play.

[9] Aileen, Carol, Jill, Jessica, and Sally are among the children who produced as many as nine to fourteen products during a single painting experience.

[10] Ruth Griffiths, *A Study of Imagination in Early Childhood* (London: Kegan Paul, Trench, Trubner & Co., 1935), 117.

The differences in the personality traits of children who sought the easel and those who sought crayons, as judged by group comparisons, are striking. The different ways in which the same child used these two media are also highly revelatory.

Children with a predominant interest in crayons have been found, as a group, to show more controlled reactions, both in terms of physical coordination and in terms of emotional control than (a) children with a major interest in easel paints or (b) children with a minor interest in crayoning.

The children who preferred crayons tended, as a group, to be more concerned with expressing ideas and with the desire to communicate with others than with finding a free outlet for their own impulses. They also showed more awareness of the environment and more concern over conforming or adapting to environmental forces. Often this attitude paralleled exposure to high adult standards or to other forms of stimulation beyond the readiness level of the child involved.[11]

That a strong drive toward control, accompanied by a predominant interest in crayoning, is not altogether healthy during these early years seems evident on examination of data. Children who were observed to have a predominant interest in crayons, to the relative exclusion of other activities in the nursery-school group—as was true of *Ann, Alan, Albert, Tilly*—tended to be inadequately adjusted and to show marked fluctuations in mood. They were inclined to be unhappy and tense. Often their difficulties were most severe when they were newcomers to the group. Possibly because all of them came from homes with high expectancies where they had had little opportunity to function at their own level or with others of their own age, they seemed ill at ease with other children. These children, especially when they first entered the group, apparently felt more at home with crayons than with other materials.

The frequent mood of children while they were crayoning was one of tension and dejection, whereas a happy, carefree attitude was often observed while children were painting.

*Aileen*, for example, who used both paints and crayons frequently, often gained obvious satisfaction from her painting experience, but at the crayon table she more often appeared dejected.[12] Three observations an Aileen at the crayon table, taken over a span of a year,

---

[11] True also of children with combined painting and crayon interests (p. 122, n. 8).

[12] Further examples on this point are reserved for a future discussion on children's use of crayons. Children illustrating this trend include Alan, Alvin, Alma, Arthur, Dorothea, Esther, Kit, Loretta, Louis, Louise, Sally, and Shirley.

point to the parallelism between working with crayons and low emotional tone: 1-19-38: Aileen's entire mood was one of dejection. 2-1-38: Aileen appeared unusually ashen pale. Her eyes were red. She drew with her head on the paper, more or less concealing what she was doing. 1-25-39: Aileen cried very hard when she accidentally tore her crayon paper. She cried easily all day. She was unusually cross when children attempted to play with her.

Children not only turned to crayoning frequently in cross, irritable moments but tended to remain tense while crayoning. This medium did not seem to provide release. Rather, it seemed to be in keeping with their mood—to reflect and perhaps even to intensify the mood. Crayons, a hard medium, require physical tension to use, and frequently, as stated above, the use of them tended to increase rather than diminish tensions.

Children who sought the crayons often to the exclusion of other media when they first entered nursery school were frequently observed to turn to easel painting as their first observed step toward freer behavior.

When *Ann*, *Albert*, and *Tilly* entered nursery school, they were blocked in all activities except crayoning. Crayons were used to draw structuralized nonexpressive patterns. These children were also blocked in speech. All three turned to easel painting as a preliminary to, or as a parallel activity to, freer overt behavior.

*Alan*, tense and unhappy throughout his first year and a half at school, during this period sought and used crayons in preference to all the other creative media. Alan began to paint one day during a play interview when he was alone with Dr. Hattwick in her office. His subsequent absorbed interest in painting in the group was paralleled by more overt aggressive behavior. For example, he sometimes kicked other children instead of following his previous pattern of aggression, which had been to irritate children so that they were challenged to kick him. He also began to carry on more co-operative play, though he still lacked the capacity for co-operation and outgoing behavior which was usual among children of his age—children who had moved beyond primary concern in their inner lives and had gone on from painting to more social and objective interests.[13]

*Peter* turned to painting after a series of play interviews[14] which apparently helped him to become progressively freer. After this period, the staff reported "better speech and social contacts," and the home reported that he was "bossing his younger sister," in desirable contrast to his earlier attitude of being overwhelmed and bossed by her.

*Floyd*, a persistent user of crayons, tended to have more social relationships following painting experiences than he had on days when he limited his creative activity to use of crayons.

That these differences between painting and crayoning experiences were widely observed is borne out by the quantitative findings. It is important, however, constantly to keep in mind the fact that individual differences exist. There were some children who enjoyed all school activities. They

[13] A positive relation between painting and sociability is apparent only in those children who turned to the easel after a relatively exclusive interest in crayoning. In general, children's interest in painting decreased as social relations and interest in the world about them increased.

[14] These interviews were held by Anni Weiss-Frankl.

sought the crayons frequently. Their crayon drawings had the same kind of varied pattern as characterized their other activities, and their behavior while using crayons was not noticeably different from their behavior during their other group experiences. Perhaps the main distinction between these children and those previously described is that for them crayoning was not the predominant or all-absorbing interest.

When we compare crayon and painting products of those children who showed a strong interest in both media, we often find contrasting patterns. It is possible to generalize on the differences:

*a*) In crayon drawings the emphasis tends to be upon line and form, upon the cooler colors, such as blue, upon representation or attempts at representation, and upon realistic naming.

*b*) In easel painting the work tends more often to be characterized by mass rather than by form and line. Emphasis is more often upon the warmer colors, there seems little conscious attempt at representation, and products are more likely to be accompanied by free association than by realistic naming.[15]

A quantitative study of the significance of the characteristics noted above (see chap. ii) reveals that these differences in crayon and easel-painting products are consistent with the differences already noted in the behavior of the individual children who seek easel paints and those who seek crayons, namely:

The child who is inclined to prefer crayons and who in his behavior is attempting self-control and adaptation to his external environment, in his products emphasizes line, form, cooler colors, and realistic representation.[16]

The child who prefers easel paints and who in his behavior is more concerned with self-expression than with adapting realistically to the world about him emphasizes warm colors and mass techniques in his products.

Children who showed contrasting themes in their crayon and painting products have often been found to have conflicting drives. Their *crayon* patterns seemed to reflect the drive currently expressed in their overt behavior, i.e., the drive that accorded with the demands and expectancies of the outside world. In contrast to their crayon pattern, their *painting* pattern tended to reflect personal drives not permitted or admitted in their overt behavior.

[15] See, for example, Fredrika, pp. 35–36, 132.

[16] Archie, Arnold, Esther, Gloria, Hall, Norman, Rachel, Robert, Sally, and Stanley were among the children in whom these distinctions were pronounced. Edward started the year with the same high representation in painting that he used in crayoning, but he soon reverted to warmer colors and mass techniques in the painting medium.

Although relatively full data have been given on this point, it seems desirable to point it up again in terms of painting and crayon usage.

Our study of products revealed that circles, delicate colors, and light strokes are likely to be associated with submissive and/or feminine qualities, while strong colors and heavy, vertical strokes tend to be associated with assertive and/or masculine tendencies.

Many children, as previously stated, are in conflict over these two drives.

*Bee*, overtly quiet and submissive, when she used crayons made representations that were delicately colored and had basically circular forms. In striking contrast to this were her heavy, full-page verticals in easel painting. Bee's paintings of this type were made during the periods when she turned to boisterous play with boys, when she showed unusual determination and intense but passive resistance to adults. Apparently, most of the time, she suppressed her strong assertive drive (expressed in the painting patterns) beneath her usual submissive behavior (expressed in her crayon drawings) (Pls. 116–20). Her ordinal position in the family—the middle child in a family of three sisters, behaving like well-mannered, rather shy little girls, may offer a clue as to why the assertive, masculine role appealed to her.

*Jocelyn, Margaret, Arlene, Sara, Patty,* and *Loretta* all emphasized circles in crayons and either verticals or conflicting vertical and circular patterns in painting. All were girls, and all expressed the "expected" girl pattern in most of their overt behavior and the "expected" girl pattern of circular response when using crayons. But these same little girls all indicated in their less guarded behavior and in their painting patterns that they had conflicting personal drives.[17] These they expressed in contrasting vertical and circular patterns.

It is of some interest to note that all these examples of conflicting circular-vertical designs (or, as interpreted, "conflicting masculine-feminine drives")[18] occur in girls. One wonders whether this may be due to two cultural factors, namely (1) Do the rather rigid standards concerning the behavior of little girls make for rebellion and conflict? (2) Does the value placed on being a male in our society also make for the conflict noted?

Comparison of crayon and painting products reveals that crayons are likely to portray a variety of realistic experiences taken from everyday life, whereas paintings are more likely to be abstract and to reflect concern with inner problems and emotional involvements.

*Fredricka* made constructive, recognizable products with crayons and gave no evidence in this medium of her interest in elimination. But this interest was clearly evidenced in her painting and clay activities—both in the products and in the verbalization that occurred in con-

---

[17] Developmentally, as before noted, children incline to make circles before they try to make straight lines and angular forms. Straight lines and angular forms are usually drawn with crayons before they are made with paints. The fact that the process is reversed in these particular cases, that is, that at the time they were still crayoning circles they were making straight lines and circles with paints, is one fact which inclined us to look for personality factors in these cases.

[18] Further defined and discussed, pp. 60–64.

nection with them. *Bert*'s crayon work was on a par with his constructive, nonrepresentative work with blocks, whereas his paintings revealed a marked conflict between assertive-submissive or masculine-feminine drives.

We should not conclude from the foregoing examples that the painting and crayon products of.all children show contrasts such as these. Many children express quite similar content or trends in their work in the two media. Where similarity exists, we have found that a given child usually fits into one of these two groupings: (*a*) He may be a well-adjusted child who uses both paints and crayons to reflect his daily, varied experiences which he is in process of integrating into himself; or (*b*) he may be a child who is in a deeply disturbed state, whose every action is colored by his impulsive emotional drives, and who tends to use crayons as he does paints (with emphasis on mass and color) to express personal feelings and problems.

*Angela*, it will be recalled, at different periods, expressed both of these trends. She alternately went through stages (*a*) of good adjustment, when her varied interests were richly and variously expressed in painting and crayoning, and (*b*) of emotional conflict, when all her creative activities reflected disturbance and preoccupation with the same problem. In her more usual periods of happy adjustment, Angela used crayons and easel paints to produce a variety of constructive or representative forms. These were usually done in predominantly cool and well-balanced color combinations. In her occasional upset periods, Angela created mass effects with both paints and crayons. The occasion for her difficulty each time was the same (a new baby expected in the family), and each time she reverted to approximately the same palette and color-mass organization of her paper, using red, orange, and yellow touched or overlaid with black.[19]

The following factors may, to some extent, account for the differences noted above between usage of paints and crayons:

*a*) Crayons are a more readily controlled medium than easel paints and, accordingly, lend themselves more readily to circumscribed usage—particularly to work in line and form.

*b*) Before they enter school groups, children are more often exposed at home to crayons than to paints. They therefore may tend to use this medium according to family standards and expectancies which are likely to include drawing of pictures.

*c*) Crayons in the nursery-school setting are provided at a table where other children may also be crayoning. Communication and social values are current. "Pictures" and "letters" are added to conversation, perhaps as another means of communication.

[19] For more detailed description see Pls. 22–23. Among the other children who showed relatively good adjustment and who used both crayons and paints for varied constructive and representative work were Alma, Bess, Dorothea, and Esther. Among the other children who were preoccupied with conflicts and who used the color-mass technique in both painting and crayoning were Danny and Glen.

### II. SOME COMPARISONS BETWEEN CHILDREN WHO PREFERRED EASEL PAINTS AND THOSE WHO PREFERRED BLOCKS

Differences again prevail in group comparisons of those children who preferred easel painting and those who preferred blocks. Differences rather than similarities in these groups are indicated in the very fact that few children in the nursery-school setting showed an interest in both media.[20]

Children who preferred the blocks stood out as a group for their spontaneous, outgoing, adaptive, realistic drives and behavior. This was in marked contrast to the predominantly subjective, impulsive, self-centered characteristics of those who sought easel paints.

Many children turned to work with blocks as they were making the transition from impulsive behavior toward adaptive reactions. Their developing interest in building with blocks was paralleled by a keen interest in discovering and interrelating facts in the world about them. This parallelism suggests that the manual relating of structural units (i.e., building with blocks) and the mental process of relating facts may be different reflections of the same developmental trend.

From the standpoint of manipulation and control, there seems to be more similarity between blocks and crayons than between blocks and any of the other media explored. But children who outstandingly preferred blocks showed more genuinely adaptive behavior and sounder adjustment than the children who outstandingly preferred the crayon medium.

Children's block products, as observed in this study, were not, as a whole, so expressive of feelings as were their products in easel painting and clay. This we might expect, since we have noted that children turned to the use of blocks as they moved away from their earlier impulsive behavior and as their interest in factual and logical material increased. Social factors which, as a rule, enter into the use of blocks in a group setting also militate against the use of blocks as a medium for expressing personal feelings. Yet, despite these facts, certain children, notably *Alan, Archie, Bert,* and *Ralph,* sought blocks in the nursery school in preference to other media as a means of expressing their emotional needs. Many other children reflected their feelings through their block usage, although they did not outstandingly seek

---

[20] Only three children showed a predominating interest in both paints and blocks: Benjy, Della, and Diane. In each of these, one or both of the following parallelisms in product were noted: (*a*) inclosures in blocks, paralleled by restricted filled forms in painting; (*b*) nonrepresentative structuralized patterns in both media.

this medium in preference to others or use it primarily as a means of expressing their emotions.[21]

Those children who, in the nursery school, preponderantly sought blocks as a means of expressing their feelings rather than using the blocks, as did most children, to express their adaptive drives showed one or more of the following trends: (a) They were likely to choose the small, unit blocks rather than the large, hollow, or drag blocks; (b) they tended to use blocks in solitary play rather than in co-operative or parallel play situations; (c) they were wont to build the same structure over and over again far more than did the better-adjusted children, who used the blocks in a variety of ways; and (d) they showed a more extreme reaction to their own products, such as long-continued and vigilant protection of their products without using them, extreme disturbance if products were destroyed or touched by other children, or else, as happened in the case of some children, they got intense pleasure from destroying their own products.

In the same way that a comparison of children's crayon and easel products was fruitful, a comparison of children's block and easel products yields some basis for further consideration. In general, we noted that children who were primarily interested in blocks and who were relatively well adjusted in their group tended, when they did paint, to produce highly structured patterns in which straight lines and/or angular strokes predominated.[22]

Among individual children there were a few whose block and painting products showed markedly similar emphases that seemingly had a common origin in their emotional life.

*Enclosures.*—*Richard* built enclosures with blocks and painted circular enclosures. During periods of emotional upset, *Sally* and *Victor* made enclosures with blocks that were paralleled by overlay in painting. The periods during which *Don* and *Ralph* built block enclosures in which to hide things paralleled the times when they were working in restricted masses with easel paints.

*Tower emphasis.*—*Sara* and *Loretta* showed vertical emphasis in painting that was paralleled by tower emphasis in blocks. A change in *Richard's* block pattern from inclosures to towers was paralleled by a change in painting pattern from circles to verticals. A pronounced focus on towers by *Archie* in block building was paralleled by such varied types of emphasis on height in painting as (1) use of verticals; (2) overemphasis on top of page in painting; and (3) such verbalized accompanying content as "Sky," "Ladder," "Chimney," "Smoke."

[21] Among these children were Aileen, Glen, Gregory, Jay, Jill, Jimmy, Joe, Louis, Margaret, Peter, Robert, and Ronny.

[22] These children included Barry, Don, Hilda, Hugh, Joe, Robert, Ross, Sheldon, and Steven.

*Destroying of products.*—Interest in destroying block structures was paralleled by smearing techniques with paints in the cases of *Glen* and *Ray*. *Bert*, who was inclined to protect his block structures at first and finally to destroy them with glee, also found enjoyment in the final smearing of his paintings.

*Other cases of parallelism in usage of the two media.*—*Bee*'s and *Fredrika*'s painting patterns changed from circular, warm-colored mass effects to structured straight-line, angular forms just at the time that they began to show interest in block building. They were using blocks during this period to carry out varied locomotion projects.

A decorative theme was pronounced in both the painting and the block work of *Paul*. Dots often provided the decorative motifs in paints. Tiny colored cubes provided the decorative motif for block structures.

Fanciful rather than realistic representation predominated in both the painting and the block work of *Aileen* (see Pl. 11).

A comparison of the amount of emotionally weighted verbalism of given children during block play and during painting reveals the fact that children tended to be more articulate about their emotions during block play than during painting. The period of generalized emotions expressed through painting seems in some cases to have prepared the way for ensuing verbal release.

*Aileen*'s comment during block building—"This is my house. Nobody can live in it. This is a house only for my people who haven't any other place to stay"—followed a very long period of much less revelatory activity when Aileen was painting the ovular red masses which she sometimes simply called "Houses."

*Angela*'s mass-painting pattern with the one comment "Old Witch" was not particularly revealing. But later, after she had initiated dramatic play with blocks, the meaning of "Old Witch," its association with "Bad Mama"—and with Angela's inner turmoil over a baby that was expected in her family—became apparent.[23]

Because self-expression is often more specific with blocks than with easel painting, blocks may offer a simpler method of understanding what is going on within the child than do paints. Dr. Hattwick's experience when she had individual children playing alone in her office during periods of controlled observations strongly suggests this possibility.

Blocks become an easier and probably better diagnostic medium when children are old enough to build structures and to verbalize freely than they are at earlier stages.[24] Case studies suggest that blocks may have special value for highly intellectual children like *Eda* and *Peter*, who needed to learn how to handle and use concrete materials as well as thoughts.

[23] See Pls. 28, 29.

[24] See Erik Homberger, "Configuration in Play," *Psychoanalytic Quarterly*, VI (1937), 139–214. It may be that, if the authors had made as extended a study of blocks as they did of painting, they would have found children's early piling and use of blocks equally revealing.

Characteristic differences that appear in easel paintings and in block products would seem to be influenced, in part, by the circumstances under which each medium was available in the nursery school and in part by actual differences in the nature of the medium. Blocks in the nursery school are seldom used without some degree of interaction or of actual co-operation with other children. Even when children work on individual projects, there is, as a rule, need for exchanging with other children, dividing, or otherwise compromising on numbers, shapes, and sizes of blocks. Painting, as a rule, is likely to be a solitary enterprise.

Blocks, by their inherent form, call for fitting and aligning. Their usage, after children pass the early "piling stage," demands controlled reactions. It would be almost impossible to work with blocks and to achieve any sort of result that would be satisfactory, with attention directed elsewhere.

Satisfactory results with easel paints can be achieved with the most casual attention. Blocks lack the fluidity and flexible color possibilities that tend to make easel paints such a good medium for expression of feelings. They are a relatively structured medium which demands more adaptation from the user than do the more readily manipulated paints.

### III. SOME COMPARISONS BETWEEN CHILDREN WHO PREFERRED EASEL PAINTS AND THOSE WHO PREFERRED CLAY

Whereas *contrasts* have prevailed between children who preferred easel paints and those who preferred crayons or blocks, *similarities* predominated between the groups preferring paint and clay. Many children, in fact, showed a strong parallel interest in both media (35 per cent of the fifty-four children who outstandingly sought the easel also showed a predominating interest in clay).

High usage of both easel paints and clay seems consistent with the early manipulative stage of development when children, as a rule, are full of unrestrained impulses toward action. Both media seem to stimulate children to symbolical expression of feelings which they are either not ready or not able to express in more articulate or overt fashion. In varying degrees at different times, both clay and paints seem to heighten and to offer outlets for emotional drives.[25]

While apparently somewhat similar in their appeal and release effect, clay and easel paints evoke certain specifically different responses. Children

---

[25] Our observations and analyses also included a separate study of finger painting. Data were too few to permit of sound statistical analyses, but the findings in general seem to parallel those for clay.

are likely to be more open and direct in their verbal and other expressions of emotions while using clay than while painting. In fact, free verbalization has been more evident during activity with clay than with any of the other media explored.

*Anita, Harriet, Harvey, Jimmy, Margaret, Peter, Ralph,* and many other children were markedly more talkative while manipulating clay than at other times observed.[26]

*Danny, Jimmy, Ray, Roberta, Rowena, Sara,* and others talked much more nonsense at clay than during other activities. The free and absurd character of the verbalization suggests an unusual degree of release.

*Frank, Gilbert, Howard,* and others talked out their emotional problems while at clay more freely than at other times, even though they did not express their problems through the clay medium.

Problems expressed relatively indirectly in painting—as was *Fredricka's* concern with elimination (Pls. 56–59)—seemed to find more direct expression through clay (and likewise through finger painting). Whereas *Ann* actively released aggressive drives through her intensive pounding of clay, she kept her aggressions and other outgoing drives covered while painting, as she overlaid red or yellow with blue and green.[27]

The following factors probably contributed to children's free expression during periods of clay usage:

1. The clay situation, more than any other in the nursery, stimulated parallel play. Clay was presented at a small table, around which four or six children usually sat rather close together. This was conducive to social interchange.

2. Clay did not require an intermediate tool as did easel painting and, accordingly, evoked a more direct response. Whereas strong aggressive feelings were often expressed through vehement pounding at clay, they were more indirectly expressed through choice of red or work in heavy vertical strokes at the easel.[28] Many children of this age, we know, are concerned with excrement. The sensory similarity between clay and excrement made clay a more direct means than paints for working out this concern.

A few parallels between clay products and by-products of play with other media, particularly easel painting, that seem worth noting have been observed. They especially indicate need for further observations.

*Breaking off of tiny bits of clay.*—*Jean* and *Tess* focused on breaking off tiny pieces of clay. They tended at the easel to produce many dots and dabs. *Floyd* also was apt to break tiny pieces from his clay, while his crayon products were characterized by minute forms and fine detail. *Hope,* Jean, and *Phyllis* were inclined to break off tiny pieces of clay, and they all were outstanding in their group for their particular interest in collecting tiny objects at play. Phyllis, Floyd, and Jean tended to break off tiny pieces of clay and showed an outstanding interest in jigsaw puzzles—not only of the type which the school provided but of the complicated, commercial types devised for adults.

[26] See Van Alstyne, *op. cit.*

[27] See p. 31.                              [28] See pp. 21–23.

*Container theme.*—*Louise* used clay to make balls or containers, and at the easel she characteristically worked in restricted masses. *Alma, Arnold,* and *Tess* also showed pronounced tendencies to work clay into balls and/or containers, and each of them emphasized circles in crayons and/or easel painting.

*Vertical emphasis.*—*Sara* predominantly rolled cylindrical snakes out of clay and showed a predominant vertical emphasis in easel painting. *Archie, Jay,* and several other boys emphasized long cylinders in their clay work and verticals in painting. *Jessica* made vertical columns at clay and showed the vertical emphasis at the easel.

*Piling.*—*Ann* broke pieces at clay and then combined them by piling while at the clay table. She characteristically "piled" (overlayed) one color upon another. She also used piling techniques with blocks and showed a strong collecting interest in general.

*Fitting pieces together.*—*Hilda, Sara,* and *Phyllis* broke tiny pieces and patted them together for a large, flattened mound at clay. At the easel each tended to produce full-page masses composed of systematic piecemeal combination of smaller masses.

### IV. SOME COMPARISONS BETWEEN CHILDREN WHO PREFERRED EASEL PAINTS AND THOSE WHO PREFERRED DRAMATIC PLAY

A comparison of easel painting and dramatic play necessitates some definition of the latter term. The expression "dramatic play" may cover a wide range of possibilities: (*a*) The simplest form of dramatic play may be the handling of play materials in a manipulative way, as, e.g., the mere holding or carrying of a doll with obvious intent to "play something." (*b*) Also on the border line of dramatic play are the imaginative tales of possible happenings which children relate but which they do not enact. (*c*) More easily recognizable as dramatic play is the handling of play materials when accompanied by monologue suggesting dramatic content. (*d*) Also more recognizable as dramatic play is the actual pantomiming or use of materials to carry out a dramatic-play theme, such as sweeping the floor, making the bed, setting the table in the doll corner—another kind of "let's pretend." (*e*) More complicated forms of dramatic play are characterized by decreasing dependence on materials and increasing reliance on content, on interaction with other children, and on specific roles. Some of the highest examples of co-operation observed at the nursery-school level come in these more highly differentiated stages of dramatic play.

In our group comparisons of easel painting and of dramatic play we have not been able to consider separately the levels of dramatic play suggested above. All of them, however, are represented in our group evaluations. The preponderance of our dramatic-play observations deal with the last three types enumerated. Observations have been heavily weighted by children's activities in three areas, viz., in the doll corner, around locomotor toys, and around block play. A more differentiated technique would obviously be desirable in further research studies.

Our group comparisons of children who preferred the easel and those who preferred dramatic play, as observed in the present study, suggest that easel painting and dramatic play had common appeals. Thirty-three per cent of the fifty-four children with a predominant interest in paints likewise preferred and showed an ever increasing interest in dramatic play. Children in both groups had particularly strong emotional drives.

Despite this basic similarity of appeal, differential factors were found to be operating in the painting and the dramatic-play situations. The chief characteristic which distinguished the children in the group primarily interested in dramatic play was their more highly developed social orientation. Children with a major interest in dramatic play, as a group, showed freer and more affectionate responses to people in general and had a more co-operative attitude toward others than did the children primarily interested in easel paints.[29]

Our observations suggest that chronological age accounts for some of the difference just cited. As children (ages two to four) get older, interest in painting decreases and interest in dramatic play increases. Social interaction and co-operative play also increase with age. The shift in interest from easel painting to dramatic play occurred gradually in many of the children observed and seemed in large part a reflection of social development.

The factors of age and social development, however, are not the only ones to consider as contributing to children's shift from easel painting to dramatic play. As children develop and mature, their interests and problems, as a rule, reach a more focalized and overt level. As previously indicated, many children like *Aileen, Angela, Gloria,* and *Esther* can and do express their feelings abstractly and symbolically through easel painting as long as those feelings are still at the level of somewhat vague and generalized disturbances. Apparently, once their problems have become specifically identified with given situations, people, or objects, many children are ready and able to express them, at least symbolically, in dramatic play. Our observations led us to believe that when the child is developmentally ready for it, dramatic play, which crystallizes in more specific and overt form than easel painting, offers children a fuller release and a more satisfying experience.

As in the case of other media, comparisons of dramatic-play activities with painting products reveal parallelisms which may be helpful in furthering our understanding of expression in both media.

*Patty* went to the easel and painted a product with a circular theme, following an absorbing dramatic-play experience in which she took a feminine role. Her usual painting theme was not circular, and many of her interests were not feminine.

---

[29] Although the foregoing was true as a general trend, we must again remember that there are always many exceptions to every generalization. Aileen (in her second year), Phoebe, and Rowena all had predominant interest in dramatic play but had poor social relations.

*Angela* engaged in dramatic play which involved the wrapping-up of a doll and the putting of "Baby," "sick girl," or "Mama" to bed at a period when she was painting emotionally weighted color-mass patterns that were related to her conflict over "Baby" and "Bad Mama."

*Gloria* played the sick, new-baby role at a time when she was depicting the container theme with both paints and crayons.

*Jay, Hugh,* and *Archie* characteristically chose the "big man," usually the father role in dramatic play, and they characteristically used a vertical painting pattern.

Children often carried on similar free associations in their painting and in their dramatic play; for example, *Ethel* was concerned with "washing clothes" in both media; *Virginia* with "eating" and "birthday cake."

### SUMMARY OF DISTINCTIONS SUGGESTED BY COMPARISON OF MEDIA

The preceding discussion of various forms of self-expression in different media suggests the following tentative conclusions:

1. That easel painting may be of particular value for expressing generalized emotions, conflicts, and difficulties which are at a nonverbal, nonovert level, i.e., for expressing felt tensions rather than problems and conflicts that have crystallized at the conscious level.

2. That easel painting may be of particular value for self-expression between the ages of two and four, when children are at the stage of interest and development at which color and symbolic representations are used with facility.

3. That easel painting may be of particular value to disturbed children who can more readily use paints (a relatively clean medium) than the dirtier media, such as clay and finger paints.

4. That use of easel painting may be helpful to children in bringing their vague disturbances into more definite form. In those cases in which children are disturbed and spontaneously seek the easel, painting is likely to bring temporary release. For deep problems, it is not likely that painting will, by itself, effect basic therapy.

5. That easel painting may be of particular diagnostic value in connection with those withdrawn, repressed, or shy children who either consciously or unconsciously try to cover over or hide their real feelings.

6. That easel painting may have unique value as a diagnostic measure because it is relatively easy to preserve and interpret the final products as contrasted with the difficulty of preserving and interpreting final products in clay, blocks, or dramatic play.[30]

---

[30] In easel painting we can preserve one phase of the situation—the painting page—and we can usually reconstruct in order the steps or processes (in terms of colors applied and strokes made) through which the child went to achieve his end-result. In clay and finger painting, the intermediate processes are lost in the final product and can be reconstructed only when those final

7. That children, in general, may express themselves more directly both with the material and verbally when using clay and/or finger paints than at the easel.

8. That clay (or finger paints) may be a particularly helpful medium for children who are in conflict over problems concerning elimination and/or overcleanliness.

9. That clay (or finger painting) may be of particular value for children who are naturally in the smearing, manipulative stage of development (a phase somewhat earlier than interest in color symbolism).

10. That clay usage in a group may tend, because of the opportunity for parallel play, to stimulate a somewhat more direct release for feelings of competition, aggression, etc., than do easel paints. For example, *Aileen* and others merely *voiced* their defiant attitude at the easel; but at the clay table defiance was often projected through such activities as outdoing others in number or size of snakes, or by grabbing and by redividing clay. There were countless examples of this sort.

11. That blocks are likely to be a specifically valuable medium for expression after children have reached the controlled, adaptive stage of development.

12. That blocks may be a relatively more valuable medium for expression and release after children have passed the stage of color symbolism and have become interested in line and form.

13. That crayons are one of the least adequate media for satisfying experiences at the two- and three-year level.

14. That crayons may become a valuable diagnostic tool at the nursery-school level if products are studied in relation to easel paintings.

15. That crayons probably become a more satisfactory medium for expression after the child has passed the impulsive stage of development, after he has begun of his own accord to accept and adapt to his external environment, and after he has reached the stage of realistic representation.

16. That dramatic play may be a particularly valuable medium for expression after the child has reached an outgoing, socially oriented stage of development (probably around four years of age and older).

17. That dramatic play may be of particular value for the release of feelings and conflicts that involve specific social relationships.

It must not be forgotten that all these suggested values for specific creative

---

products are accompanied by observations that offer a parallel description of process. We should also note that the advantage which easel painting provides, as far as interpretation of final product is concerned, is accompanied by a hazard: there is always danger in attempting to interpret products if they are abstracted from their original setting.

media have grown from observation of their use in group situations. There is little doubt that, from time to time, the relative value of these media shifts for the individual child. The value of any of the media discussed will depend, in part at least, upon the circumstances under which it is used, e.g., whether in a group of other children or when alone. From the total of group and individual observations, it would seem that no one material is in itself better than any other. Choice and value apparently depend in large part upon the age, maturity level, and makeup of the child and upon the problem (if any) that the child is at the given time trying to resolve. It is, accordingly, important not to focus on any single medium but to offer all of them to children at appropriate times and to keep in mind that responses in any one area can be understood only if seen in relationship to activities in other areas and to all aspects of the child's life.

# CHAPTER VII

## EVALUATING CHILDREN'S PAINTINGS: AIDS AND SAFEGUARDS, RELEASE AND THERAPY

### AIDS AND SAFEGUARDS

GENERALIZED findings of the sort presented throughout the foregoing discussion, like other generalizations, hold only within certain limits. They are subject to many exceptions and modifications, and this is especially true of a study wherein findings are based upon and related to human factors. Findings in such cases should be regarded as clues to deeper understanding rather than as axioms on which to base further conclusions. Discriminatingly used, however, these findings can be valuable in heightening teachers' sensitivity to the content and value of children's creative work, they can help to document analyses of children's needs and problems and can give direction to guidance.

It has been abundantly illustrated throughout this investigation that, long before paintings are recognizable in a realistic sense, they are full of significant content of which the child himself is often quite unaware. Content of this sort is most readily identified in the work of children who are emotionally disturbed. But careful and systematic study of the paintings and other creative activities of practically any child is rewarding either in substantiating what is already known of him or in some way further increasing understanding of the child's inner life. In some cases examination of his work will reveal the child as a soundly developing youngster expressing a variety of interests, and in other cases his creative work—particularly his paintings—may reveal that the child is troubled, suffering, and in need of special consideration and help.

Our findings, we believe, have practical implications for workers in various fields. Safeguards for discriminating use of them warrant discussion. As different as is the role of the educator from that of the psychiatrist is likely to be their use of this material. Educators, like parents, will realize that some difficulties indicated in children's paintings can be quite simply handled in any one of a number of ways. Wise educators, like wise parents, will distinguish simple or passing problems, often characteristic of particular stages of development, from deeper problems that require more expert help than most educators are prepared to give.

Educators, as well as others who wish to use this material meaningfully, will observe a child's general behavior and activities over a period of time before making inferences or interfering in any way with his creative efforts. Manifest relationships and objective evidence in other areas of his living should be observed and related to what is felt to be significant in his paintings before conclusions are warranted. It is only as supplementary evidence is found that interpretations of paintings as outlined can be properly formulated and used. It will also be important to keep in mind that constant flux and resultant change within both child and environment must continuously modify thinking and conclusions about any given child. Suggested bases for analyzing children's paintings may be considered—like various tests of intelligence—as diagnostic tools particularly useful in contributing to the understanding and guidance of young children.

### I. THE NEED FOR AN INDIVIDUALIZED APPROACH

As previously stated, any generalization pertaining to human beings will, when applied, vary from child to child and will, of necessity, be modified for the same child under different conditions.

Any single observed phenomenon, as we have stated in connection with focus on the color red, may have quite varied significance for different children. For one child a focus on red may symbolize a craving for love and may become identified with the desire for a stable home. Another child, focusing on red, may be expressing symbolically his need and longing for the supporting affection of a particular individual. In other cases red may be used as an outlet for feelings quite counter to these—namely, aggression and hatred. In all these situations, red is used to satisfy the individual's active need of expressing his driving emotions. In such cases recognition of the particular need is obviously important.

Similarly, it should be noted that the same child may vary his painting pattern because of purely temporary factors, such as (a) happenings that for the day or hour colored his mood when he came to the easel; (b) immediate physical conditions, such as kind of paint, size and placement of painting page, type of brush, indoor or outdoor setting; (c) immediate social situation, such as whether or not adults are present or about; (d) whether or not other children are present and interacting with him; or again the particular activity that some other child is engaged in may influence his work. All of these seemingly extraneous factors must have due consideration if there is to be intelligent understanding of a child's painting.

The same child may display more than one type of pattern in a given medium, each pattern consistent with a particular set of circumstances. Differentiated responses of this sort were pronounced in *Aileen*'s block building. Aileen often produced symbolical, abstract, pedestaled effects when withdrawn from the group and when absorbed in fanciful play, and she frequently built platforms on which to stand or act and thrones on which to sit when stimulated toward overt dramatic play in which she had the opportunity to take the lead. In contrast to these, for a period of time when she was particularly happy in her play with George, she geared in with his interests and built tracks, bridges, and other structures that afforded her opportunities to play with him.

Before we can adequately evaluate a painting or any other creative product, we must be aware of, and take into account, circumstances such as the foregoing, which may have influenced what was done.

We have already discussed a variety of happenings of the kind that tend to modify the child's mood. Expectation or birth of a new baby in the family, sibling rivalry, parental pressure, and high standards, particularly in regard to cleanliness, are other factors which in either transitory or more permanent ways may affect the child's mood when he paints or initiates other creative activities. Even in certain transitory situations we have found some general tendencies. Birthdays and Christmas, for example, are heartwarming experiences for children, and our observations have suggested a tendency among them to turn to freer use of warm, "happy" colors, particularly yellow, at these times.[1] A stay at home often precipitates a change in painting pattern. In children subjected to high home standards, for example, we have frequently observed a swing to overlay, particularly with blue, after a stay at home.[2] A number of times it has been noted that children, on returning from a test situation in which a good rapport was established with the tester, have evidenced a kind of release that enabled them to initiate new and freer expression in painting, as well as in other activities.[3]

If analysis of paintings is to deepen insight into the dynamics of individual children, observers must remain continuously aware of every sort of situation which may affect any particular child's feelings and his consequent painting products. Educators and others will wish to keep themselves free not only from the desensitizing effects of wholesale generalizations but from fixed attitudes of prejudice about any given child.

Illustrative of transitory experiences of the sort which alert observers may note and utilize as clues to guidance are the following:

Danny, Jessica, and Phoebe each produced paintings which were noticeably freer in color and space usage when their mothers were away from home. Each changed again to an overlaid and otherwise repressed pattern upon the mother's return. The freer painting

---

[1] See pp. 32–33.         [2] True of Edward, Phoebe, Elinor, et al.

[3] True of Paul, Peter, and Polly after play interviews with Dr. Hattwick. This was apparently also the situation that freed Alan sufficiently so that, although he had not used paints before his play interview with Dr. Hattwick, subsequently painting became one of his regular activities in the group.

during the mother's absence paralleled freer behavior in other areas and helped to substantiate the belief that each of these children felt restrained under the mother's influence.

*Philip* and *Polly* each gave up painting for more articulate overt activities during their mother's absence from home. They went back to painting and became less outgoing upon their mother's return. The related circumstances again suggest restraint under the mother's influence and a particular, self-expressive value in painting for these children.

We have noted how *Angela* at three different periods consistently returned to her particular pattern of mass technique, using warm colors somewhat overlaid with black during expectation of a baby in the family and around the times of subsequent miscarriages. The consistent reversion to an earlier pattern gives clue and support to the supposition that Angela was, in reality, deeply concerned, despite her tendency to behave as usual in all situations except those creative-play situations or activities which encouraged free symbolic expression of her underlying disturbance.

*Perry* turned to crayons and produced three products with cutoff verticals on the day following a threat by an older boy that "the doctor will cut off your ears." Perry also had night terrors following this threat. The crayon pattern, with the symbolic cutoff verticals, along with the night terrors, supports the belief that Perry was deeply disturbed by the threat, which, according to psychoanalytic theory, may have assumed the significance of a castration fear.

*Erwin*, instead of having a self-expressive individual painting pattern, tended consistently to copy the pattern of whatever child was painting at the opposite side of the easel. Erwin was outstandingly imitative and lacking in self-expression in all activities. The paintings provide a record of Erwin's dearth of creative quality and capacity for self-expression even in the medium most likely to stimulate expression of those qualities.

II. THE INDIVIDUAL'S CHARACTERISTIC PATTERN MUST BE SOUGHT THROUGH A
LONGITUDINAL OR RELATIVELY LONG-TIME APPROACH

Paintings can be safely interpreted as related to the individual only as each child's products are observed day after day and compared with one another, as well as with reactions in other areas. In this way only can the common, persistently recurrent features be discovered. As previously stated, the individual's characteristic pattern or deviations from his characteristic pattern will be found only through a longitudinal or relatively long-time approach. Such an approach is a safeguard against being misled by either extraneous or transitory circumstances.

As a longitudinal study of each child's work is made, different degrees of similarity or variability in successive paintings will be noted. These offer one of the first clues to understanding. The more emotionally involved the child, the more likely is he to be focused on a single problem and the more repetitive or even stereotyped is his pattern likely to be. The better adjusted the child is at any given time or at all times, (a) the more likely are his paintings to show a clear-cut developmental sequence; (b) the more likely are individualized features, such as his own palette, to be interwoven among variable techniques and content; and (*c*) the more likely are his varied daily experiences to be reflected in his paintings. Sudden drops in the usual level of work, as from form to mass and/or smear, may offer a clue to the fact that the child has run up against an emotional problem.

If, over a period of time, recurrent or persistent events which parallel a given child's painting pattern are observed, these may be considered as clues to the child's paintings and to whatever deviations may be evident. If, for example, change in usual painting pattern is consistently paralleled by aggressions, by night terrors, or by persistent sibling conflicts at home, then possibilities are suggested that warrant investigation. If, along with these difficulties, increased tension while painting, an intense expressed desire to paint and/or continuous, accentuated use of one color, such as red, black, brown, or purple, are noted, it is probable that the given child needs carefully considered guidance.

It is the existence of repeated, persistent relationships, such as those outlined, that has justified the thesis of the present book and that lends objectivity to the generalized statements that have been made.

The fact that a child used yellow on a day when he was happy would not in itself necessarily be significant. But the finding that various children who showed striking ups-and-downs in mood consistently turned to the use of yellow and often to bright sweeps of yellow or its equivalent on days when they were happy and that on days when they were unhappy or subdued they turned to black, purple, and other somber colors gives us a basis for believing that a relationship between mood and color usage exists. If a child consistently and repeatedly used blue, as many did after a stay at home, whereas his characteristic pattern at school was not blue, then again the repeated evidence seems to justify the assumption that there was a relationship between use of blue and the home experience—an assumption obviously not justifiable on the basis of single incidence.

The foregoing discussion does not imply that single, differing products may not be important. Once the child's characteristic painting pattern is recognized, then a *single differing product may be highly important*, particularly if it is the beginning of a new painting trend and if the attendant circumstances are known. In fact, it may be such a single product with the unusual associated events that may help to prove, disprove, or vary interpretations previously held: for example, the fact that *Elaine* for the first time verbalized about the coming baby on the first day that she did not overlay with black (this was after a long series of black-overlay painting) lent more weight than all previous evidence to the belief that her full-page black paintings were somehow related to repressed feelings concerning the coming baby. The fact that *Andy, Anita,* and *Jeff* each produced rare sporadic products at a form level far higher than their characteristic pattern gave pictorial evidence for the belief that these children ordinarily functioned at a level below their true ability. Shifts in pattern and behavior—as, for example, the tendency for children to make a parallel shift from red to blue as they change from highly charged emotional to more controlled behavior or the tendency for children to shift from work in restricted areas to work all over the page as they make the transition from self-contained and re-pressed to outgoing behavior—provide stronger and more dynamic evi-dence of the apparent relationships between painting patterns and per-sonality than are likely from any number of static factors or comparisons.

### III. OBSERVATIONS ON PAINTING MUST BE CONTINUOUSLY INTEGRATED WITH OTHER CHARACTERISTICS AND REACTIONS

If a true understanding of the relatedness between children's paintings and their personalities is to be secured, not only must an individualized ap-proach be made and each child's characteristic pattern and tendencies be noted, *but observations on painting products must be continuously integrated with all other known and observable characteristics and reactions of the child in all areas.*

This involves, as previously stated, (*a*) comparison of all aspects of the painting pattern with one another for similarities and differences that are suggested or implied and (*b*) establishing of possible relationships between the painting product and the child's behavior, including verbalizations and other reactions while painting. In addition, (*c*) characteristic painting pattern and behavior while painting should be compared with other be-havior, particularly in social situations, and (*d*) comparison of activities while painting with activities during the use of other creative media should also be made.

Murray makes an interesting statement and analogy in this connection:

A single significant response may be likened to one piece of a picture puzzle. The latter has a certain shape and exhibits certain colors, but these items per se are of little interest or importance. They only become meaningful when it is known how they are related to the attributes of other pieces and how together they contribute to the total unity. . . . . By observation of many parts one finally arrives at a conception of the whole and, then, having grasped the latter, one can re-interpret and understand the former.[4]

Like the search for persistent or repeated responses and tendencies, at-tempts to understand the child's reactions as a meaningful whole help to avoid many false conclusions. Human personality and its dynamics can be understood only if approached not as a random accumulation of attributes but as a whole made up of certain perseverating, related traits and trends. If an interpretation of a child's paintings cannot be related meaningfully to

---

[4] Henry A. Murray *et al.*, *Explorations in Personality* (New York: Oxford University Press, 1938), p. 605.

other facts and events of his existence, judgment and action should be reserved until substantiating evidence is found.

A certain consistency within the framework of the painting products as a rule offers important clues to integration and interpretation. Our observations suggest that if a child shows a consistently restricted pattern in all areas of expression—as, for example, use of cold colors—and, along with these, evidences of some or all of the following characteristics: overlay with cold colors, closed forms, forms which are circular and filled and/or work in a restricted area of the painting page, then the chances are more than likely that we shall find evidence in the child of a consistent tendency toward withdrawn feelings and withdrawn overt behavior. If, on the other hand, different aspects of a given child's painting reflect conflicting trends, then the chances are more than likely that we shall find conflicting and less predictable parallels between feelings and overt behavior.

Behavior while painting may be in harmony with the painting pattern, while the child's general overt behavior is quite otherwise.

*Margaret*,[5] for example, produced a series of paintings in heavy, vertical strokes, suggestive of strong assertive feelings. She also displayed aggressive behavior toward other materials and individuals while she was painting. Throughout this same period, however, Margaret in her other activities in the schoolroom continued to be withdrawn and given to crying.

*Glen*[6] similarly reflected aggressive drives through heavy red vertical strokes with paints and crayons. He was, at the same time, extremely submissive and retiring in the group. (Follow-up information indicated that Glen subsequently became free and expressed the strong aggressions that were evident, or at least implicit, in his nursery paintings.)

In instances such as the foregoing, in which both painting product and painting behavior are a contrast to usual overt behavior patterns, opportunity and encouragement for release through the painting medium seem indicated. Such contrast may also indicate need for psychiatric guidance.

While contrasts such as these are not infrequent, they have not been usual among two-, three-, four-, and five-year-old children. As already stated, children of these ages are inclined to be impulsive, and they tend to express what they feel rather directly in overt behavior, as well as in their use of creative media. Accordingly, similarities rather than differences between painting and overt behavior trends tend to be the rule. Such analogies, for example, as *Aileen's* closed red-mass paintings paralleled by withdrawing behavior, *Archie's* emphasis on height in painting paralleled by "big" drives in other areas, or *Kit's* delight in dirt and mud play while indulging in dirty, smearing painting are more frequent than are contrasts such as we mentioned for *Margaret* and *Glen*. We offer the consistency of trends in our qualitative findings as substantial evidence for the foregoing statements.

[5] See also p. 126.         [6] See also pp. 21–22.

The majority of children whom we observed, including *Aileen*, *Archie*, and *Kit*, also tended to show parallelism between painting products and products in other media. But sometimes, particularly in the comparison of easel paintings and crayon products, we found interesting and enlightening differences. Such differences are as valuable as similarities in giving insights into the individual child. By and large, contrasts helped us to remain aware of this very important fact: that paintings tend primarily to reflect feelings and that only secondarily do they mirror overt behavior. Paintings may reflect feelings which are not finding expression in more overt reactions. When differences between painting trends and more overt reactions or between painting trends and trends in crayons are found, it is advisable to consider the possibility that the easel paints may be serving as a special and meaningful medium of release; and further evidence should be sought that will either verify or nullify the interpertation that might be given the paintings if considered by themselves.

### IV. ADEQUATE PERSPECTIVE

A fourth invaluable aid to study and interpretations is adequate perspective. One kind of perspective includes *knowledge of usual developmental trends in painting*. Observations of the individual child should be studied in relationship to usual performance of other children at the same stage of development.

Knowledge of developmental expectancies is essential to proper interpretation. As has been previously reported, emphasis on any one color, such as red or blue, may, from the standpoint of adjustment, have a certain significance at the nursery level and a quite different significance for an older child. Responses of a child at a given period may or may not correspond to his stage of development; for example, high usage of red in the early nursery period is usual, whereas persistent usage throughout the nursery-school years is unusual and likely to have special significance. Only by knowing what is typical and what is atypical at given periods can one make proper distinctions between what is primarily unique and individual and what is characteristic of the particular stage of development.

We should like to deviate from our findings at this point to suggest that perspective on children's paintings may be further heightened by knowledge of the findings derived from such specialized techniques as those used by psychoanalysts and Rorschach workers. Although our basic study was undertaken without inclusion of these two techniques, Rorschach tests were later given thirty of the children as part of our follow-up study. Our own awareness, our limited knowledge, and our belief in the underlying validity of both Rorschach and psychoanalytic approaches to the understanding of human behavior and of children's paintings have been supported and have increased progressively as a result of our present investigation. While indiscriminate application of the generalized trends derived from these techniques may be exceedingly harmful, the authors believe that an understanding of the objective relationships suggested by these methods may provide helpful clues to understanding of individual children. These relationships can be objectively tested. Actually, many of the findings in this study support, and are supported by, relationships established by Rorschach and psychoanalytic workers.

### V. OTHER PHASES OF BEHAVIOR

Besides the aids to interpretation outlined above, several other phases of behavior seemed to offer fruitful fields for further study. They include *verbalization, children's reactions to their own products, the paintings they wish to take home*, and *their self-portraits*.

*Verbalization.*—The field of verbalization offers rich opportunities for study.[7] The child's spontaneous naming or description of his creative product, as has frequently been noted, plays an important part in facilitating adult interpretation, and it frequently augments the release or therapeutic value of the painting experience for the child.

Since the name or descriptive designation of the product may have been planned when the child projected his painting or while he was doing it, since it may have been a response to some chance superficial environmental stimuli, or since it may perhaps have derived from some deep emotional source, it is highly important to discover, if possible, the real motive or stimulus for the designation given, if we are going to try to understand the significance of the content in relationship to the child's personality (Pl. 112).

Designations or verbalization about their work that have proved most valuable to us in interpreting pre-representative paintings are those which apparently have sprung spontaneously from the emotional core of the child. In such cases the designations tend to take the form of free association or monologue not obviously related to the task at hand. Designations under these circumstances "unfold" as the child is painting. It is, as a rule, quite clear to the observer that the content of the painting has been the subject of previous preoccupation and that the child has "painted out" something about which he has had strong feelings. The designation or verbalization often appears to be a significant, though seemingly unrelated, accompaniment of the painting experience.

---

[7] We have already noted how tendencies toward relevant or "personal" verbalizations (often seemingly irrelevant) accord with other factors in our statistical analyses. We have also indicated how children's verbalizations have given clues to the symbolism and the unconscious significance of their products (see, e.g., Bert, p. 22; Barry, pp. 25, 26 on overlay; or the children's comments on circles and verticals, p. 74).

An uninitiated observer would be inclined to dismiss this type of verbalization as not applicable to the painting product, since the child seemed to be talking quite casually, unrelatedly, and apparently without conscious intent. Yet our observations have shown that it is just this type of designation which, together with the painting pattern, is most likely to emerge from a common focus. Both seem to rise directly from the core of the being.[8] Often it is this type of naming or designation which gives a clue to the underlying emotional problem. Sometimes it is the last bit of evidence necessary to an understanding and interpretation of the basic emotional difficulty; and it supplies, along with the rest of the data, what is needed in order to see all the known facts as a meaningful whole.

*Aileen's* association of "House" with the closed red forms that she painted[9] and *Angela's* remark of "Old witch" during the painting of her overlaid, emotionally expressive paintings[10] were important factors in validating the interpretations given to the painting patterns of these two children.

We have observed that many children, when they first began to express their repressed feelings through painting, did not verbalize. If asked quite casually, "Do you want to tell me about your painting?" these children were likely to attach the name of whatever happened to catch their eyes, or sometimes they offered a name suggested by something just said by another child. At such periods their designations were prompted by external stimuli. Later on, however, as their feelings became more clarified, they would frequently and spontaneously offer a free-association sort of verbalization. Achievement of this verbal level seemed to offer a release and apparently helped children to be free of their erstwhile preoccupying and disturbing emotions.

It was only after *Aileen* was able to verbalize her concern about her family situation with the words, "This is a house for my people who have no other place to stay," that her disturbed preoccupation concerning her home perceptibly declined. (It did not disappear.)

It was only after *Angela* had sufficiently clarified her hostility that she could talk about "Bad Mama" that her emotionally weighted painting pattern ceased.

*Will* lost his fear of the school mascot after a series of paintings which culminated with the remark, "It ain't no dog."

---

[8] Griffiths offers a discussion of levels of attentiveness that perhaps elucidates this statement: "The most attentive level involves the most logical or intellectual processes. The less attentive levels increasingly reflect impulsive or emotional processes (see Ruth Griffiths, *A Study of Imagination in Early Childhood* [London: Kegan Paul, Trench, Trubner & Co., 1935]).

[9] See Pl. 3.                              [10] See Pl. 29.

*Sally* seemed to have fewer conflicts with her younger sisters after she had revealed her feelings through a number of paintings, to which she gave such designations as "Little girl walking down the street talking to her mother. The baby is following but they don't know it."

*Elaine*[11] and *Howard*[12] have already been discussed as less preoccupied with their personal conflicts once they had begun to verbalize about them. The painting experience seemed to help each of these children to bring his problem to a verbal level. Once this had occurred, these children were apparently better able to handle their difficulties, as in each case the previously felt need to use paint as a medium for expression and release ceased and marked strides in personal adjustment occurred.

Observations such as the foregoing have indicated not only the value of spontaneous verbalizations but also the futility, and perhaps the blunder, of stimulating names and comments and the attaching significance to such responses when given.

*Children's reactions to their own products.*—Such reactions have given many helpful clues to guidance, as, for example, the following: (1) The young child who is still developmentally in the stage of keen interest in *process* seems likely to show little or no interest in his finished painting or other product. (2) The child who is eager—perhaps overeager—for adult approval is likely to call attention to his work. (3) The child who is too burdened with adult expectancies and with standards beyond his level is likely to be ashamed of and to hide or destroy his products. (4) The child who is insecure and greatly absorbed in his emotional life may be especially protective about what he has made, even though he wishes to put it to no functional use. His work is apparently a projection of himself which he feels he must shield. (5) The child who has gained release through the painting experience may, like the child who is primarily interested in process, show no interest in the final product; or sometimes his gleeful destruction of his product is an indication of the release afforded by the painting experience.

*Paintings made to take home.*—Paintings are sometimes made with the expressed desire to take them home or as gifts for specific individuals. In such cases the exact nature of the painting, perhaps its deviation from the child's usual pattern, may be revelatory of the child's feeling toward his home or toward the particular person involved.

*Dora*, a child from a home which placed great importance on high standards, took a crayon product home to her mother on May 20, 1938. It was made up of controlled blue strokes that seemed to accord with the home expectancies of highly controlled behavior. Support for this interpretation was given a few days later (May 26, 1938), when Dora made two paintings: (*a*) a smeary product in green, orange, and blue, with green

[11] See pp. 38–40.                    [12] See pp. 60–63.

predominant in smeary strokes and many heavy verticals, the whole suggestive of assertive drives; (b) a second product in which blue predominated and was used to overlay green, in which circular strokes predominated, and in which the cleanliness of the final product was pronounced. Dora left the first painting at school and chose the second one to take home.

*Peter*, like *Dora*, took a clean blue painting home on February 6, 1939, and left a painting with contrasting treatment of blue and brown at school.

*Aldo* took home his first blue painting, which was also his first attempt at form.

*Jay* and *Rita* each tended to select those products with the highest form level to take home.

*Jill* took her cleanest product home (January 11, 1939), with the query, "Will Mother like it?"

*Archie* took his more multicolored, more warmly tinted products home to mother, suggesting a warmth of attachment to her that was not ordinarily revealed by him.

*Aileen* tended at specific times (October 12, 1937; January 4, 1938; January 6, 1938; May 9, 1938), when her relationship with her mother was happier than usual, to take home her less restricted paintings.

*Anita* took home her fullest paintings. These were made during periods of better home relationships.

*Elinor* took home those paintings that had content which she thought would please her mother, such as "Fairy Queen" and "Princess." She left at school those that she felt would displease her mother, such as "Boys and Girls Dancing."

Ordinarily all these children were disinterested in taking their work home. Each time they chose to do so, the product of their choice seemed significantly related to immediate home circumstances.

*Self-portraits.*—A fourth clue to interpretation of paintings was to be found in children's self-portraits. These paintings, whether in the form of striking abstractions or in the form of realistic portrayals of the child's feelings and drives, often have seemed to bring together in a single product the dynamics which were otherwise to be found only in a variety of sources.

Children's self-portraits are evidently made with the urge to express their inner feelings about themselves. They are not self-portraits in the ordinary sense of the term. Children are very likely to attach their names or some identifying symbol to these portrayals of self. They may print their initials; they may produce horizontal, wavy, scribbling lines which they say are their names; or they may ask the nearest adult to write their names on the products. It is as though the children felt the identity between the products and themselves. The desire to attach their names particularly to these products seems to spring spontaneously from the same emotional core as do the free associations previously described and as do the self-portraits to which they feel their names should be attached.

*Aileen*'s pedestaled effect and her "Crying eyes" are both meaningful and illustrative of self-portraits (see Pls. 1 and 9).

A painting which *Archie* produced on February 27, 1939, with a relatively huge head and overemphasized hair and teeth, seemed to be identified with his oft repeated wish to be ever so much bigger than he was. Emphasis on teeth seemed significant, as at that time Archie was, with relative frequency, attacking other children through biting. "Teeth" was also a recurrent response made by Archie in a later Rorschach test (Pl. 14).

*Ruth* frequently carried on fanciful play around "Susie," an imaginary character whose activities paralleled Ruth's or else represented things Ruth desired or had not yet attained, such as the opportunity to attend kindergarten regularly. "Susie's activities" as depicted on the painting page, as well as through verbalizations and pantomiming, were clearly representations of Ruth-as-she-felt and may be considered as another type of self-portrait.[13]

Sometimes a child's abstract reflection of a conflict going on within him gives such a clear-cut picture of the opposing forces that are known from other sources to be at work within him that the abstraction warrants the designation "self-portrait."

*Ronny*, with his differentiated use of drippy, dirty brown on one side of the painting page and clean blue on the other side, gave us a striking portrait of his conflicting drives to smear and to be clean.

*Rita*, through her left-right paintings, also portrayed her conflicting drives (see p. 29).

*Jocelyn*, in a product of May 8, 1939, in which red was sandwiched between vertical masses of blue, seemed to be reflecting her strong emotional drives, which were quite restricted by the conventional demands and expectancies that characterized her daily life. A painting made two years later, a recognizable self-portrait of a little girl in red, bounded on both sides by relatively large heavy masses of blue, lent weight to the interpretation and significance attached to the earlier painting.

*Ray* produced a picture suggestive of conflict on May 25, 1939—a picture with heavy, purple verticals on the left, yellow and red verticals on the right. He seemed to feel this was a self-representation, for he said: "It's about me."

As children reach the stage of recognizable representations, there no longer remains any doubt that many of their paintings are self-portraits. We have already described some of the parallels between the physical appearance or other identifying characteristics of the child and his painting products (pp. 7–9).

Children frequently reveal something of their feelings about other persons, as well as about themselves, in the abstract paintings to which they attach the name of another person.

*Richard* named a painting that consisted of a relatively small black and blue mass made up of short vertical and horizontal strokes "My daddy." He named a product "Mother" that consisted of yellow and orange masses spread over most of the page and heavily overlaid with blue.[14]

[13] Self-portraits in the feeling-about-self sense have also been suggested by products in other media; for instance, in blocks: Sandy clustered several blocks in a precariously balanced relationship on one very small block. This might well have been an abstract representation of her insecure, fanciful, unrealistic, poorly balanced orientation to life. Archie's continuous block-tower structures were a kind of projection of the towering self he wished to be.

[14] The impression that portraits such as these were meaningful has been substantiated by observation of the paintings of children outside of this study, e.g., Larry, approximately Richard's

*Betty*, on April 29, 1938, painted "Myself with Mommy." Mommy consisted of a dirty orange mass. Betty was represented by a larger blue mass. Betty's feelings at that period about her mother in counterdistinction to those about herself seemed to be reflected in this picture.

*Gloria*, in a crayon product of concentric circles, placed herself in the center, father on the outside, and mother in between. She quite omitted her brother. Her own known desire at that period to be in the center of things and her desire to leave her brother out of the family unit are suggested by this painting.

*Gilbert*, on November 22, 1938, produced a crayon product in which he represented himself as the center vertical in a series of verticals made to represent the rest of the family. The strokes which represented "Mommy" were filled in so that they lost much of their vertical effect (see Pl. 113).

### RELEASE AND THERAPY

Since this study was first undertaken, the quest in two areas has been continuous: (1) What can observation of children's painting and study of their paintings mean *to adults?* (2) What does the painting experience mean *to children?* Much more has undoubtedly been learned about the potential meaning for adults than for children. With a distinct sense of the limitations of our knowledge in this field, we should like to suggest some criteria for judging whether or not the painting experience is, or seems to be, providing release or therapy for children.

Before we can know with any degree of accuracy the extent of release or therapy that children may be gaining from their experience with easel paints, many more careful observations will be necessary. In any consideration of therapeutic and release possibilities, we must realize not only that painting serves different purposes for different individuals but that it may serve quite different purposes for the same individual at different times. Some suggested clues that we believe warrant further investigations follow.

*a*) Some children are so thoroughly restrained or repressed that they use easel paints (ordinarily a medium for free self-expression) much as they use crayons, viz., to reflect their obviously controlled thoughts and their overt behavior. Evidence of release, of therapy, or even clues to basic feelings are not to be found in their paintings. *Alan* (Pl. 65) in his constructive, nonrepresentative forms and *Louise* (Pl. 75) in her rigidly separated color masses seem illustrative of this way of painting.

*b*) There are other children who, like *Alan* and *Louise*, reflect their daily happenings and overt experiences in their easel paintings, but they differ from them in that they are children who are making wholesome adjustments. Their feelings and their conscious behavior patterns seem to be health-

---

age, on being asked to make drawings for Daddy and Mommy, produced crayon pictures almost like Richard's. Daddy's drawing consisted of elongated cylindrical forms done with dark blue crayons, and Mother's was made of orange and red circles with the remark, "I'll make Mommy's with a nice color." Both boys were evidently still in the stage of strong identification with their mothers.

ily integrated. Such children tend to represent their daily experiences in painting, and they usually reveal considerably more variety, in both the content and the techniques of their work, than do children like Alan and Louise.

*c*) There are some children who use easel paints as a means of expressing their personal needs and problems, but they seemingly get no basic release from doing so. In these cases the children may be so entirely absorbed in their problems that evidences of them are to be found in practically all other areas of expression, as well as in their painting. *Aileen* gave expression to her craving for adequate affection in her almost daily painting of isolated red masses. She reflected the same need in her withdrawn, unhappy behavior in the group, in her insistent self-centered demand for attention, and through her projection of herself into her block and clay projects. Apparently at times she obtained temporary release from all these activities, especially painting, but her basic problems remained unsolved. Her problems were probably so deep and hurtful that without adequate psychiatric help she could not clarify and face them and, through understanding, turn her energy into constructive action.

In contrast to children like these, who express their all-absorbing difficulties in almost all their activities, there are children like *Rita* who only with easel paints feel free enough to express their "base" desires. Rita was a model of control and cleanliness at the overt level, but that she had conflicting desires to smear seemed evident when one looked at her right-left painting pattern as well as at her smeared dots (Pls. 47–49).

Many children, like *Aileen* and *Rita*, expressed their conflicts through the painting medium. The painting experience for these children apparently never eventuated in clarification or real release. For them, painting could perhaps be compared to the adult experience of communicating troubles to a sympathetic listener. The act of expressing or communicating in such cases is likely to be useful in that it offers temporary easement, but of itself it cannot be considered basically therapeutic. This merely defines and in no way denies the value of painting for these children. For them, under these circumstances, painting offered temporary release. In cases such as Rita's, this may be all that is necessary. If there are observant adults about, the child's paintings and accompanying behavior, although not a solution, may well offer clues to guidance. (Such guidance may or may not be available within a school situation.)

*d*) For other children, easel painting is a more basically therapeutic experience. It is a medium which carries them from passive portrayal of their problems to active expression at the verbal level. Frequently these children then dramatize or in some other active form work out the new-found crystallization of their problem, and thereby their difficulties seem to be past. We have already seen how *Howard, Elaine, Angela,* and others first expressed their problems through abstract painting patterns; how they gradually came to verbalize about them; how, in time, they turned to more active projection of their problems through dramatic play; and how, once the level of verbal and overt action had been achieved, the problems seemed to be resolved. It is when easel painting leads to genuine release, as in these cases, that its therapeutic values may be very real.

Easel painting also seems to have genuine release or therapeutic value for children who find in it a medium for symbolic expression and use it as a means for sublimating feelings and concerns that are not permissible in more direct and overt form. When *Rita* painted over her precise blue pattern with smeary dabs of brown, for example (see Pl. 50), she was, no doubt, actively satisfying her desire not only to smear but also to react against the controlled behavior pattern exacted by her mother. The paints enabled her to express her resistance in a manner that was socially acceptable. In this definitely expressed negation of accepted standards she probably gained satisfaction and release to a greater degree than when she merely portrayed her conflicting drives in her sharply defined right-left presentations. We have also noted how *Glen* and *Margaret* (Pl. 75), though overtly withdrawn and submissive in their groups, symbolically expressed their aggressions at the easel. *Fredrika* (Pls. 56–59) and several other children, like Rita, found that they could use the easel to express and work out interests in smearing, in being dirty, in sex, and in elimination activities that were not permitted them in overt behavior.

We have outlined some clues by which we may be able to determine the effect of the easel-painting experience on a given child. We have suggested that the child's attitude toward the easel, his craving for the paints and easel, his long periods of work at it, his expression of satisfaction while painting,[15] might indicate that this medium may be meeting a real and felt need. Other perhaps more specific evidence on the value of the painting experience for a given child comes from comparing behavior while painting with behavior in other situations, particularly with behavior during free-play periods within a nursery-school group.

Differences either in kind of behavior, in emotional quality, or in quantity of expression, while in the situations outlined above, may offer clues to the meaning of the painting experience to the child. Release is suggested when the child behaves more freely during the painting situation than during other activities. Suggestive of greater freedom may be: more verbalizing; a more subjective or personal type of verbalization; more social interaction, such as initiating contacts or calling attention to self and to work; more

[15] See listing, p. 127.

laughter and expression of pleasure, such as "I feel like painting," "I'll never be through painting"; more open demonstrations of affection, of aggression, and/or of hostility.

It is likely to be impossible to judge the value of painting for the individual child without understanding and taking into account his previous or usual overt behavior pattern. What might indicate release for one child may very well indicate tension for another. A quiet, withdrawn child like *Ann*, for instance, who became more talkative and active while at clay and paints, seemed to be finding release in these situations. But the hypertense children, such as *George*, *Carol*, *Jessica*, and *Arline*, who became increasingly talkative and active while at painting and clay, seemed more often to be developing hypertensions than to be gaining release.

Also helpful in gaining clues as to the release value of the painting experience for the given child is a longitudinal study of his painting pattern. Progressively freer painting patterns, such as increased use of warm colors; wider use of space; less restricted lines and forms; evidence of increased freedom to dab and smear; to intermingle colors rather than to use them quite separately or to overlay them—all these changes in usage, especially when paralleled by freer verbalization and less restrained behavior while painting, suggest release value in the painting experience. Often such progressions in painting pattern do not require long spans of time. They may be observed as progressive changes from first to last paintings in a series made on a single day.

Reactions after painting may provide helpful clues for evaluating the effect of the painting experience on the child: *Jessica* tended to have happier social relationships and fewer conflicts following times spent at the easel; *Audrey* had noticeably calmer rest periods on days when rest followed a satisfying painting experience; *Loretta* and *Phyllis* became perceptibly more absorbed in dirt, clay, or finger-painting experiences when they followed painting periods. These and other indexes of freer and more relaxed behavior following painting would seem to indicate the releasing effect that frequently accrues from painting experiences.

The foregoing discussion, we believe, indicates that painting provides varying degrees of release and therapy for young children. As children develop and make the transition from impulsive toward reasoned behavior and as their interests turn outward, they increasingly depict their environment rather than their inner life. We should expect paintings of environment to be less of a release than paintings of one's emotions and inner life. This last statement is obviously a conjecture. It is our hope that further investigations will provide additional knowledge in the field of release and therapy through painting.

# CHAPTER VIII

## SOME EDUCATIONAL IMPLICATIONS

THIS study, we believe, has offered full and significant evidence that young children of the ages studied are basically driven, both from within and by external circumstances, in much the same way as are mature human beings. Among the children, pressures of hostility, anger, fear, jealousy, and love, and need for ego-preservation and ego-satisfaction, as well as need for dependence and independence, were frequently evidenced. These pressures turned into action were primary factors in the behavior patterns of the children studied. Actually, these same drives are commonly found among individuals of all ages everywhere. Integrated in a mobile sort of way, as they are in human beings, they constitute the core of personality, which in each individual is consistent, unique, and yet ever subject to modification by pressures both from within and from without.

That children feel the full force of these pressures is indicated in their behavior and in their choice and usage of materials. As we noted recurrent tensions and hostilities; as we observed children who felt isolated and unloved; and as we gathered evidence of their inner life from their paintings, block building, and dramatic play, we realized more keenly than ever that if the term "happy childhood" is used to convey the impression that childhood is an altogether happy, untroubled period, it presents a quite oversimplified and untrue picture.

One cannot study the lives or even the summarized biographies of one hundred and fifty unselected children without realizing that acute problems characterize the lives of young children just as they do the lives of adults. An alternating current of events brings happiness and unhappiness to daily living. All too frequently life is weighted in ways that make young children exceedingly unhappy. Many of their difficulties are probably unavoidable. They occur because of qualities inherent in human development and in our way of life. As our insights increase, we shall perhaps become less prone to attach blame either to adults or to children. We shall know that objective analysis rather than blame or guilt is in order and that such analysis will be far more effective in resolving difficulties.

It is toward objective analysis and subsequent guidance that this study leads us. Our findings indicate that certain problems occur with particular frequency between the ages of two and five. Because they were encountered so frequently in this study and because they are likely to be found wherever children are, we believe they warrant consideration at this point.

Foremost among these problems seems to be the conflict between the child's inner impulse to do as he wishes and the external demand on him for controlled behavior that implies conformance to the wishes and standards of others. Very frequently the child overtly conforms to the controlled pattern expected of him, but he continues to struggle inwardly with his suppressed desires to behave in socially unaccepted ways. Our day-by-day study of children suggests that the struggle between these opposing forces most often takes the form of a major conflict because concerned adults tend to push the developmental process. Parents generally are likely to be over-anxious to have children educated and advanced along physical, social, and intellectual lines.

A second difficulty that was quite frequent among the children studied was apparently brought into focus by the ordinary developmental changes that occur between two and five years of age. In one form or another many children indicated their ambivalent desires to be assertive in one situation and submissive in another. This conflict often can be specifically identified as we watch children cling or revert to infantile dependent roles, while at the same time they are resistant toward authority and are striking out with great self-assertiveness.

Sibling relationships and the arrival and absorbing of a new baby into the family often seem to ignite assertive-submissive conflicts. On the occasion of the coming of a new baby and of his taking his place in the family, the older child wishes to keep the infantile role in which the new baby has supplanted him, while at the same time he wants and is being urged to "grow up now that he's the big brother or sister." The assertive-submissive conflict also appeared many times when children were ambivalent in their feeling about their sex role.

The conflicts outlined above, although likely to be sharp and troublesome when they occur, can, as a rule, be guided into constructive outlets more readily than can a third difficulty, which we wish particularly to cite because it carries with it very dire potentialities for character deformation.

A number of children were basically disturbed and their development was both blocked and distorted because they felt unloved and rejected by their parents. Our records indicate that children were likely to feel unloved, insecure, and unaccepted not only when they were actually rejected but when parents were overcritical and had too high standards in such matters as elimination control, social behavior, and general expectancies. Acceptance, approval, and affection, on the other hand, were obvious assets among children who were adjusting and developing in wholesome fashion. A fact well known but not sufficiently taken into account is that the child's love or hostility for the adults who care for him during his first years directs—or misdirects—the stream of his emotions. Although this occurs, as a rule, before the child becomes a part of group life, the pattern of his affectional life is likely still to be in a formative stage when he enters his first group. Accordingly, a school for young children has a particularly important function. Observing and sensitive staff members can note whether or not a youngster feels loved and loving or rejected and resentful. Not only can good educators of young children be sensitive to what is happening and guide school programs in terms of the child's needs, but they often can be extremely helpful to parents who are more likely to be flexible and eager for help when the children are young than at later periods.

This study has revealed that just as urgent as is the child's need to receive affection is his need to express affection and all other emotions—especially those that are disturbing him.

The need for release and the release values of the various media studied have been so fully discussed in other sections of this work that we shall only allude in passing to the fact that each one of the materials seems to be particularly suitable under certain circumstances and/or for certain children. For children whose emotional surge is still unchanneled and largely undefined, easel paints seemed to be a particularly good medium. For the same and other children, when their feelings were ready to be projected more clearly and directly, blocks, crayons, and dramatic play often had specific values. Some children found more satisfaction in blocks than they apparently ever found in easel paints—and the reverse was true. For children trying to clarify elimination and certain other problems, paints and clay were of particular value. Crayons at around five years were much used by children ready and anxious to communicate ideas to other people. Although the above media were the only ones studied in detail, many other materials, such as dolls, representative family figurines, animals, tea-party materials, and a variety of equipment for water play are known to offer excellent opportunities for enriching and releasing experiences.

In the course of this study we became ever more mindful of the fact not only that children reveal themselves, their problems, and their needs in their choice and usage of materials but that, to sensitive eyes and ears, they reveal themselves in practically every aspect of their behavior. Observation of voices, choice of words, posture, and way of walking, to name but a few behavior manifestations which we ordinarily pass by without consideration, can, if thoughtfully analyzed, contribute to adult understanding of children and of their immediate and long-time needs. As has been previously stated, the nursery-school years lend themselves particularly to this type of observation because the children are full of drives and emotions which they are constantly and unself-consciously expressing.

In the process of offering various materials to children, special consideration should be given to the question of when, how, and how much direct stimulation is desirable.

Before considering these questions, we wish to call to mind the fact that the emotional climate in which materials are offered must be healthy and conducive to usage if children are to express themselves freely and use creative media as meaningful outlets. Schools have certain advantages over most homes because other children engaged in like pursuits offer natural stimulus and because it is, as a rule, easier for teachers than for parents to maintain a friendly interest without trespassing on the inner life of the child. Parents and schools alike can be richly helpful in a variety of ways. They can offer sturdy, thoughtfully selected materials. They can try to provide sufficient space, uninterrupted opportunity for experimentation, and a sympathetic (but not obtrusive) interest in what the child is doing. As far as possible, acceptance of the form of the child's activity as well as of the product is essential if the child is to be helped to develop his own creative quality. Because adult standards and ability are very high as compared to children's, adults are often tempted to show the child how to improve his way of doing things. They want to show the child how to make the engine or airplane really look more like an engine or an airplane. As previously indicated, although giving the child patterns may improve his form, it is likely to paralyze his creative impulses. His erstwhile impulse to explore and experiment will too often be replaced by "You show me how to paint [or it may be 'build a house,' or 'model'], I don't know how to do it." One cannot reiterate too often that an adult-given push toward true pictorial or representative form often gives satisfaction to adults, but the child's creative quality may be lessened or lost in the process. As has been observed throughout this study, when children turn toward creative media to express feelings, concerns, and anxieties which ordinarily are not permissible in more overt form, it is particularly important that they feel quite uninhibited in action and accompanying speech. Suggestions for change of content or technique are likely to stifle the impulse for self-expression.

Perrine[1] and Dixon[2] both offer stimulating material to adults wishing to nourish creative expression among children. Dixon suggests that techniques should be introduced not when we see the need, but when the child shows he feels the need. Let the child experiment widely before giving ready built forms, but don't withhold knowledge of skills and of techniques with materials. Let experience take the form of expression, not *how* to express self. "It is not art forms that we are after but art experiencing."

[1] Van Dearing Perrine, *Let the Child Draw* (New York: F. A. Stokes & Co., 1936).

[2] C. Madeleine Dixon, *High, Wide, and Deep* (New York: John Day Co., 1938), p. 137.

Dixon suggests that "at four or whenever we give children art materials they have a right to a few incisive rules about the handling of them, techniques that will keep them from mechanical defeat in expressing some clearer idea."[3] She suggests, as an example of helpful techniques, "indicating the amount of water on the paint brush that will work best and showing the child how to keep the water in which brushes are washed from getting muddy." She adds: "If a child is not ready for it, your ideas just will not take. Also if he is sold to some idea of his own he lends you only deaf ears." Up to a certain point we concur with Dixon on this matter. When presenting the materials or after allowing the child full opportunity to explore their usage, such suggestions as these can be followed to advantage.

But Dixon is obviously speaking of four-year-olds or older children. She is discussing the expression of *ideas* and not the vague generalized expressions of children whose feelings are unbounded by ideational content of the sort with which this study has largely dealt. A highly sensitive child quite absorbed by his emotional problems may feel the need to paint drippy pictures. Any suggestion about using his brush and paint to better advantage would be likely to frustrate his efforts and to diminish the value that the painting experience might otherwise have.

In connection with the introduction of techniques, the question is often raised as to the extent to which children should be encouraged to verbalize about their work. If the adult is truly objective and not unduly concerned, sometimes a casual remark such as "Do you want to tell about your painting?" indicates friendly interest and gives the child an opportunity to express himself verbally. He may or may not wish to do so. He may say: "This is no good" or "I want to take it home" or "I want to paint all day"; or he may not answer. As previously indicated, any one of these responses may be meaningful. The adult in learning to accept and understand rejoinders such as these will gain greatly in his understanding of the child.

What, then, shall be our criteria for determining when a child is being hampered for lack of techniques? Interest in children and sensitivity to their changing and developing needs will probably be our soundest guide. For more specific suggestions, we again refer our readers to Perrine and Dixon. Both of them offer inspiration and help through their published works. While certain implications came out clearly in our findings, specific suggestions beyond those already given were not among them.

Our findings, however, did continuously impress us with the uniqueness and the complex quality of every human being. Because, above all, we respect that individuality, we urge that the deductions and generalizations presented be used with great care and perception. The variation of purport in our findings is as infinite as is the variation within human beings.

[3] *Ibid.*, pp. 197–204.

# BIOGRAPHICAL SUMMARIES

T HE descriptions of individual children here given summarize the most pronounced and the most consistent tendencies of each child with special reference to those factors that pertain to this study: the child's place in the family and in school, along with his use of the creative media. Each aspect is telling in relationship to the total concept of the child and his work.

The reader will find that many of these summaries indicate constellations of traits which are reported and described in other parts of the study. As we have worked with the material over a period of years, insight and understanding have continued to develop. Nevertheless, in a number of summaries, a coherent picture is still lacking. In studying the material the reader may gain clues to relationships that we have not seen. We again wish to call attention to the fact that this study was done within the limits of an educational and not a psychiatric framework.

## AILEEN

*B.D.:*[1] *5-20-34    I.Q.: 115, Stanford (L)    A.D.A.:*[2] *3 years, 5 months, to 5 years, 1 month (obs. 2 years)*

A sad, dejected-looking little girl, with deep-set brown eyes, straight blond hair, and slender build. Aileen was an only child, whose parents had been divorced and had remarried other people. She alternated between the parents' homes and the home of a grandmother. In none of these homes did she find adequate and consistent affection.[3] Her father had two foster-children by his second wife. Her mother was interested in a career. Her grandmother was suffering from despondency and an incurable illness.

At school Aileen's feelings were easily hurt, and she was inclined at such times to' withdraw, cry, sulk, and suck the third and fourth fingers of her left hand. A typical observation: "Aileen became upset and had a tantrum

[1] B.D. (birth dates) are given so that the reader may, if he wishes, determine exact age of any child at the time of specific observations by comparing date of observation with date of birth.

[2] A.D.A. (age during attendance) represents age from time of first to time of last nursery-school observation. Dates given do not include follow-up material later obtained on many of the children.

[3] It is very difficult for children who come from broken homes to feel as though they are getting enough affection. "The sum of the whole [where parents are together] is greater than the parts." Children from broken homes some for a time, and some always, remain affectionally unsatisfied.

167

when it was time to give up the sled. She wandered around alone. She went inside to take off her wraps. She started to cry. She began to push other children away from her. She said she did not like them and did not want to come to school any more. She screamed and yelled until she finally was isolated. She somewhat later returned to the group, still sobbing and unhappy. For awhile she played alone in the doll corner. Then she went to the easel and painted 'A House.' " Aileen increasingly sought other children during her two years in nursery school. Her attitude toward children tended to be dictatorial, superior, condescending, and at times ingratiating. From adults she sought much attention and affection. Aileen found a real outlet through use of creative media: easel painting was her preferred medium when first observed; dramatic play was her greatest interest during the second year; clay was another favorite; and she especially enjoyed music. She was strongly attached to her pets and literally loved three of them to death. During her use of materials Aileen showed marked fluctuations in mood. Sometimes she worked with great intensity and absorption, at other times she appeared flighty and more interested in happenings around her. She actively sought materials and was inclined to hold on to them after her apparent use for them was past. She objected violently to anything she considered interference, whether by children or by adults, and usually resorted to tears or wails or both. Aileen's most recurrent painting pattern was an ovular red mass, often identified verbally as "House." In dramatic play Aileen focused on household activities, especially those involving eating and entertaining. Enclosures characterized her fanciful block structures. Her crayon and clay products reflected the interests shown in other media but were relatively more varied.

## ALAN

*B.D.: 4-25-34     I.Q.: 116     A.D.A.: 3 years, 6 months, to 5 years, 2 months (obs. 2 years)*

An attractive boy, with delicate features and an appealing smile, which was too rarely seen. Alan's parents had been divorced, and he lived with his mother and foster-father. A baby sister was born into this home during the summer of the second year of observation. The school staff felt that both the mother and the foster-father attempted to be "too kind and sweet" in their handling of Alan. They lacked firmness and attempted to hide any unpleasant feelings, even those natural to all human beings. Actually, the mother was easily annoyed and upset by Alan, who reminded her, in disposition, she said, of her first husband. Alan's own father kept in close contact with Alan.

At school Alan gave the impression of being inhibited in movement and in his manner of speaking. He was extremely upset by change, any deviation from the regular school program causing frustration, confusion, and crying. His mother reported similar behavior at home when any change occurred, as, for example, when the furniture was rearranged. During the first year of observation Alan made no contacts with others. When children approached him, they usually interfered with his activity, with the result that he became upset and gave way to loud crying. In the second year Alan occasionally joined others, especially in block constructions, or he permitted them to join him. He could be extremely thoughtful, sympathetic, and kind upon occasion. He tended to be quite verbal and a perfectionist in his use of materials. During the first year at school Alan's major interests were the crayons and the tricycle. In the second year he began with a strong interest in blocks and developed an interest in easel painting. Alan began to paint during the second year, following controlled observation during which he had an opportunity to use the easel alone in a room with the psychologist. His paintings tended to be characterized by full-page effects, usually painted with cold colors, green especially predominating. Later, his work was dirty, heavy, and wet. Often structuralized forms could be detected underlying the full-page mass. Frequently, cold colors were seen to overlay warm-colored strokes. Alan used crayons much less the second year than the first; but when he did so, the cold-colored, structuralized pattern which had characterized his first year's work still persisted.

Alan used clay the second year, as he had the first. It was an apparent release for verbal and social behavior. He seemed much more interested in the setting which the clay table provided than in the medium itself. Blocks were Alan's greatest interest during the second year of school. His products were characterized by a widely extended solid block base, unlike the structures of any other child; and one or more tall towers usually appeared somewhere in his structure. He often engaged in dramatic locomotor play around these structures but did not engage in dramatic play with others, which required him to take a role himself.

## ANDY

*B.D.:* 3-14-35    *I.Q.:* 98, *ambidextrous (follow-up shows this was not a full measure of his ability)    A.D.A.:* 3 *years,* 1 *month, to* 4 *years,* 3 *months (obs.* 2 *years)*

An attractive, dark-haired boy, with a sunny smile and happy disposition. Andy had an older sister, who was very possessive with him. His contacts with his father were few and superficial. His mother felt helpless in her handling of Andy, was unfriendly, often cruel, in her attitude toward him, and gave other signs of rejecting him. She resented giving up her personal freedom and personal good times for her home life. She was tense and characteristically functioned at a superficial level. She reported home problems with Andy which included night terrors and running away.

At school Andy was overactive, scattered, and distractible in play. His greatest interest was in the locomotor toys and in parallel play activities. He also liked mud and sand play. Whenever the opportunity presented itself, he ran away from the schoolroom or playground. During the first year of observation Andy's paintings were characterized by all-directional lines scattered over and off the painting page. He mixed colors indiscriminately, with results which suggested a tangled mass of varicolored yarns. During the second year he spent more time at the easel and ended with smeary masses spread over the page, usually made up of diagonal and circular swing scribbling and with colors indiscriminately mixed. The only suggestions of a symbolic pattern were recurrent appearances of yellow overlaid with blue. He smeared his most constructive paintings. Circular stroking became pronounced during the second year. His attention was distributive, and he carried on much social interplay while painting. Both years his interest seemed more in the motor activity and manipulative exploration of the material than in constructive work. Naming of products seldom occurred and then was clearly secondary. Andy seemed to like the feel of the clay, and, as with paints, he functioned largely at a manipulative stage. His most frequent product in this medium he called "cakes." These he sometimes embellished with candles to represent "birthday cakes," and he would then pretend, or at times actually try, to eat the clay. Andy showed little interest in blocks and in crayons. His dramatic play was chiefly of the locomotor type. Here he usually assumed the role of engineer. He frequently pulled the chairs together and used them for his train. His rare moments in the doll corner were, as a rule, spent playing with the tea table and doll dishes in dramatizations of eating situations.

All-directional work, 81, 109, Pl. 94    Indiscriminate mixing, 47
Color-mass technique, 16    Paint all over page, 89
Easel painting preference, 121    Paint beyond page, 88

[*Continued on next page*]

## ANGELA

*B.D.: 10-25-34    I.Q.: 141    A.D.A.: 3 years, 0 month, to 4 years, 8 months*
*(obs. 2 years)*

A long-legged, tall child, with blond pigtails and a "lantern" jaw, which during the period of observation was being corrected with braces. Angela was an only child whose parents took great pride in her high ability and intelligence. The family standards resulted for Angela in tensions and inner conflicts, which, after some difficulty, she apparently managed to resolve within herself. During the course of observation, Angela's mother had three miscarriages. Angela knew of the expected baby in each instance and showed changed patterns of behavior both during the months when the baby was expected and after it miscarried.

At school Angela was an outstanding leader. On entrance she showed a bossy, dominating, highly critical attitude toward others but was sought by them in spite of this because of her good ideas for play. During the years of observation she became less bossy, more constructive as a leader, and increasingly popular in her group. During both years of observation there were periods, however, when she was extremely tense and high-strung and did not play well with others. Angela liked all the creative media, especially dramatic play, blocks, and paints. In Angela's dramatic play household activities centering around sleeping and being sick were most recurrent. Sometimes Angela played the baby role, sometimes she chose a doll or child for baby and was herself the mother. In a few instances she played "Bad Mother" and "Old Witch." In her most upset times Angela gave up very active dramatic play and went around carrying a doll wrapped in a blanket. Her interest in blocks always led to dramatic play. Sometimes she built houses which she could use herself, at other times she built small replicas which were used in play with miniature toys (Pl. 28). Angela enjoyed the clay at school and used it to make many recognizable and varied products. She also enjoyed the social stimulation at the clay table. "Snowmen," "beds," and "baskets" were her most frequent clay objects. In her easel paintings one can catch a remarkably continuous picture of Angela's changes in feeling in relation to events at home. Full-page masses, with black partially overlaying red, yellow, and orange, recurred during each upset period. Structuralized and varied representative paintings appeared in happier moments. During the two years of observation Angela came to express her emotional problems in representative and verbal terms, as well as in the symbolic mass effects. In Angela's case a striking parallelism between her painting and her crayoning patterns existed (Pls. 22–23).

## ANITA

*B.D.: 5-24-35    I.Q.: 118–29 (tested one year apart)    A.D.A.: 2 years, 11 months, to 4 years, 1 month*

A large, outgoing girl, with blond hair, plump face, and a "peaches-and-cream" complexion. Anita was the older of two children, her brother having been born the summer preceding the beginning observation of Anita in the nursery school. Anita's mother reported herself at a loss as to how to deal with her daughter. She was upset by Anita's large physique and attempted to compensate for it by selecting undersized clothes for the child and by enforcing a diet. Around the time of enrolment, the mother reported a long list of destructive activities which Anita was carrying on at home, such as smearing the walls and furniture with lipstick and breaking her father's watch. She also reported an unusual series of self-injuries: Anita had cut her head in a fall from the davenport, had been hit by an automobile while on a walk, had swallowed the baby's nipple, had upset scalding water on her head, had pushed gum up her nose, had run through a window glass. The mother at this time obviously rejected her daughter.

When she first entered school, Anita was aggressive and bossy. She was much more aware of people than of materials. Children did not seem to care for her, and she had no special friends. She made many friendly advances to adults and sought their attention. During the first year in school Anita showed little interest in materials, and, when she used them, it was at a relatively low, manipulative level. Music was her strongest interest outside of personal contacts. With paints she at first made scattered, all-directional strokes, with colors indiscriminately mixed into multicolored effects. She sometimes worked off, as well as on, the painting page. Sometimes she seemed to "dirty" the page with but a few dry strokes. During the second year in school she painted with more absorption and did full-page work, often in brown and black. During one period of heavy smearing with red she renewed her earlier destructive and hostile behavior at home. Anita seemed to like the social interplay which the clay situation provided and to get enjoyment from the violent pounding of her clay. Blocks held no interest for Anita until the end of her second year in nursery school. Then she began to build tiny enclosures, platforms, and towers and to show particular interest in balancing the blocks. Her work at that time was comparable to that usually observed in a child a year or more younger than she was at that time. Anita took a dominant role in dramatic play. Usually she made herself the mother and lavished her attention and care upon a doll.

## ANN

*B.D.: 7-4-34     I.Q.: 118 (no response to test 1st year; only partial rapport 2d year)*
*A.D.A.: 3 years, 3 months, to 4 years, 11 months (obs. 2 years)*

On entrance, Ann was a chubby little girl who was frequently observed in a withdrawn position from the rest of the group. At such times her facial expression was likely to be sullen and her eyes downcast. Ann was an adopted child. An adopted foster-brother, two years older than herself, had been the family's major concern during Ann's infancy because of his retarded development. Thyroid injections had been begun with him at the time that Ann was beginning to talk and had produced excellent results in speeding his development and adjustment. At the time of her entrance into nursery school the parents reported that Ann had always refused to talk in the presence of anyone not belonging to the immediate family circle. However, she spoke with facility at home when she chose to do so. Ann's mother returned to her professional work as soon as she had enrolled Ann in nursery school. She was reticent in discussing her relationship with the children, and the dynamics of the family relationships were never actually determined.

At school Ann made no verbal responses, nor did she initiate any activities until the spring of her first year in the group. This was more than six months after entrance. When directed into use of any material by an adult —as, for example, use of the swing, the tricycle, or the crayons, which adults selected because of the interested glances Ann cast in their direction—she would cling to these activities day after day until once again she was led into another activity. Her earliest crayonings were either abstract structured patterns or cold-colored, restricted, circular forms in which yellow was smeared over (as though to overlay) with colder colors. Ann avoided other children until the spring of her first year at school, when she made her "debut" with sudden aggressions, such as kicking others or snatching and throwing their hats about. She began to talk at the same time, and her first verbalizations were such negations as "No," "Good-bye," "You dumb sing."

In her second year at school Ann reverted to a considerable extent to her earlier withdrawing, repressed behavior. Her few contacts took the form of attacks on others. Her contacts with adults were attempts to get attention through negative behavior. She did talk occasionally, however, and initiated a few activities—an advance over the extreme repression evidenced in her earliest months at nursery school.

Ann's first paintings were made in the weeks just preceding and accompanying her aggressive outbursts at school. They were characterized by a strongly persistent theme: a well-defined, usually tight mass of yellow was overlaid with blue and with green. This same theme persisted in her crayon drawings. Her last painting of the year was the only one that did not show the overlaid technique. It was a wide mass of yellow, quite clear and unsmeared. She became increasingly aggressive after this work. In her second year at nursery school Ann seemed freer in her use of easel paints. Full-page masses in dirty color effects, particularly in brown, were produced. She ·went through a lapse in bowel control during the period in which she painted most intently. In contrast to her easel painting in her second year in nursery school, Ann was apt to use crayons in highly structuralized, nonrepresentative designs. Her characteristic pattern was to make a frame and work within its boundaries. Ann seemed happiest when using clay. She pounded her clay violently and smiled frequently while using it. Twice she wet herself at the clay table. She carried on some social interplay, including grabbing and giving of clay.

During her first year in school Ann showed no interest in blocks except to destroy others' products. The second year she built compact inclosures or piled blocks. She was observed sometimes to build while pretending to put blocks away. She used miniature figures and decorative effects on her tiny, compact block structures. Ann engaged in no dramatic play, with the exception of imitating others in the role of a dog and a goat (Pls. 50–54).

## ARCHIE

*B.D.: 10-28-34    I.Q.: 117    A.D.A. 3 years, 3 months, to 4 years, 8 months (obs. 2 years)*

Archie, conspicuous for his unusually small stature, was a serious, intent, bespectacled little fellow. Archie was the youngest of four children; there were eight years between him and the next-youngest sibling. The family placed a premium on grown-up behavior, and at home Archie vied with his two older brothers.

At school Archie's dominating drive, often expressed verbally, was to be big, to be a man. He stressed strength, height, power, and the masculine role in all his activities. Archie was independent of adults. With children he displayed a ruthless drive for power. He dominated, attacked, and bit others to get his way. Archie showed a strong interest in creative materials and in locomotor activities. He liked to be the engineer in locomotor play or the father in household play. With blocks he built high towers, often using blocks or a chair to make a taller structure than was otherwise possible. He used clay to make varied and recognizable products. The names he gave his products showed consistent masculine symbolism. Archie did relatively little painting; but when he painted, his products were characterized by vertical strokes, emphasis on the top of the page, and choice of cold colors. During one period he showed a tendency to overlay with black. The names he gave his products suggested height, for example, "Sky," "Star with a String." In his crayon products, where cold colors also prevailed, he progressed from heavy smearing to recognizable forms.

Avoidance of warm colors, 16

Block interest, 134

Crayon interest, 131

Parallels, 150, 151; between painting and block work, 135, Pls. 15–17; between painting and clay, 139; between painting and dramatic play, 141

Self-portrait, 156, Pl. 14

Tendency toward: differential right-left work, 70; emphasis at top of page, 92, Pl. 15

Use of: black, 37–38; green, 36; heavy strokes, 80; red, 19, 21; verticals, 59

Other references, 13, 90, 128, 155, Pl. 111

## BEE

*B.D.: 7-10-33    I.Q.: 132 (Minn.)    A.D.A.: 4 years, 3 months, to 4 years, 11 months*

A dark-haired girl, with bangs and a particularly sweet smile. She was very timid and shy. Frequently she showed physical pallor and had cold hands. Bee was the middle child in a family of three girls. The entire family was reserved and sensitive. The mother, an intelligent, effective person, had had professional training. She was a perfectionist and did most of the planning for the girl. She described Bee as having a "stubborn streak" but as being "extremely generous, thoroughly honest, and very independent."

Bee tended to watch but to avoid other children. Shortly before the close of the school year, a neighbor (boy) was enrolled in school, and thereafter Bee followed him in activies of a boyish, constructive type (especially block building; follow-up studies also show a preference for boyish play, with boys). Bee displayed a strong will and was frequently negativistic with adults. At other times she sought adult attention and went to adults with criticism of others. Bee's preference at school was for the creative-play materials, especially the easel paints. Her earliest paintings were characterized by full-page masses of vertical strokes and heavy, warm colors. These were followed by a period of amazing designs (suitable for wallpaper or cloth patterns). In contrast to her paintings, when working with crayons Bee attempted recognizable representations with dainty strokes and pastel colors. She did not engage in active dramatic play. At clay she found satisfaction in the social situation.

## BENJY

*B.D.: 1-4-34    I.Q.: 115 (Minn.)    A.D.A.: 4 years, 2 months, to 4 years, 6 months*

An attractive boy, with brown eyes and curly brown hair. Benjy was an only child, whose mother was overattentive and held standards which were much too high. At the time of his enrolment, she listed eating problems, fears, negativism, whining, crying, dawdling, dependence, attention-seeking, grabbing, and a host of other problems, as prevalent in the home.

When he first came to school, Benjy was very quiet and shy, although obviously alert and observant. He played alone or with one other child, an older girl whom he followed. His speech was indistinct. In a few months Benjy's behavior had changed to the opposite extreme. He became aggressive, hitting and punching others. He defended himself firmly and was proud and satisfied when he won a battle. Benjy preferred the creative materials, especially blocks. He was also much interested in the story periods. With easel paints he progressed from small filled forms to widespread interrelated forms which were not filled. His crayon work paralleled his easel painting. He displayed no interest in clay and initiated no dramatic play.

## BETTY

*B.D.: 12-13-33    I.Q.: 126 (Minn.)    A.D.A.: 3 years, 10 months, to 4 years, 6 months*

A dainty, delicate child, with long curls and blond complexion. She was obviously aware of and impressed with her own feminine charms. Betty was an adopted child who lived with foster-mother, foster-father, nurse, and two aunts. She was "made over" by all the members of the family. She had been strictly schooled in the social amenities of "Please" and "Thank you," but her basic habit training was spotty and inconsistent. Her mother described her as temperamental, obstinate, and hard to manage.

At school Betty was, at first, shy, talked little and frequently played alone. Gradually she began to play with a few selected friends, whom she tended to follow. Her attitude toward other children seemed sympathetic, friendly, and affectionate. With adults she easily became self-conscious and hung her head. Betty seemed to prefer the creative materials, especially the easel, clay, and dramatic play. At the easel Betty's characteristic pattern, at first, consisted of dotted designs primarily in green with a recurrent circular design. At the time of her nurse's dismissal she reverted to heavy mass techniques. Following a trip to Florida, she began a period of constructive blue painting, followed by a period of overlaying blue on green. Betty's crayon products differed from her paintings in their higher form level. Attempts to make alphabet letters were recurrent in her crayon products. She seemed most outgoing and free at the clay table. Here she reacted happily with other children. Recurrent names for her clay products were "Snake" and "Tiger." Although Betty frequently took part in dramatic play, she always seemed to accept a role as follower. No strong individual theme appeared in this medium. Blocks did not seem to have any appeal for her, and no prevailing pattern was apparent in this medium.

## BRIAN

*B.D.: 1-18-34    I.Q.: 117 (Minn.)    A.D.A.: 3 years, 9 months, to 4 years, 5 months*

A slender boy, with blond hair, whose face usually wore an expression of daydreaming. At home Brian was surrounded by feminine influences: his mother, the servants, two older sisters, and girls who were neighbors. At this time Brian's father was away from home on business for long intervals. Brian's mother and her relatives were gifted artistically, and all the children were very highly stimulated, probably beyond their years.

At school Brian sought the girls in play, particularly one of the neighbors who also attended nursery school. With these children he engaged in dramatic activities in which he would take a feminine role. Sometimes a self-assigned female role would absorb him for days at a time, and he would answer to no other name than the one he assumed in play. In keeping with his dramatic leanings, he was interested in impressing adults. Brian's keen imagination and verbal interests carried him along in play. He had apparently no need for, or interest in, concrete materials. Of the research materials, he used paints most, but he produced only thirteen products during the school year. Brian's paintings were smeary and dirty. He alternated between use of warm and cold colors. Tendencies to differentiate treatment of verticals and circles (see references below) suggest conflict. His only recognizable representation was a human figure with several legs dangling from the left side (Pl. 2). (Brian had a deviate left foot and was wearing a corrective shoe.) He used crayons only one day during the year. On that day Brian made three products, all very clean and in somber black, brown, and purple. At clay and blocks Brian's interest was always in the social situation rather than in the medium which he was using.

Differential use of circles and verticals, 69, 72    Use of: green, 36; purple, 42
Self-portrait, 7, Pl. 2                              Other references, 74
Tendency to: alternate color periods, 49; make
    dirty paintings, 84

## CHARLOTTE

*B.D.: 11-8-31    Mental test: subnormal level    A.D.A.: 5 years, 11 months, to 6 years, 3 months*

A small, thin child, with medium coloring, vacant expression, and listless attitude. Charlotte was an only child. Her parents had been concerned, from her birth, about her mentality. They were especially sensitive, because a cousin of Charlotte's age possessed superior intelligence and was often compared with Charlotte by the relatives.

Charlotte tested at a subnormal level. Her large and small co-ordinations were very poor. She was listless, tended to stay near adults, and passively to watch others. When children did play with her, they usually assumed a protective, mothering attitude, and she passively accepted their attentions. Her only spontaneous interests at school were in the easel paints and in the group story and music periods. Charlotte's paintings were characterized by an almost stereotyped pattern of short, vertical strokes done in pallid colors with no seeming vitality. There were perhaps four or five such lines scattered sparsely across a given painting page (Pl. 107). Her crayon products were also characterized by short and sparse strokes, but here the direction was apt to be horizontal rather than vertical (difference due to [a] standing at easel for painting and [b] sitting at table for crayoning). Blocks, clay, and dramatic-play materials seemed to occupy no place in Charlotte's sphere of interests.

Preference for paints and crayons, 121        Short, broken, scattered strokes, 108, Pl. 107

## DANNY

*B.D.: 5-1-33    I.Q.: 112 (left-handed)    A.D.A.: 4 years, 6 months, to 5 years, 2 months*

A blue-eyed, light-haired boy of slender build, who frequently wore an expression of sullenness and defiance. Danny was the youngest of three boys, while a fourth child was expected in the summer. Danny's mother reported continual competition among the brothers at home.

Danny had many difficulties with other children at school. His general attitude toward children was one of competition and rivalry. He was inclined to harbor resentment, and he showed a very determined will. He was easily upset at changes and fussy over details. He resisted most routines, especially those connected with the toilet, including bowel training. He said once, in reference to sitting on the toilet, "Only girls do that." Danny liked music and most of the creative materials, particularly the finger paints, clay, and easel paints. He did not take part in dramatic play. At clay Danny rolled snakes and was verbally competitive with the other children at the clay table. With blocks he built enclosures for himself and resisted interference. In both easel painting and crayoning, Danny produced brown smeary masses while resistant to bowel training and turned to clean, constructive patterns in blue and varied colors after his conflict over bowel control had been resolved.

Balanced use of colors, 49
Parallels in painting and crayoning, 133

Use of: blue and brown paralleling cleanliness conflict, 28, 41, Pls. 43–46; verticals, 58–59
Other references, 128, 146

## EDWARD

*B.D.: 4-8-34    I.Q.: 127    A.D.A.: 3 years, 6 months, to 4 years, 10 months
Left early in second year*

A large-boned, well-proportioned boy, with a pallid complexion which was in striking contrast to his dark hair and eyes. Edward was an only child. His parents and grandparents stimulated him toward intellectual attainment that was far above his readiness, for example, the recitation of poetry. Edward's mother expected a baby at the end of the first year of observation, and the family openly hoped for a girl. (A brother arrived during the summer.)

In school Edward was a preoccupied, anxious-appearing child, tense and excitable. He carried on long monologues, colored with such sayings as "Don't put your face up by the window, the glass might cut you, the glass might cut you" or "You mustn't hurt the guinea pigs; you mustn't say 'Boo,' it would scare them." At first Edward avoided contacts with other children. He sought adults, asking them many questions and attempting to draw their attention, often at rest time. Toward the end of the first year Edward sought the less assertive children, with whom he engaged in silly play. Erwin was one chosen companion, and with Erwin he pantomined sex and elimination activities. He frequently identified himself with the feminine as well as the masculine roles. Once he protruded his abdomen, saying, "Baby in here."

The second year of observation, Edward came to school a more assertive boy. He now rejected feminine roles and took the father or big-man part in dramatic play. Crayons were the earliest creative materials used by Edward. With them he at first drew circles or paired ovular forms. He carried on a monologue suggestive of many fears while at the crayon table. At this time Edward showed persistent use of both verticals and ovals in easel painting. Two rare products revealed his ability to make recognizable human representations, though he characteristically functioned at a much lower level, often with color-mass techniques. He used much blue and said that this was his favorite color. During the first year of observation Edward refused, at first, to touch the clay or finger paints. Later he threw himself wholeheartedly into their use and seemed to get intense satisfaction from the smearing which he did with these media. With blocks Edward tended to build towers, which he destroyed, or bridges or enclosures when alone. With others he built roads for locomotor play. Edward's dramatic play is suggested by comments given above. Usually the play involving feminine or masculine roles did not go much beyond the designation of roles. Edward spent much time in fantasy rather than in overt dramatic play. During the second year of school he went through a stage of great interest in being a repair man. Edward was transferred to kindergarten after only a few months of his second year of attendance in nursery school. He had used paints and crayons little before his transfer, spending most of his time in more active play. The few paintings and crayon products made were characterized by warm colors, attempts at writing and at representation, and by an absence of circular forms.

## ELAINE

*B.D.: 3-22-34     I.Q.: 112     A.D.A.: 3 years, 10 months, to 4 years, 3 months*

A sturdily built girl, with blond coloring, who often came to school in colorful peasant costumes. Elaine was an only child. The mother expected a baby in the summer, however, and spent much time in bed to forestall a miscarriage, which was feared because of a fall. Elaine was excluded from her mother's room during these days in bed. Elaine spoke two foreign languages, and her mother attempted to continue these by speaking to Elaine only in German and by asking the governess, who had returned with them from an extended trip abroad, to speak to her only in French. Elaine's father was highly intellectual. Her mother was ambitious and had high aspirations for herself and for Elaine. The home reported persistent night terrors for Elaine during the year of observation.

At school Elaine displayed a passive attitude. She accepted changes as they came and took almost no initiative in play. When she did play with other children, she seemed to regard them as puppets, to be handled as she chose, and not as living individuals with ideas of their own. She presented an enuresis problem both at school and at home. Elaine spent much of her outdoor time in the sand pile. Indoors she was most often at the easel or in the doll corner. Elaine's paintings were characterized by persistent full-page masses of black, which frequently overlaid touches of other colors. Often she began with a border around the edge of her page. Her verbalization, including "Night," "Wall," and a mention of "Blackie" (a school rabbit which had been killed by a dog), as well as talk of the expected baby, gave some clues as to the significance of her paintings. In dramatic play, which increased in frequency after Elaine had begun to verbalize while painting, her own bedtime activities were acted out.

## ELINOR

*B.D.: 10-24-33    I.Q.: 133 (left-handed)    A.D.A.: 4 years, 0 month, to 4 years, 8 months*

Elinor was a slender girl, with long dark hair, who strikingly resembled Snow White (as portrayed by Disney) and who consciously assumed this role. Elinor was an only child. Her mother stressed the feminine, the dainty, the "nice," and the beautiful and from time to time expressed hostility toward what she termed the "rough" and the "masculine." A revealing incident occurred when Elinor's mother brought a puppet monkey to school. The children gathered around. Elinor's mother said, in the voice she used for the puppet, Clippo: "I don't like these boys. These boys are too rough." Elinor's mother repeated it in several variations, until finally some of the boys began to kick at Clippo. Elinor's mother had had dramatic training, and the father reported that she and Elinor sometimes assumed fairy roles for days at a time. At school Elinor played alone, often in an imaginary role of Princess, or she engaged adults in adult-like conversations. Easel painting and crayoning were Elinor's major interests among the materials at school. At first, she used both to make stylized human representations, which she identified as fairy queens and princesses. Occasionally, she slipped from this pattern into a portrayal of "Boys" or "Boys and Girls Dancing." In these instances she would whisper the title, feeling evidently that one does not talk about such things. During a brief period of resistance at home, Elinor broke into freer social behavior at school. Her paintings changed at this time from human representations to color-mass effect of beautiful aesthetic quality. Other tendencies are suggested in the references.

## ESTHER

*B.D.: 9-27-34    I.Q.: 139    A.D.A.: 3 years, 0 month, to 4 years, 8 months (obs. 2 years)*

A small girl, with light-brown hair, blue eyes, a round face, and pallid complexion. She seemed to lack physical resistance and was frequently ill. Esther's mother and father were professionally employed. The mother, interested in intellectual pursuits and in writing, drove herself continuously and was far too greatly absorbed in her activities to give much thought to the personal appearance of herself or her children. As a result, the family usually looked tousled and unkempt. Despite this physical neglect, there was much devotion between members of the family, and both Esther and her younger brother felt much wanted and loved. Esther's mother took an active part in her training and provided many enriching experiences. She set a rather high pattern for the children; for example, Esther was toilet trained at 3 months. The father took an assertive attitude toward the children and was inclined to be firm and rigid in his discipline. The children became tense and indicated fear of him at these times.

At school Esther revealed an unusual sensitivity to people and things. She showed marked resourcefulness and spontaneity in play. Esther was eager to be accepted and adapted readily to external expectancies. Teachers observed: "Esther always does the socially acceptable thing. She is an excellent influence in the group because of her friendly, sympathetic, co-operative relations to all." She was obviously happier in a close relationship with one other child than in larger-group activities. She sometimes lacked self-assurance in social situations, despite her abilities. Esther was obviously fearful in various situations, including the use of the high climbing apparatus. She tended to drive herself to perform these activities in spite of her fears. Esther liked all the creative activities. In dramatic play she frequently chose the "big-sister" role—her true life position. Her dramatic play also included the baby role, an interest in eating situations, and animal roles. During one period of observation she carried on much chasing and wild-animal play. In her pastel blending of colors at the easel, in her rather unusual ability to portray movement in her paintings, Esther revealed aesthetic qualities. Her names for products, such as "Moonlight on the Snow," suggest her sensitivity to nature. She went through a period in painting when she overlaid with cold colors. Simultaneously, she went through a period of enuresis, and the mother reported many home upsets because of a change in housekeepers. Esther began her second year of nursery school with heavy, dirty, and wet masses of red in her easel painting. She was reported more generally assertive at this time. Her crayon work differed from her easel painting in the more deliberate and persistent attempts at representation and at making alphabet letters. With clay Esther showed marked ability to mold and made such recognizable objects as "Cradle for Baby." Usually, however, she was so interested in the activities at the clay table that she preferred to join in these and to imitate others rather than to function at the higher level of which she was capable. Esther liked the blocks and used them to make realistic structures, such as beds, seats, and steps. Her block structures usually had decorative effects.

## FRANK

*B.D.: 5-3-33    I.Q.: 123 (Minn.)    A.D.A.: 4 years, 6 months, to 5 years, 2 months*

A tall, slender, reserved boy, with relatively fine features and pale coloring. Frank was a middle child and the only boy in a family, of three. A baby was expected during the year of observation, and the entire family, including Frank, said they hoped for a boy. The baby turned out to be a girl.

Frank displayed many nervous tensions at school. He lacked self-confidence and avoided adults. In the fall he played with girls; but he increasingly sought boys in the spring. Frank frequently daydreamed and told imaginative stories. He used most of the creative materials. With blocks he built enclosures with decorative effects. His greatest use of easel paints followed the baby's arrival and reflected a conflicting treatment of circles and verticals. His only crayon work was at this period and consisted of diagonal scribbling over circles. Frank liked the feel of clay and seemed most relaxed when using it. He first openly talked about babies during a clay experience.

## FREDRIKA

*B.D.: 5-20-33     I.Q.: 135     A.D.A.: 4 years, 5 months, to 5 years, 1 month*

A large, dark, curly-haired girl, with boyish appearance and mannerisms. She was jovial and active, inclined to take the lead in initiating adult-like conversations with adults and to be overly boisterous in most situations. Fredrika's eight-year-old brother was her ideal. She resembled her father in her build and boisterous mannerisms. Her mother, who was small, tense, and anxious for perfection in Fredrika, was disturbed by her "unladylike" mannerisms.

At school Fredrika preferred play with boys in rough-and-tumble activities. Sometimes she engaged in giggly, elimination pantomiming with Gloria. Although she was assertive, she tended to be accepted by others. She had no close friends and seemed to be neither strongly liked nor disliked. Fredrika preferred persons to materials and large motor activities to constructive work with material. Of the research materials she most often sought the clay and easel paints. In these she expressed, and to some extent worked out, her strong elimination interest. Her painting theme gradually changed from dirty black and greenish masses, to which she gave such names as "Garbage," to clean, constructive designs. At about the same time she gave up her giggly interplay concerned with elimination and turned to constructive block work with a group of other children.

### GILBERT

*B.D.: 2-8-35    I.Q.: 133 (left-handed tendency)    A.D.A.: 2 years, 8 months, to*
*4 years, 4 months (obs. 2 years)*

A chubby, sturdily built boy, with brown hair and eyes and a straight-backed, assertive carriage. Gilbert had two older sisters. A baby brother arrived two months after observations began. Around this time Gilbert showed considerable jealousy toward his sisters and indicated concern over the arrival of the new baby. The parental relationship seemed a happy one. The father was rather an assertive individual.

At school Gilbert stood out as a happy, slow-geared boy with much determination, and with practical, realistic interests. He led other boys in constructive block projects or in locomotor play, despite the fact that he was one of the younger children in the group. Gilbert was inclined to tease or to be negativistic with adults. Occasionally, he offered demonstrations of affection not in keeping with his usual behavior. Gilbert sought the easel paints, clay, and crayons only in times of emotional stress. One such time was the period shortly before his brother's birth. At this time Gilbert's pattern and conversation in each medium suggested his concern over the coming event (Pl. 114). Following his brother's birth, Gilbert's main interest was again in the blocks and in dramatic play involving cars, garages, and trains and frequently involving the idea of delivering and cooking things. He was a leader and often the "big boss" in these activities. In follow-up observations Gilbert was found again to have developed an interest in easel painting. This coincided with another emotional involvement brought about by a prolonged conflict with an older sister.

Color emphasis, 16
Overlay yellow with blue, 30, Pl. 115
"Portrait" with crayons, 157, Pl. 113; with
   paints, Pl. 114

Shift to painting and crayoning, 125
Verbalization at clay, 138

### HOWARD

*B.D.: 11-29-35    I.Q.: 111, ambidextrous    A.D.A.: 2 years, 10 months, to*
*3 years, 6 months*

A plump little boy, with a cheerful countenance and a fun-loving disposition. Except for certain inconsistencies in handling and a tendency on the part of the father to be too strict, Howard's home relationships were happy ones. A sister was born during the course of observations (1-18-38) and his only tensions of the year paralleled and followed this event.

At school Howard showed friendly and affectionate relationships with both children and adults. At first, he led his cousin Hope; later, in the spring, after his sister's birth, he became rather dependent upon her. In general, Howard had a wealth of play interests. He was especially interested in active motor play, in dramatic play, and in play with blocks. With the exception of the weeks preceding and following his sister's birth, his play was constructive and varied. Near the time of the impending birth, Howard began to use the easel paints with a contrasting treatment of circles and verticals. Conversations in other situations at this time revealed concern because he was not a girl. In dramatic play at this time he gave up his usual roles to push the buggy or to go around with a doll blanket on his head.

Circular-vertical theme, 60–63, 67, 69, 76, Pls. 80–83

Release: through painting, 60–63, 126, 154; verbal 138, 154

Tendency toward paired effects, 76

Use of: green, 36; yellow overlay, 33

Other references, 73

## IRVING

*B.D.: 12-9-35     I.Q.: 70, left-handed     A.D.A.: 2 years, 3 months, to 3 years, 3 months (obs. parts of 2 years)*

A blond, curly-haired boy, with delicate features and a vague, blank expression. Irving's parents were both disturbed by his hyperactivity and his general lack of responsiveness to themselves or others. They reported that he had almost no contacts with his twelve-year-old brother.

At school, as at home, Irving met attempts at contact or communication with a vague expression. It was impossible to establish rapport with him. Children tended to disregard him, and he, in turn, paid no attention to them except for occasional unprovoked and unexpected attacks on others. Irving spent most of his time in aimless activity. He used the large-muscle equipment, the locomotor toys, the easel paints, and the clay most often. He seemed to enjoy music. Irving was highly distractible. He followed a rather stereotyped pattern with all materials. In easel painting his products were characterized, during the first year, by short, scattered, all-directional strokes (Pl. 106). The second year, they were characterized by horizontal swing scribbling (horizontal rather than diagonal because he sat to paint). The products from beginning to end of a given year were so similar that any single one might have adequately represented all the rest. With clay Irving tended to sit fingering the mound in front of him or breaking off tiny pieces, which he did not combine. He frequently put the clay to his mouth. This oral interest was also suggested in the doll corner, where he always sought the miniature cups and saucers and played at tea party.

Illustrative work, Pl. 106

Preference for paints, 121

Tendency toward: indiscriminate mixing, 47;

short, scattered strokes, 96, 108; work all over page, 89

Use of horizontals, 77

## JEFF

*B.D.: 12-10-34    I.Q.: 102    A.D.A.: 3 years, 10 months, to 4 years, 6 months*

A tall, thin boy, with dark curly hair, a slouching posture, and loosely jointed movements. Jeff was an adopted boy whom the foster-parents had emotionally not accepted. His foster-mother admitted that she was horrified by his sex interests, questioned his mentality, and said that she sometimes wondered if he had Negroid blood. Jeff was intensely jealous of the adopted foster-sister, who was two years younger than he. His feelings were so intense that the foster-mother feared he might kill the sister if left alone with her. Staff observations indicated that this foster-sister was showing some of the same retarded tendencies displayed by Jeff.

At school Jeff shrank from adults and was disregarded by children. He had no strong interests and no seeming drive to express himself. He frequently wet himself, sat to urinate, and displayed many other infantile mannerisms. He spent much time masturbating and daydreaming. He became only slightly more outgoing and boyish at the end of the second year of observation. At that time an interest in displaying his sex organs and in examining other children became pronounced. Jeff used the locomotor toys and the clay more than other materials. He seemed to like activities calling for large co-ordinations. He was highly distractible and scattered in all his activities and performed at a low level for his age. With clay Jeff tended, the first year, to break pieces from the larger lump and to scatter or overlap these on the clay table. Twice he was observed to place these overlapping bits of clay in a straight line and to call his product "train." He was never ready to leave the clay table. During the second year of observation, he displayed a persistent interest in holes and the ramming of "snakes" in and out of these holes.

Jeff's easel paintings and crayon products during the first year were characterized by all-directional lines of many colors, scattered over and sometimes off the painting or crayon page. He made one or two products of interrelated forms at a developmental level strikingly in contrast to and above his more usual pattern. On some products he differentiated between smeared and constructive use by putting each on a different side of the painting page. During the second year of observation he worked over and over the same area in diagonal or circular strokes, a pattern more or less typical of a beginner with this medium. Some of his products showed heavy overlay of red with black, a tendency which recurred during follow-up observations. Jeff used blocks little, and then his interest seemed in knocking down rather than in constructing. His few constructions were flat and sprawled. His only dramatic activity was in locomotor play, in which he took no preferred or obvious role.

## JESSICA

*B.D.: 4-22-35    I.Q.: 102    A.D.A.: 3 years, 6 months, to 4 years, 2 months*

A girl of average size, with dark hair cut in a Dutch bob, she was usually garbed in boyish clothes and looked much more like a boy than a girl. Jessica's father traveled and was almost never at home. Her older brother was a problem both to the mother and to the school because of his extremely effeminate behavior. The mother seemed to regard Jessica as the boy—if not the man—of the family.

At school Jessica displayed highly impulsive and aggressive behavior. She was usually unco-operative with children, though she gave occasional evidence of her potentialities for warmth of affection and gentleness, particularly in her concern for plants and pets. She had boundless energy and was easily overstimulated. She tended in play to seek the other more assertive girls, as, for example, Arline. Jessica's aggressive behavior soon made her an outcast among the children. She came to desire their acceptance, however, and from time to time she would try hard to build co-operative play relationships. At such times she would frequently ask: "Will you play with me?"

Of the research media Jessica sought the easel paints most. She also showed a strong interest in the clay. With easel paints Jessica revealed marked ambivalence (*a*) in her use of blue and yellow; (*b*) in her handling of verticals and circles; (*c*) in the overlay and separate placement of colors; and (*d*) in a tendency toward differentiated, left-right treatment of the painting page. Her crayons also reflected a contrasting treatment of circles and verticals. Crayon products tended to be in the colder colors, especially black and purple. With clay Jessica seemed to find much satisfaction in pounding. "Snakes," "holes," and "candlesticks" were among her more frequent named products. When she did engage in dramatic play, Jessica always took the dominant role, usually of mother. She loved to dress up. Eating and sleeping situations were those most often dramatized. Jessica had a vivid imagination, and she frequently went about imagining or acting without the aid of materials. Her few uses of blocks tended to emphasize the element of height and consisted of products (house, seat, step, bed) which could be adapted to her own use.

## JILL

*B.D.: 11-28-34    I.Q.: 122    A.D.A.: 3 years, 10 months, to 4 years, 6 months*

A heavily built, slow-moving child, with soft, light-brown hair, blue eyes, and intelligent, sensitive features. Jill was an only child who, with her parents, lived in a relatively secluded, hedged-in home—virtually in a world of their own. Jill's parents held high, rigid standards, and she lived the part of a "nice little girl" at home. Her cleanliness training had been begun early and was particularly strict.

At school Jill was inclined to stay near adults and to be reticent and shy with children. She was orderly and neat in all routine activities. She tended to prefer work with creative materials to all other activities at school, and she particularly sought the easel paints. At the easel, regardless of colors used, Jill tended very often to achieve green and dabby effects. Sometimes she used dotting techniques. She expressed a dislike for brown. She only once chose it as though to use it and then quickly replaced the brush before she had touched her painting page. Circular forms and pastel colors were recurrent in her work. She produced quantities of paintings, sometimes as many as twelve at a time. She almost never named her products. Her one most spontaneous description was "Bird Tied." Jill gradually came to like clay at nursery school. In the group she used it almost entirely in a manipulative way. During controlled observations in Dr. Hattwick's office she used it to make a house and a yard with a fence "to keep the dog in." With blocks Jill built tall, ladder-effects, often higher than her head, or enclosures which she called "houses" or "garages." Her work was frequently decorative. She seemed sometimes to use her tall block structures as walls to hide behind. Jill showed little interest in dramatic play and she made little use of the crayons at school.

## KENNETH

*B.D.: 7-27-34     I.Q.: 80     A.D.A.: 4 years, 3 months, to 4 years, 11 months*

A tall, thin boy, with dangling limbs, who had a history of spastic paralysis and who displayed marked hyperactivity and poor co-ordination. Kenneth lived with his own mother and foster-father, who admittedly had difficulty in accepting Kenneth. A brother was born into the home in the fall of the year of observations.

At school Kenneth was avoided by other children because of his unintentional interference with their structures and activities. He continued eagerly attempting to contact others, despite their pointed rebuffs. With adults he was dependent, often negativistic, and inclined to seek undue attention. Outdoors, Kenneth liked the large apparatus. Indoors, he most often sought the blocks and crayons. He built by himself—never with others—and spent tedious, painstaking minutes in trying to balance his blocks one on another in vertical forms, with the large blocks perilously placed on the smaller ones. He used crayons with jagged, saw-tooth strokes. He most often chose the cold colors, such as blue and black. His few paintings were much like his crayon products in the jaggedness of the strokes and the choice of cold colors. He tended to overlay in easel painting. He used clay at a manipulative level, often breaking or pinching off tiny pieces, while he took part in or observed the social interplay of others at the clay table.

Tendency toward balance, 95, Pl. 102          Use of: black, 37, 38; blue, 27

## LORETTA

*B.D.: 12-4-34     I.Q.: 120     A.D.A.: 3 years, 11 months, to 4 years, 7 months*

A sturdily built girl, with brown eyes and brown hair cut in a Dutch bob. She strongly resembled her mother in build. The mother reported that Loretta's keen competition with her seven-year-old brother and the dissension between the two children were continuous difficulties at home. Bedtime was also a particular problem.

At school Loretta stood out as an assertive, colorful, dramatic child. She was always conscious of clothes, was especially proud of new things, and keenly enjoyed dressing up in clothes from the school costume box. Music and dramatic play were her outstanding interests. She often led others in play and was usually co-operative, friendly, and generous with those with whom she chose to play. Jocelyn and Angela were her favorite playmates. Loretta tended to stimulate rivalry feelings between those children whom she selected for play and other children in the group. This attitude spread until "We aren't playing with you" became a frequent expression among a large number of the children in the nursery-school group to which Loretta belonged. In addition to dramatic play, Loretta showed a strong interest in clay. Although she used easel paints little, she was apt to seek them on upset days. Blocks also were a relatively minor interest. Her dramatic play was characterized by richness and variety of content and roles. In it she usually took the lead. House play, in which Loretta was mother, nurse, or cook, was more frequent than any other single theme. Clay seemed the medium through which she worked out the home problem most directly. She went through a period of making beds with clay, and it was while using this medium that she verbalized on her relationship with her brother. With blocks Loretta sometimes built houses in which to play. Several times she showed the unusual tendency of building her structure with the blocks lying on their sides and then, when through, of turning each block up on end. At other times, Loretta chose the tiny blocks, including colored cubes, and built highly decorative structures with the exception of the period of conflict mentioned in the text and references. Her paintings tended to be full-page masses in colorful, patchwork effects. Decorative dotting was sometimes used. There was no overlay. This same interest in blocked-color effects appeared in Loretta's crayon products and persisted, despite the fact that she could do excellent representative work when she so desired.

## LOUISE

*B.D.: 10-14-34     I.Q.: 121, ambidextrous     A.D.A.: 4 years, 0 month, to 4 years, 8 months*

A plump little girl, with thick, dark pigtails, who always appeared freshly scrubbed and who often came to school attired in a pinafore. Louise was the youngest of three girls in a rather conventional home. The older sisters, the mother, and the nurse were all more or less continuously impressing Louise with the "proper thing to do."

At school Louise was more aware of adults than of children. She often initiated sophisticated, adult-like conversation. When in the doll corner, she would sit at the "tea table" or at the telephone, carrying on a patter that bore the home imprint. Louise tended to seek other girls in play. She was domineering in her contacts, and was apt to have difficulty in making and keeping friends. Louise showed only a mild interest in school activities. Her preferences lay in the direction of dramatic play and easel painting. She resisted clay at first but showed much enjoyment in this medium after she began to use it. She had almost no interest in blocks. In dramatic play Louise often introduced sick play, in which she took the nurse or doctor role. She also enjoyed playing cook or imitating the social amenities which she had seen her mother carry on while entertaining in the home. At first, Louise used each painting color in a small restricted mass, each mass widely separated from every other one on her painting page. As she became more outgoing and expressive in the group, she began to mix and smear her colors. During one especially unhappy period, she showed a recurrent tendency to overlay yellow. She used crayons to make forms or recognizable representations, and here she used varied colors and worked freely over the page. Louise began to use clay when she was becoming more outgoing in overt behavior. She enjoyed the social give-and-take at the clay table. Tiny balls or container themes (vases, baskets, fences) were recurrent in her clay activities.

## MARGARET

*B.D.: 10-15-34    I.Q.: 128    A.D.A.: 3 years, 10 months, to 4 years, 6 months*

Margaret was a thin, pale girl, with long, straggly brown hair and, more often than not, a tear-stained face. Margaret's mother was in poor health, was very tense, and openly rejected Margaret in favor of the two-year-old brother who was "more the type we wanted." The mother reported Margaret to be extremely negativistic, to have long crying spells each night when put to bed, and to be tense, unhappy, and crying much of the daytime. In apparent overcompensation for her feelings, the mother expressed excessive concern over Margaret's physical safety and for her routines.

At school, as at home, Margaret was usually crying. She seemed to hurt herself almost daily. Others soon began to regard her as a crybaby and to tease her in order to provoke her tears. Margaret usually played alone or in silly interplay in the sandbox with Jimmy. She frequently stood or sat masturbating and daydreaming. She often sought the doll corner. She liked to dress up in costumes. Margaret frequently played at going to bed. Often she had an imaginary playmate in the doll corner. She would punish this imaginary playmate by putting her to bed. One time our observer caught the comment, "You are my favorite, so Daddy will take you out." Margaret also tended to seek the easel paints and the crayons. A similar theme was observed in both media. She mixed colors indiscriminately and produced dark brownish-green effects regardless of the colors selected. Her muddy-palette period was paralleled by a time when she was defying bowel control at home. At this time overlay was frequent. During another period she worked in heavy vertical strokes. Twice her products were called "A Fraidy."

## PERRY

*B.D.: 10-36-34   I.Q.: 123   A.D.A.: 4 years, 0 month, to 4 years, 8 months*

A husky, determined, independent boy, with fair skin, blond hair, and blue eyes. Perry had a brother and sister, each more than ten years older than himself. His father was in the Army, and his mother had given him the feeling that he was a "big boy who took care of mother." (This was the mother's own statement.)

At school Perry showed a drive to play the big-boy or big-man role. He was independent with adults. He showed excellent co-operative ability with children and was extremely generous in sharing materials and responsibilities. Perry's special interests at school were in such activities as "making roads" or "being repair man." He also enjoyed dramatic play in which he could take the daddy or big-brother role. He often commented while playing, on what a hard worker he was. Perry used blocks in well-built structures related to his other play interests. He showed no interest in clay or paintings. His crayon products were limited to the days following a fearful experience: He had been told by bigger boys that in his forthcoming visit to the doctor the latter would cut off his ears. He had night terrors following this "revelation," appeared nervous and upset the following day when he came to school, sought the crayons, and made three products, each with cut-off verticals.

## RITA

*B.D.: 4-25-35   I.Q.: 102   A.D.A.: 3 years, 6 months, to 4 years, 0 month*

A tall, blond girl, who looked, as one teacher said, "as though she had eaten too many sweet rolls." She was reticent and easily lost in a group. She had a mincing walk and affected gestures. Rita's mother held extremely high standards for Rita, who was the only girl and the youngest of three children. The mother devoted most of her daytime to Rita and shared all the daughter's play experiences at home. She also slept with Rita. She was particularly proud of her own drawing ability. (To the teachers she bragged about her drawing achievements of former school days and she demonstrated how quickly she could draw Mickey Mouse.)

Rita spent much of her time at school in standing and watching others. She was dependent, lacking in initiative, and tended to show unimaginative, repetitive patterns in play. She was obviously not at ease in free-play situations with children. She was most confident in adult-directed situations. Rita preferred the easel paints to all other school activities, apart from adult-directed group periods. She also liked the doll corner, when she could play there alone. In the doll corner she spent most of her time in repetitive, "tidying-up" activities. At the easel she began with representative work. As she became freer, she broke from strict representation and alternated between structuralized or representative patterns and smeary, dabby, orange-and-brown effects. Sometimes she vehemently smeared over precise blue patterns with red or brown. She frequently sought the crayons for representative work or for systematic filling of space. She did not bring out in crayoning the blue-brown conflict expressed in easel painting. Rita used clay little. She seemed to choose it in freer moments, and her behavior while at the clay table was more outgoing and happy than at other times. The opportunities which the clay table provided for parallel play and social interplay seemed to please her, and usually her handling of the clay itself was at a manipulative level not in keeping with her real ability. Rita used blocks very little. Her few structures tended to be tiny, ornamental affairs, not adaptable to play.

Contrasting blue-brown or blue-orange palette, 29, 41, 42, Pls. 47, 48, 49*A*
Preference for easel paints, 122
Product taken home, 155
"Self-portrait," 156, Pl. 48

Tendency toward: circular emphasis, 56; differential right-left treatment of page, 71, 94, Pls. 47, 48; emphasis at top, 92; scatter, 97
Other references, Pl. 49

## SALLY

*B.D.: 6-30-35    I.Q.: 118    A.D.A.: 3 years, 3 months, to 3 years, 11 months*

A pale, slender girl, who wore her hair drawn sleekly back in two tight braids. She appeared so clean and neat that one suspected much fussiness over this point at home. Sally had a younger sister, aged one and one-half years, who constantly interfered with her activities and whom Sally was forever trying to avoid. The mother held high standards. She disciplined on an emotional plane, with such admonitions as "Do this, or mother won't like you."

For many months Sally gave way to hysterical weeping when her mother left her at nursery school. This ceased as soon as her mother had gone. At school Sally usually played alone, often seeking high places, such as the window ledge, on which to play. She displayed restless, discontented, quarrelsome, and lonely tendencies. Her attitude toward adults was possessive and demanding. When with children she was bossy, "teachery," critical. Her only happy moments seemed to be when she was the center of attention. Sally showed a special interest in dramatic play and easel painting. Her dramatic play consisted of highly repetitive and exact reproduction of daily routines at home and in nursery school. She played alone or with one or two children whom she would try to boss or direct. Easel painting seemed the medium through which Sally gained the most release. Her products were characteristically overweighted at the top of the page and dripping wet. She was frequently observed to turn to the easel and to paint vehemently after an incident which had incited anger or jealousy on her part. Such products were in heavy strokes and mass effects. At other times Sally characteristically produced human representations, often faces of girls (self-portraits) and often with crying eyes. Much original content also appeared, as "A Cemetery," "A Garden Plot." About some of her products she made revealing remarks (see p. 154). With crayons Sally worked in lines and recognizable forms. Her representations here (as "Faces," "Boats," "Chickens," "Pumpkins") reflected adult stimulus. They lacked the originality and freedom of her painting products. Sally seemed to gain much satisfaction from the pounding and the social interplay of the clay table. Products were of minor significance. Imitation and attention-seeking were pronounced. Sally seldom used blocks at school, except in a group, usually in a dramatic-play situation. Her few individual products consisted of low, compact structures.

# REFERENCES[1]

ALLEN, GRANT. *The Color Sense—Its Origin and Development*. London: Kegan Paul, Trench, Trubner & Co., 1892. Pp. 282.

BEST MANGARD, ADOLF. *Method for Creative Design*. New York: Alfred A. Knopf, 1927.

BIBER, BARBARA. *From Lines to Drawings*. New York: 69 Bank St., 1930.

CAILLI, RUTH KENNEDY. *Resistant Behavior of Preschool Children*. ("Child Development Monographs," No. 11.) New York: Teachers College, Columbia University, 1933.

CAMERON, N. "Individual and Social Factors in the Development of Graphic Symbolizations," *Journal of Psychology*, V (1938), 165–84.

COLE, N. R. *The Arts in the Classroom*. New York: John Day Co., 1940.

DANZ, LOUIS. *It Is Still the Morning*. New York: William Morrow & Co. 1943. Pp. 273.

DIXON, C. MADELEINE. *High, Wide, and Deep*. New York: John Day Co. 1938. Pp. xix+300.

DUMMER, ETHEL S. *Why I Think So: The Autobiography of an Hypothesis*. Chicago: Clarke-McElroy Pub. Co., 1937. Pp. 274.

ENG, HILDA. *The Psychology of Children's Drawings: From the First Stroke to the Color Drawing*. London: Kegan Paul, Trench, Trubner & Co., 1931. Pp. viii+223.

GESELL, ARNOLD, and OTHERS. *The First Five Years of Life: A Guide to the Study of the Preschool Child*. New York: Harper & Bros., 1940. Pp. xiii+393.

GESELL, ARNOLD; ILG, FRANCES L.; and OTHERS. *Infant and Child in the Culture of Today: Guidance and Development in Home and Nursery School*. New York: Harper & Bros., 1943.

GOODENOUGH, FLORENCE. *Measurement of Intelligence by Drawing*. Yonkers-on-Hudson, N.Y.: World Book Co., 1926. Pp. xi+177.

——— *Developmental Psychology*. New York: D. Appleton–Century Co., 1934. Pp. xvi+619.

GRIFFITHS, RUTH. *A Study of Imagination in Early Childhood*. London: Kegan Paul, Trench, Trubner & Co., 1935. Pp. xiv+367.

HARMS, ERNST. "Child Art as an Aid in the Diagnosis of Juvenile Neuroses," *American Journal of Orthopsychiatry*, XI, No. 2 (April, 1941), 191–209.

HATTWICK, LA BERTA A. "Sex Differences in Behavior of Preschool Children," *Child Development*, December, 1937.

HOMBERGER, ERIK. "Configuration in Play," *Psychoanalytic Quarterly*, VI (1937), 139–214.

HURLOCK, E. B., and THOMSON, J. L. "Children's Drawings: An Experimental Study of Perception," *Child Development*, June, 1934, pp. 127–38.

JACOBS, MICHEL. *The Art of Color*. New York: Doubleday, Doran & Co., 1931. Pp. 90.

JACOBY, H. J. *The Handwriting of Depressed Children*. London: New Era, January, 1944.

KLOPFER, BRUNO. "Personality Differences between Boys and Girls in Early Childhood: Report before the American Psychological Association," *Psychological Bulletin*, XXXVI (July, 1939), 538.

———. "Rorschach Reactions in Early Childhood," *Rorschach Research Exchange*, V (1940), 1–23.

KRÖTSCH, W. *Rhythmus und Form in der freien Kinderziehung*. Leipzig, 1917. Reported by VIKTOR LÖWENFELD. *The Nature of Creative Activity*. New York: Harcourt, Brace & Co., 1939.

[1] "References" include those publications to which we have made specific reference. "Other Suggested Reading" covers books and articles which have contributed to our thinking, but to which no specific reference has been made. For more extensive bibliography, see Oldham, Read, *Review of Educational Research*, Sachs, and Schilder, listed in "Other Suggested Reading."

LARK-HOROVITZ. "On Art Appreciation of Children," *Journal of Educational Research,* XXXIII, No. 4 (December, 1939), 258–85.

LERNER, EUGENE, and MURPHY, LOIS BARCLAY. *Method for the Study of Personality in Young Children.* ("Monographs of the Society for Research in Child Development," Vol. VI, No. 4 [1941].) Pp. xiii+289.

LEVY, DAVID M., and TULCHIN, SIMON H. "The Resistance of Infants and Children during Mental Tests," *Journal of Experimental Psychology,* VI (1923), 304–22.

LISS, EDWARD. "The Graphic Arts," *American Journal of Orthopsychiatry,* VIII, No. 1 (January, 1938), 95–99.

LÖWENFELD, VIKTOR. *The Nature of Creative Activity.* New York: Harcourt, Brace & Co., 1939. Pp. xvii+272.

MURRAY, HENRY A., and OTHERS. *Explorations in Personality.* New York: Oxford University Press, 1938. Pp. 761.

PAULSEN, A. "Rorschachs of School Beginners," *Rorschach Research Exchange,* V (1941), 24–29.

PERRINE, VAN DEARING. *Let the Child Draw.* New York: F. A. Stokes & Co., 1936. Pp. 88.

PETTIGREW, JAMES B. *Design in Nature,* Vol. III. London: Longmans-Green, 1908.

READ, HERBERT. *The Meaning of Art.* London: Faber & Faber, Ltd., 1936. Pp. 224.

RIVERS, W. H. R. "Primitive Color Vision," *Popular Science Monthly* LIX (1901), 44–59.

SCHMIDL-WOEHNER, TRUDE. "Formal Criteria for the Analysis of Children's Drawings," *American Journal of Orthopsychiatry,* XII, No. 1 (1942), 95–103.

STAGNER, ROSS. "Visually Determined Reactions in the Vertebrates," *Psychological Bulletin,* XXVIII, No. 2 (February, 1931), 99–129.

STAPLES, RUTH. "The Responses of Infants to Color," *Journal of Experimental Psychology,* XV (1932), 119–41; also *Psychological Bulletin,* XXVIII, No. 4 (April, 1931), 297–308.

STEWARD, JULIAN H. *Petroglyphs of California and Adjoining States* (Berkeley, Calif.: University of California Press, 1929), Pls. 23E and 59E.

STODDARD, GEORGE D., and WELLMAN, BETH L. *Child Psychology.* New York: Macmillan Co., 1934.

VAN ALSTYNE, DOROTHY. *Play Behavior and Choice of Play Materials of Preschool Children.* Chicago: University of Chicago Press, 1932. Pp. xii+104.

WALTON, W. E. "Exploratory Experiments in Color Discrimination," *Journal of Genetic Psychology,* XLVIII (1936), 221–22.

WARDEN, CARL; JENKINS, THOMAS; and WARNER, LUCIEN H. *Comparative Psychology,* Vol. II. New York: Ronald Press, 1936. Pp. 1070. See esp. pp. 685 ff.

## OTHER SUGGESTED READING

ADAM, L. *Primitive Art.* New York: Penguin Books, 1940.

APPEL, K. E. "Drawings of Children as Aids to Personality Studies," *American Journal of Orthopsychiatry,* 1931.

BERRIEN, F. K. "A Study of the Drawings of Abnormal Children," *Journal of Educational Psychology,* XXVI (1935), 143–50.

BUCK, MARIA. "Mental Hygiene Value of Children's Art Work," *Journal of Orthopsychiatry,* XIV, No. 1 (January, 1944), 136–46.

BURT, CYRIL. *Mental and Scholastic Tests.* London: P. S. King & Son, Ltd., 1922. 3d impression, 1927. See esp. pp. 319–22.

*Encyclopedia of Educational Research.* New York: Macmillan Co., 1941. See esp. "Art Education," pp. 59–65; "Child Development in Drawing," pp. 147–60.

LORAND, SANDOR (ed.). *Psychoanalysis Today.* New York: International University Press, 1944.

LOWENFELD, MARGARET. *Play in Childhood.* London: Gollancz, 1935.

MATHIAS, MARGARET C. "Encouraging the Art Expression of Young Children," *Childhood Education,* XV, No. 7 (March, 1939), 293.

OAKLEY, C. A. "The Interpretation of Children's Drawings," *British Journal of Psychiatry,* XXI (1930–31), 256–70.

OLDHAM, H. W. *Child Expression in Form and Color.* London: John Lane, 1940.

READ, HERBERT. *Education through Art.* London: Faber & Faber, 1944. Pp. xxxiii+320.

*Review of Educational Research* (Washington, D.C.: National Education Association of the United States, 1201 Sixteenth St. N.W.), Vol. XIV, No. 1 (February, 1944), chap. vi.

SACHS, HANS. *The Creative Unconscious.* Cambridge, Mass.: Sci-art Publishers, 1942.

SCHILDER, PAUL. *The Image and Appearance of the Human Body.* ("Psychic Monographs," No. 4.) London: Kegan Paul, Trench, Trubner & Co., 1935.

*The Visual Arts in General Education: Report of Committee on Function of Art in General Education, Progressive Education Association Commission on the Secondary School Curriculum.* New York: D. Appleton–Century Co., 1940. Pp. x+166.

## SUPPLEMENTARY BIBLIOGRAPHY

Free expression through painting and other creative media has become an accepted research tool and a valuable aid to therapeutic work with both children and adults. The following selected references will open the door to further exploration of this field.

### GENERAL REFERENCES

ABT, LAWRENCE EDWIN, and ABT, BELLA K. *Projective Psychology: Clinical Approaches to the Total Personality.* New York: Grove Press, 1959. Pp. xvi+485.

ANDERSON, HAROLD H., and ANDERSON, GLADYS L. *An Introduction to Projective Techniques.* Englewood Cliffs, N.J.: Prentice-Hall, 1951. Pp. xxiv+720.

HAMMER, EMANUEL. *The Clinical Application of Projective Drawing.* Springfield, Ill.: Charles C Thomas, 1958. Pp. xxii+663.

MURPHY, L. B. "Art Techniques in Studying Child Personality," *Journal of Projective Techniques,* XIII (1949), 320–24.

MUSSEN, PAUL H. (ed.). *Handbook of Research Methods in Child Development.* New York: John Wiley & Sons, 1960. Pp. x+1061.

NAUMBERG, MARGARET. *Dynamically Oriented Art Therapy: Its Principles and Practices.* New York: Grune & Stratton, 1966. Pp. xxiv+168.

PRECKER, JOSEPH A. "Painting and Drawing in Personality Assessment," *Journal of Projective Techniques,* XIV (1950), 262–86.

RABIN, ALBERT I., and HAWORTH, MARY R. *Projective Techniques with Children.* New York: Grune & Stratton, 1960. Pp. xiii+392.

### REFERENCES CONTAINING CONDENSED VERSIONS OF "PAINTING AND PERSONALITY"

ALSCHULER, ROSE H., and HATTWICK, LA BERTA A. "Easel Painting as an Index of Personality in Preschool Children," *American Journal of Orthopsychiatry,* XIII (1943), 616–25.

EISNER, ELLIOT W., and ECKER, DAVID W. *Readings in Art Education.* Waltham, Mass.: Blaisdell Publishing Co. [Division of Ginn & Co.], 1966. Pp. xii+468. See chapter ix, pp. 117–30.

NOTE: The general references by Abt and Abt, Anderson and Anderson, Hammer, Murphy, Mussen, and Precker also discuss some of the findings in *Painting and Personality.*

### References Illustrating the Use of Creative Media in Therapeutic Work with Children

Axline, Virginia Mae. *Play Therapy: The Inner Dynamics of Childhood*. Boston: Houghton Mifflin Co., 1947. Pp. 379.

Reports on play therapy sessions involving a wide variety of play and creative media, including easel painting, finger painting, crayons, clay, and blocks.

Axline, Virginia M. *Dibs: In Search of Self*. New York: Ballantine Books, 1967. Pp. ix+220. Paperback. (Originally published by Houghton Mifflin Co., 1964.)

A moving account of how the personality of one small boy emerged with the aid of expression through creative media. For references to easel painting, see pp. 43, 54–55, 94, 127–28, 184, 203.

Kalff, Dora M. *Sandspiel: Seine therapeutische Wirkung auf die Psyche*. Zurich and Stuttgart: Rascher Verlag, 1966. Pp. 104. (An English version of this book is in preparation.)

Dora Kalff has helped many persons, both children and adults, overcome personality disorders through the technique of sand play, or the spontaneous creation of "sand pictures." This first book deals with the creations of children. The plates, both black-and-white and color, make it an especially vivid account of how the unconscious reveals itself through expression in creative media.

Kramer, Edith. *Art Therapy in a Children's Community*. Springfield, Ill.: Charles C Thomas, 1958. Pp. xvii+238.

Report on seven years of work with six- to twelve-year-old boys at the Wiltwyck School for Boys. Tempera paints were found to be the best art medium available for fostering emotional maturation in these boys. The orientation of the book is strictly Freudian.

### References Illustrating the Therapeutic Value of Drawing and Painting in Work with Adults

Adler, Gerhard. *Studies in Analytical Psychology*. New York: W. W. Norton Co., 1948. Pp. 250.

Case material, together with color plates of paintings, illustrates the value of painting in the ongoing development of adults and in their wholesome adjustment.

Jung, C. G. "A Study in a Process of Individuation" and "Concerning Mandala Symbolism." In *The Archetypes and the Collective Unconscious*. Bollingen Series XX. New York: Pantheon Books, 1959. Pp. 290–384.

Reports from individual analyses, which illustrate with both black-and-white and color plates the significant role played by drawing and painting in Jungian analysis. (The reader who finds this account stimulating will want to explore the other volumes in the Bollingen Series.)

Naumberg, Margaret. *Schizophrenic Art: Its Meaning in Psychotherapy*. New York: Grune & Stratton, 1950. Pp. viii+247.

Well illustrated and a rewarding testimony to the therapeutic value of free expression in drawing and in painting.

Note: The Naumberg book listed among the General References also contains helpful case material. See also the Naumberg article "Spontaneous Art in Therapy and Diagnosis" in *Clinical Psychology*, I (1952), 290–311.

# INDEX

Names of children given here are those whose paintings are illustrated. Page references are to the biographical summaries, where further references will be found.